Contents

1
The boy in the box

Darkness beat upon his senses and his heartbeat pounded in his ears. The cuffs were cutting into the flesh of his arm and he couldn't feel his feet. Knees thrust down into forehead, he waited, foetus-like in the hard womb of a steel lined trunk. Just one more minute....

Fifty eight, fifity nine, sixty.

That's it. He had to get out, had to suck air into his starved lungs and unwind his cramped limbs.

The escapologist eased open the lid and rolled sideways from his tiny prison. Slowly he unpeeled himself, stood up and pulled down his ruffled waistcoat and rolled shirt sleeves. He glanced over at the clock.

Three hours and ten minutes. Not bad at all, he thought, stretching his arms up to the attic ceiling and smiling. He threw down his cast off hancuffs, smoothed down his hair, and wrote himself a note:

"Endurance test 1913. Remained in steel trunk in upside down position 3 hours & ten minutes. The only means of getting air; through the hinge gaps in the trunk! Rather cramped but no worse for my 'seige'."

And with that, the great liberator bounded down the attic stairs in search of tea.

Randolph Robert Osborne Douglas, aged 18

Buxton Museum and Art Gallery

2

The determined escapologist in the steel trunk was not Houdini - he just wanted to be.

Eighteen-year-old Randolph Robert Osborne Douglas was an eager follower of the famous Harry, and the Great Mystifier was encouraging him all the way.

By the time of his trunk endurance test, Randolph had already met his hero, who sent him letters, locks and postcards as he travelled the world. Houdini, the Handcuff King, a world famous man who dined with Royalty and stars, was sure to write to his his young friend in Sheffield. How incredible it must have been for the young pretender to meet his hero and become his friend - a friend sharing the same fascination for the art of escape and all its secrets.

Randolph's head was full of dreams and ambition, as was that of the young Ehrich Weisz - later to reinvent himself as Houdini. Ehrich, as a child, had been entranced and inspired by a German high-wire act he tried to emulate. And now he had inspired in turn another young man, watching with eyes full of wonder.

Young Randolph was determined to make his way in the world of locks, straitjackets and illusion. He filled books and papers with ideas and diagrams, invented daring new escapes and designed stage sets.

A sketch by Randolph
Buxton Museum and Art Gallery

But as the great Harry grew more and more famous, becoming a household name and a byword for amazement, young Randolph's life took a different path. Houdini is as famous as he ever was, but Randini? No one has heard of him. He did a final disappearing act as fate carved out another life for the would-be liberator, that of museum keeper, and miniature model maker. Houdini lived out his dream. Randolph had to shelve his, and watch as his friend astounded the world.

From his small museum, a House of Wonders in the Derbyshire village of Castleton, Randolph followed the career of his friend Harry Houdini.

As Houdini plunged into a water tank, was buried in a coffin and squeezed himself into a tiny milk can, Randolph poured his refocussed talent into tiny models. Houdini embraced and challenged the world; Randolph attempted to bring the world to him, reproducing it in every perfect detail.

As well as his models, Randolph collected an eclectic assortment of objects, from crystals to seahorses, stalactites to skeletons. And of course there was a grand collection of locks and keys, some of which were given to him by Houdini.

So what is the tale of this man of wonders, now a footnote in the life of the world's most famous escapologist, the man he wanted to imitate?. Some of the details of his life are lost or forgotten, disappeared behind the curtain of time and circumstance. But we can piece together much of his stay in the world, see a little of the world through his eyes, dream his dreams. We all need a little magic in our lives, don't we?

Robert Strachan Douglas, Randolph's father

Private Collection

4

2
The bonds of love

Robert Strachan Douglas sat back in the chair of the living room and looked around at his fellow artists and craftsmen. He stroked his ample moustache and thought over the evening's debate.

The handsome Scottish silver chaser and designer was pleased with the results of the meeting at Shrewsbury Road, Sheffield, to 'talk over the desirabilty of forming a society for the Arts Crafts of Sheffield and District.' He was already eager to work on the code of conduct he had volunteered to write and full of ideas for the future of the venture.

But what also filled his mind were thoughts of the woman who had maybe brought him all the way from Scotland to the city of steel. It was March 1st 1894 and in just over four months they would be married.

Margaret Helen
Osborne.
June 17,1894
Private Collection

Family tradition tells that Robert had met Margaret Helen Osborne when they were at the same art college in his native Edinburgh. He was born in 1868, the son of a wine merchant, from the ancient and historic Douglas clan. She was a painter, born 1872, and one of the Sheffield Osborne family, famous for file manufacturing, which was her father's trade. It was perhaps still a little unusual for a woman to go away to study, but if they met at the Trustees Academy at the heart of historic Edinburgh, on the Mound, it was possible, as it had been policy there to accept 'the daughters of tradesmen and manufacturers' since 1797. Maybe their eyes met over a fine art evening class, maybe during a lecture, but wherever it was, it was the beginning of love.

Creativity, artistry and vision, perfect qualities to produce an unusual and imaginative child like Randolph. For these two people were his parents.

The lovestruck couple were married in Margaret's parish, Norton, then in Derbyshire, on July 19th, 1894.

The same year, just less than a month earlier on June 22, Harry Houdini married his beloved Bess, whom he had met when she was performing with the Floral Sisters, a song and dance act.

Two families, destined to be brought together by a young boy.

The church of St. James in Norton was already famous as the final resting ground of another artist, the sculptor Francis Chantrey, whose body had been brought from London with much pomp, in 1841. But now it would be special to two more artists, Robert and Margaret.

As Margaret's bridal carriage drove past the obelisk erected forty years earlier to Chantrey's memory and up the path to the church that July day, Robert waited inside. His bride walked in under the ivy covered Norman arch, past the font with its carved salamander, and up to the altar to meet him.

St James Church Norton

Most of the two families would probably have been there. Perhaps some of Robert's siblings Anne, James, William and Elizabeth made the long journey from Scotland to the tiny Derbyshire church.

Margaret's little sister Katherine, eight years younger than the blushing bride, would almost certainly have been there watching, as their father Henry George Osborne led her big sister, fondly known as Peggy, to her new role in life.

The couple set up home in the village of Greenhill, where Margaret was from, with her family living close by. Greenhill is now swallowed up by the city to be a suburb of Sheffield, but was then a quaint village of dusty tree lined streets. Even today, though the heart of the village is hidden amongst new buildings and busy roads, it is easy to imagine the idyllic place Randolph and his family would have known.

The Douglas family home (left end of row) around 1910

Sheffield Local Studies Library

Robert and Margaret had a fine house on what is now Greenhill Main Road, in a prime site opposite the beautiful old Greenhill Hall and its stables. The historic hall, sadly demolished in 1965, dated from the 14th century, but was mostly a 16th century building with 19th century additions.

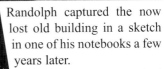

Randolph captured the now lost old building in a sketch in one of his notebooks a few years later.

The hall's stable block had a sculpture of a phoenix on the rooftop, now lost.

Robert had secured a job as farm manager for the hall, perhaps helped by his in-laws who would most likely have known the hall's owners in such a small village. Living opposite he was in an ideal spot to play this role until he could begin working as a silversmith and chaser and expand the skills gained at art college.

Greenhill Hall and above, the stables with the phoenix on the roof   Sheffield Local Studies Library

The marital home on Main Road was known as Yew House. Ivy covered the end gable and crawled around the windows, with their decorative finials, and a little railing along the terrace kept it apart from the road. It stood at the end of a row, just down from the recently restored church

It was very different to Havelock Street in Broomhall, where Robert had been living since his move to Sheffield, and the warm stone of many of the cottages in the village were a contrast to the tall grey stone buildings of Edinburgh.

So the newlyweds pushed open the little gate and stepped into their life as Mr and Mrs Douglas. Margaret loved the house, with its view out the front to the stately old hall and out the back over towards the recently enlarged school. She loved their pretty little garden and looked forward to days taking tea out there, sitting talking over the days to come with her new husband.

It was a fine village to walk around, up past the old hall, by the other picturesque cottages and past the water pump to visit Margaret's parents. They could wander past the other old and grand building in the village, Greenhill Manor, then by the White Swan public house and down the little lane to the forge, looping back by the school and church and home again.

By 1895 Robert's work with the Artcrafts Guild was going well, with exhibitions planned, lectures attended and trips for members to various historical places. In February, 45 members and friends went out to Hardwick Hall, the fine house 'more glass than wall' built by one of history's female stalwarts Bess of Hardwick.

They were met at the station by Wagonettes and after the tour of the hall were back in Sheffield for 7pm.

Maybe Margaret joined Robert on the excursion, but more likely she stayed in their cosy cottage and waited for his return, as by then she was almost eight months pregnant.

Greenhill Manor Sheffield Local Studies Library

Greenhill village pump Author

8

3

A little Douglas

Randolph Robert Osborne Douglas made his appearance on March 31st 1895. More than likely it would have been at home in their Greenhill cottage, with Robert waiting nervously downstairs until he heard he had a son.

That same year the first screens flickered into life as the Lumière Brothers initiated the birth of the cinema and the Empire Theatre, Sheffield, later to play such a big part in Randolph's life, raised its curtain for the first time.

The Oscar Wilde trials were in the news and the rapidly growing town of Sheffield had lately been promoted to a city.

It was also the year that Houdini began to grow into the persona he would become famous for. The determined and driven young Harry had moved on from the vaudeville acts and wildman routine that was paying the bills. Instead he had perfected a handcuff act and began orchestrating challenges to escape, from police cuffs and cells. It was the birth of the Handcuff King.

Randolph's early years were busy ones for the nearby newly classed 'city' of Sheffield. Another theatre, the Lyceum, opened in 1897. It was a new venture after the popular Stacey's Theatre had burned to the ground four years earlier. Robert and Margaret had been sad to see the place destroyed. They had enjoyed visits there just before their marriage, seeing such things as The Fatal Beauty Company. But disaster had struck when a fire lit on stage in one of the productions had got out of hand and sealed the fate of the old place. In its stead, there was the new Lyceum.

And there was a flurry of excitement the same year as Queen Victoria visited Sheffield on May 21st to open the grand new town hall. Perhaps the little two-year-old was amongst the huge crowd, peeking out at all the noise and bustle from his mother's arms as the royal carriage drew up outside the ornate gates.

A programme for Stacey's Theatre

Private collection

9

If he was, he would have witnessed his first piece of stagecraft and illusion.

When the old Queen officially opened the building, it seemed like magic. She merely pressed a button in her hand - and the fine metal gates swung open. But what appeared like an early version of remote control was a trick worthy of a magician.

The button did not open the gates at all. What it did do was light up an electric bulb inside the Town Hall. When this bulb went on it was the cue for people hidden from view to pull open the gates the old fashioned, manual way, but it looked as if they swung apart by themselves. Delightfully theatrical misdirection.

Queen Victoria opening the Town Hall on May 21st 1897
Courtesy Sheffield Newspapers

This was all just about two months after Randolph's second birthday and to commemorate the event, Robert had given his son a silver spoon. At the top were images of a young and old Victoria, and the date 1837. Halfway down was the date 1897; 60 years of her reign remembered. Randolph's name adorned the front and 'March 31st', his birthday, was written on the back, together with the year. The spoon was made by the firm William Hutton and Sons Ltd, of West Street Sheffield, renowned for arts and crafts silverware and where his father was perhaps working at the time.

It was an exciting time to be born into, a time of new wonders and inventions, when the giants of the age were pushing the bounds of knowledge ever further at an incredible rate. But there was still time for pleasure, with theatre and the arts an important part of life. People loved the music halls, the excitement of footlights brightening the stage, illuminating a world that felt a million miles away from the mills and factories. They loved the larger than life acts that trod the boards.

And in America, the audiences were starting to take notice of one of these acts. A new face appeared on the front page of the Chicago Journal as Harry Houdini amazed the police by escaping with ease from their best handcuffs.

The year after this publicity-generating feat, in 1900, Houdini crossed the ocean to conquer new ground. In June he set foot in England, performing his crowd pleasing escape act in London.

His brother Theo 'Hardeen' got in on the act too, even touring on his own, after Harry's invitation and instruction.

The Empire Theatre, Charles Street, Sheffield

By 1901, a year subdued by the death of Queen Victoria, but enjoying the pomp of a King's coronation, the Sheffield Empire was booming. Acts such as George Lockhart and his Performing Elephants amazed the crowds who poured through the door of the theatre with its exotic minarets.

Another act that amazed them was Houdini's brother - Theo Hardeen played there on July 29th.

Sheffield Newspapers Library Archives

Away from the bustle of the city centre, in leafy Greenhill, Randolph's parents would most probably have seen the Empire advert as they perused the newspaper. But even if they were intrigued, it was hard to get out to the theatre so much with an active six-year-old to look after.

He was a curious boy, and it was a fascinating and creative home for a child to begin his life and explore. His mother still painted and his father would work at

home sometimes on his silversmithing, carefully creating sculptural forms for the cups and trophies he produced

Little Randolph was fascinated by his father's workshop. He looked up at the model hands dangling above in the shadows below the shelf - they always scared him a little. But he loved to play with the tools, to watch the way his father created people and animals with a touch of his knife or a sweep of his pencil. He loved the smell of the polish and clay and the sketches pinned along the walls. They stirred in him his own creativity. It was a happy time

Robert Douglas in 1904   Private collection   in this first house of wonders.

11

It was a summer afternoon The sun was a little too warm and the high collar was sticking into Randolph's neck.

They had all dressed up a little for the photo, father in his best straw boater and mother in one of her finest lace collars and fancy hats. Aunt Katherine, who was also living at the Greenhill house, joined them, and had put flowers in her dress front for the occasion. The best crockery and lace tablecloth had been brought from the house after the table and chairs were set out in readiness, by the ferns.

Randolph sat as his mother's feet and looked pensively out as the person with the camera took the shot. The sound of tea splashing into cups and the twitter of birdsong filled his ears.

He didn't want to dirty his kilt and it was a little cold on the floor, even with the rug to sit on. But he loved wearing his Scottish clothes with the Douglas tartan, though they were a bit itchy. He loved the little sporran with its lions crest and the hat with its badge. He liked the big buttons on the sleeves and pocket..

The tartan made him think of all the Douglas clan before him and the stories his father entranced him with. Tales of his ancestry. Stories of a warrior's heart, a terrible shipwreck and a new start in a foreign land.

A sedate family scene at Yew House. Randolph in his Scottish outfit, Margaret in one of her best hats, Robert in his boater and Katherine with flowers in her dress front   Private collection

The heart was there on his cap badge, crowned and winged. The Douglas crest.

  He had seen it, too, on the brooch his father had made for his mother before they were wed, with her initials MHO at the bottom and the Douglas clan motto 'Forward" in an eggshell blue banner at the top.

  He could remember the story very well.

An earlier member of the Douglas clan, Sir James, was a lifelong friend of the famous Scotsman, Robert the Bruce. On his deathbed, Robert requested, as he could not go on a crusade, that they should take his heart to the Holy Land instead.

Margaret's Douglas crest brooch
Private collection

  'Good Sir James' took the heart on crusade, in a leaden casket, to follow his friend's dying wish. But James had died himself carrying it. The heart in the Douglas crest was a reminder of this long dead man and his deed.

  It was an exciting tale that seemed a world away from the sedate tea on the lawn. Randolph smiled up at his mother, adjusted his position a little, then fell into a reverie again.

Another photo session, this time with relatives. Again Randolph is wearing his outfit with the Douglas tartan kilt. Private collection

This time his inner gaze was over a stormy sea. It was a terrible scene. He could picture his lost relatives trying to scramble from the waves into little wooden lifeboats as the cold waters sucked at their heavy clothes, pulling them under. He shuddered in spite of the sun.

It had been on June 26 1857.

His grandfather's brothers Thomas, Alex, John, Peter George and William, had left Scotland with their father, James, their mother, Lillie and an aunt. They were going to join their other brother, James, already living in Canada. His grandfather Robert had stayed in Edinburgh to look after his wine selling business.

They had boarded the ship 'John McKenzie' at the Clyde on May 18th, full of hope of a better life in a new world. On the same vessel were 250 or so other Scottish folk following the same dream.

After a long and uncomfortable voyage, they had arrived at Quebec City.

But the journey was not over. They boarded another ship for the last leg of the voyage, a steamer named 'Montreal', bound for the city of the same name, 180 miles up the St. Lawrence River. They left Quebec about four in the evening

James Douglas, (son of the James which the people drowned were going to join in Canada), in 1913
Private collection

on June 26th, and were just twelve miles out when a dreaded shout went up - "Fire!"

The blaze was discovered in the wooden panelling around the ship's boiler. The crew fought madly to stop the flames and sparks igniting the rest of the vessel. But it was no use. The only hope was to ride the flaming ship up to shore and beach her, letting the souls aboard flee to land.

But the plan failed. Instead, the ship struck a rock and was stuck fast, just 800 feet from the shore. Robert, Lillie and their children were forced on deck by flames and smoke and gazed around at their fate with all the other panicking passengers. They clung to each other in terror.

With a fiery death or a watery chance of life to choose from, the people took the latter, and jumped. But some had felt the pain of being burned before they could be made to dare the terrible leap into the waves. And some were burned to death before they had the chance.

For those who had jumped, just two lifeboats were to be had, and they were quickly overfull and swamped. But if they had managed to curb their panic and had not swamped the boats, causing them to sink, some more people may have lived.

For just half a mile ahead of this tragedy was another ship, the 'Napoleon' also full of emigrants and heading for Montreal. The crew had seen the flames and the captain turned her around to assist.

They dropped a large boat in the water to pick up the cold and wretched survivors. But in the twenty minutes it had taken for this act of rescue, 200 people had already drowned. Amongst the dead were all Randolph's relatives - except one. William, the youngest at just ten years or so old, had survived.

Randolph's father had told him the sad story in hushed tones; told him of how little William had joined his grieving older brother at last. Randolph wondered how he would have felt, a small boy alone in a strange land, all your kinfolk lost to the sea.

He remembered the part about William's mother Lillie loosing her grip of the rescue boat her son was in, and being plunged down to the depths by the weight of the family fortune- gold nuggets sewn into the hem of her skirt. He felt the hem of his mother's skirt brushing softly against his back and snuggled in a little closer. He would hate to lose her.

Robert had drawn a sketch of his wife that Randolph liked to look at. He had captured her heavy Pre-Raphaelite lids and delicate neck, her hair swept up into a bun.

What the six-year-old didn't know just yet was that this delicate beauty was expecting again. For 1901 was a year later marked by the arrival of another little Douglas, Randolph's sister Margaret, who was born on November 27th.

Family tradition says that she came into the world at the old Greenhill Hall, where her father was working and not in the home of her parents just opposite. It would certainly have been a grander entrance.

But wherever her life began, she was welcomed into the arms of her mother, father and big brother Randolph.

Sketch of Margaret, by Robert Private collection

Randolph, Margaret and their mother

Private Collection

4
A curious eye

The fine silver Art Nouveau style clips held their mother's lace shawl in place as she settled down for another family photo. Maybe Robert had crafted them at Huttons as a gift, and she was wearing them especially. Randolph's little sister Margaret perched on a table and wondered what all the fuss was about, quizzically open mouthed as she took in the unfamiliar surroundings of the portrait studio at 46 Pinstone Street, Sheffield. Randolph himself stood in-between the two, looking surprisingly protective for such a little boy.

But he was already growing up. He was intelligent, gentle and extremely curious. He liked collecting, liked to find out about things. His father encouraged this wonder and enthusiasm, glad his son was gifted with creativity. Randolph enjoyed sketching and from an early age began to keep notebooks of drawings and ideas. In one is the sketch of Greenhill Hall, drawn perhaps whilst sitting atop the little wall along the front of their house opposite, book balanced on his knee and a pot of ink by his side.

He liked to draw old buildings and had a great eye for detail. As they left the photographic studio and came out into the noisy street, he looked at the fine old St Paul's church opposite. He took in the soaring clocktower of the town hall, topped by Vulcan, and the frontage, covered in a stone frieze of figures representing the various city industries. Everywhere were elegant buildings, with wonderful carvings. It was a proud and booming city. The bustle of carts and people seemed a little overwhelming after the quiet Greenhill village. There was so much to see.

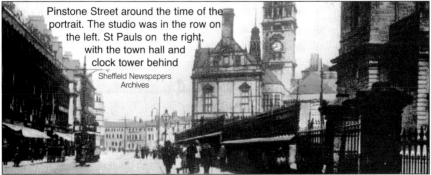

Pinstone Street around the time of the portrait. The studio was in the row on the left. St Pauls on the right, with the town hall and clock tower behind
Sheffield Newspapers Archives

And with his young mind full of ideas and in search of wonders, it is easy to imagine that Robert and Margaret would have had trouble keeping their son away from the draw of the theatre - the enchanted world of magic and spectacle.

The ornate and eastern looking Empire Theatre was just a couple of streets away from the photo studio. It stood on the corner with Charles Street, an enticing palace of varieties.

To a small boy the advertisements for the Empire Theatre, for acts like Captain Woods Sea Lions and Seals, or Chung Ling Soo, the famous 'Chinese' magician were probably irresistible.

Some of the fine work by Robert. S. Douglas
Private Collection

And the newspapers were filled too, with intriguing adverts and reports concerning the amazing American, who could escape from any set of handcuffs - Houdini.

The title filled Randolph with a sense of excitement- such an exotic sounding name. The man of mystery was visiting England again, doing a tour of the English provinces, and was playing Blackburn in October 1902.

A report of this appearance was pasted carefully into young Randolph's scrapbook. Did the seven year old get taken on a trip to see the master mystifier?

AN EPISODE IN HOUDINI'S LIFE.

Star, Blackburn, England, Saturday, Oct. 25, 1902.

MANACLED BY A STRONG MAN.
TRUSSED TILL MIDNIGHT.

Unparalleled Scenes at the Palace Theatre.

Never in the history of Blackburn or music hall life has there been witnessed so remarkable a scene as occurred last night. Houdini, the Handcuff King, and Mr. Hodgson, principal of the School of Physical Culture, provided a big sensation for the patrons of the Palace Theatre, Blackburn.

Houdini, who has been appearing at the Palace during the week, claims to be able to release himself from any of the regulation shackles or irons used by the police of Europe or America,

Did he carefully trim out the report at the time, type it up after seeing the event, or was he even sent the account later by the man himself?

An account of Houdini's Blackburn appearance in 1902, from Randolph's scrapbook
Buxton Museum and Art Gallery

18

It was the night a man called Hodgson had taken up Houdini's offer of £25 to any challenger who had handcuffs he could not escape from. Hodgson trussed Houdini so tight with chains and cuffs (which Houdini later declared had been plugged), that the exhausted escapologist almost didn't escape at all.

But when he did, over an hour later, he had ripped his clothes and torn chunks of flesh from his arms. He bore the scars for the rest of his life.

Whether little Randolph witnessed this evening of near failure first hand is open to conjecture, but he was certainly taking notice of Houdini and following, his escapades.

He was storing them away in his mind and turning them into future adventures for his budding alter ego. Later they became springboards for his imagination as he drew himself into these same escapades in his sketchbooks.

Randolph in the garden at the family home in Greenhill
Private Collection

As Randolph began to feed his dreams, Houdini was already following his, and they took him far and wide - even to Russia.

In 1903 he was there, baffling the Russian police by escaping from a Siberian transport cell used for transporting prisoners. He didn't get out through the door by opening the locks, instead he had seen that the weak spot was the floor of the carette and smuggled tools in to saw through the bottom and make his escape.

Ingenious and exciting episodes and a larger than life personality- Houdini was a perfect hero for a romantic child like Randolph.

In December, as 1903 came to a close, the first powered flight by the Wright brothers amazed the world. No doubt Randolph was impressed. But he didn't want to be an aviator, he was beginning to think about a slightly more down to earth occupation - escapologist.

And it was in 1904 that he had a perfect chance to see his role model. Houdini visited the Empire Theatre in Sheffield twice that year.

PRISON BREAKING EXTRAORDINARY
HOUDINI ESCAPES FROM A TRIPLE LOCKED CELL

Harry Houdini the world-famous prison breaker and handcuff expert, who is this week performing at the Empire Palace of Varieties, was yesterday given an opportunity of showing his skill in the police cells at Water Lane. He presented himself to the Chief Constable with the idea of arranging a private display during the week, but Commander Scott unexpectedly asked him to try what he could do at once. He was marched off to the cells on the upper corridor and was stripped of the whole of his clothes, which were placed in an adjoining cell, the door of which was then triple-locked with a master key. The apartment in which he was to be locked - the redoubtable one, by the way, in which Charles Peace was placed after his apprehension - was then thoroughly searched and the door was triple locked upon Houdini. At the artiste's request the whole of the cells on the corridor were also locked and the iron gate at the foot of the steps which is secured with a seven-lever lock, was secured. Houdini, previous to being incarcerated, asked that if he was not out in twenty minutes the door should be opened for him, but to the surprise of the Chief Constable and the few other people present, the prison breaker joined the party on the bottom corridor exactly five minutes after he had been left. In this marvellously short space of time he had got out of the cell, opened the apartment where his clothes were secured, dressed himself with the exception of his collar and tie, unfastened the remaining cells in the row and burst open the iron gate. Before he left the prison Houdini was presented with the following certificate:

"This is to certify that Mr Harry Houdini was this day stripped stark naked and locked in the cell which once contained Charlie Peace. The cell was searched and triple-locked, but Mr. Houdini released himself and re-dressed in five minutes, having also opened the iron gate of the corridor.

Charles J. Scott, Commander (R.N)
Chief Constable, Sheffield.
Witness to the foregoing feat,
George H. Barker (Deputy Chief Constable)"

Houdini, seen by a Sheffield Daily Independent representative last night, said that the cells were remarkably good ones, and as difficult as any he had been locked up in in England....This Sheffield cell, he remarked, was the 59th he had escaped from in the course of his travels... "In Birmingham," he added. "I wanted them to lock me up but they would not do so. I said to the Chief Constable. Then I will do something for which I shall be locked up and then escape. He told me, however, that if I did I would get six months for prison breaking."...

At the Empire last night Houdini freed himself from several pairs of handcuffs more than one pair of which were of peculiar design and won enthusiastic applause from a crowded house.

Sheffield and Rotherham Independent, January 20, 1904, page 8

20

5
On stage with Dink

T he crowds were crushing in under the filigree arches of the Empire Theatre, everyone determined to secure their ticket for the Saturday matinee. Arms were thrust out, waving to pay and the buzz of excited conversation filled the foyer. It seemed most of Sheffield wanted the chance to see Harry Houdini in January 1904. And with his knack for drumming up publicity, Houdini had surely hit the jackpot.

A few days earlier, he had caused a stir with his amazing escape from the police cell at Water Lane that had once held the notorious Sheffield murderer Charlie Peace. It was a publicity stunt that Houdini had used to good effect in other towns and cities- go to the police station and declare an escape from their best lock-ups.

In Sheffield, on January 19, Houdini had presented himself to the Chief Constable, Commander Scott. He was 'marched off to cells on the upper corridor' and was 'stripped of the whole of his clothes', which were placed in an adjoining cell, the door of which was then triple-locked with a master key. He was then triple-locked in the murderer's former cell and an iron gate on the steps was secured. Of course Houdini was out through the lot in a matter of minutes.

Houdini began his Sheffield Empire run on the 16th, sharing the bill with the delightful sounding

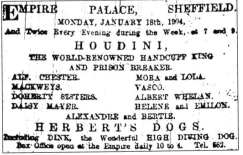

'Herberts Dogs, including Dink, the wonderful high diving dog'.

Now, the police cell stunt having grabbed column inches and a challenge to escape a straitjacket or pay a £50 forfeit filling the latest edition of the local newspaper, crowds were flocking in. The Empire ads for the show declared: 'thousands turned away nightly!' owing to 'huge success.'

Sheffield Independent ads, January 1904   21

The manager had added an extra matinee and the audience was arriving in droves, ready to see the great Houdini take up the challenge. It had been made by George Wale, a one time attendant at the Wadsley Asylum, who knew how to 'thoroughly strap any man in."

It was likely that Houdini had pre-arranged the stunt with Wale, as this was his usual pattern when he had a challenge.

And having a man from the insane asylum do the deed was much more evocative. Houdini was always conscious of getting the most out of publicity and knew how to set up a good story for the press. And they obliged.

Again it is supposition that nine-year-old Randolph was one of the eager throng taken along to the Empire that week. Though how could he have resisted if he had seen the enticing ads and articles in the newspaper?

One can imagine his father Robert mulling over headlines as he sucked on his pipe, with Randolph straining for a better view of the intruiging tales of challenge on the other pages. They must have seen or heard of Houdini's daring escape from the murderer's cell.

It was such a hyped-up event that this and the Empire shows were surely a great topic of conversation. And perhaps Robert too was taken with the tales of illusion and escape. He always liked to entertain and intrigue a little himself, with a touch of magic sprinkled into family life.

He was fond of sending cards and messages in mirror writing. To read the words, they had to put be put up to a mirror to reverse them. Other members of the Douglas family followed Robert's example. It was like a secret language for them to discover, a novel and delightful thing to do.

> **THE EMPIRE.**
> **THE EXTRAORDINARY CHALLENGE TO HOUDINI.**
> As announced in the "Daily Independent" the other day, Houdini, the jail breaker and handcuff king, has accepted a novel challenge, and the event has to be decided at a matinee to be held at the Empire this afternoon. The following are the terms of the challenge, and the acceptance of the same:—
>   "Sheffield, Jan. 21. 1904.
> "Mr. Harry Houdini, Empire Theatre, Sheffield,
> "Dear Sir,—Having in my possession a strait jacket that was in former years used to restrain the murderous insane, but which has now been abolished as being brutal, I would like to strap you in it. to test your escaping abilities. Having been nearly twenty years (20) official attendant of the South Yorkshire Insane Asylum, I know how to thoroughly strap any man in."
>   "(Signed)   GEORGE WALE."
> "No. 1, Shepperson road."
> Houdini accepts this challenge for Saturday matinee. If he fails to release himself in less than 25 minutes he forfeits £25, and if he cannot release himself he forfeits £50, the money to be paid over to the Lord Mayor's fund for the unemployed.

> "Mr. Harry Houdini, Empire Theatre, Sheffield,
> "Dear Sir,—Having in my possession a strait jacket that was in former years used to restrain the murderous insane, but which has now been abolished as being brutal, I would like to strap you in it. to test your escaping abilities. Having been nearly twenty years (20) official attendant of the South Yorkshire Insane Asylum, I know how to thoroughly strap any man in."
>   "(Signed)   GEORGE WALE."
> "No. 1, Shepperson road."
> Houdini accepts this challenge for Saturday matinee. If he fails to release himself in less than 25 minutes he forfeits £25, and if he cannot release himself he forfeits £50, the money to be paid over to the Lord Mayor's fund for the unemployed.

Two articles about Houdini's Empire challenge, January 1904 Sheffield and Rotherham Independent

A postcard with mirror writing from Robert to his daughter Margaret on February 24, 1904 Private collection

Houdini stepped onto the stage of the Empire to take up his challenge. He was by now used to escaping from a strait-jacket in full view of his audience. It was his brother Hardeen who had suggested this change to the act, which before had seen Houdini's struggle's being done out of view in a little 'ghost house' tent. Now they could all see him as he pushed up his elbows, thrashed around like a madman to get his arms over his head and in front of his body and undid buckles with his teeth. The effort looked, and was, exhausting. It is bizarre to think that the restraint, invented around 1770 by a French upholsterer at an asylum near Paris, ended up as the highlight of a show, with a willing victim putting himself through the ordeal. But the audience lapped it up.

As well as this feat Houdini escaped from handcuffs, 'many of which were of a 'peculiar design' and the Empire's capacity crowd applauded with enthusiasm. High tension escapes, a high-diving French poodle - it was a great show. And if Randolph was there, he would have loved it.

Houdini must have been satisfied with his success at Sheffield too, for in late April he was back there again, playing the Empire Theatre a week before the bizarre sounding act of 'Fred Karno's Mammoth Troupe of Speechless Comedians' trod the boards. There were certainly some fabulous entertainments to divert the masses in Sheffield's Empire. Staley's novelty Transformation Company were another act whose name sets the imagination wandering and also, in September 1904, Chung Ling Soo, the famous 'Chinese' conjuror amazed the crowds.

But in April it was Houdni's turn, and he returned with an even bigger reputation of being the Handcuff King than before, after having made headlines all over England in March. He was almost defeated by a challenge from newspaper the 'Daily Mirror'.

It was on his continuing UK tour, in London's Hippodrome on March 17, that the 'Mirror Cuffs' escapade took place. The handcuffs the 'Daily Mirror' challenged Houdini to escape from kept him captive for more than an hour, but after cutting off his coat, and working furiously, he was finally free.

The audience were so delighted he was carried shoulder high by some of them. As a token of his success the newspaper presented Houdini with the cuffs and a silver replica of them. The publicity generated for both Houdini and the 'Daily Mirror had been immense and it is thought by some that the whole thing had been yet another elaborate publicity stunt orchestrated by Houdini in collaboration with the 'Mirror'.

Whatever the truth, it sealed Houdini's reputation and no doubt encouraged more curious readers to catch his next act. The Empire in Sheffield would have been crowded that April. And Randolph was quite possibly amongst the sea of bodies filing in to their seats, holding on to his father's arm so they didn't get parted and impatient to see the man of the moment. It is tempting to think so.

If he was there, at the second house on the Friday night, he would have seen Houdini challenged by another local 'handcuff king,' a lad named Tom Sharp. He locked Houdini into an extraordinary set of cuffs that took an hour to escape from. And it would have been even more exciting if he had been there on Saturday. A representitive of Sharp came on stage, and the cuffs he gave to Houdini that night were tampered with. Houdini was outraged and recognised him as a man named Brown, who had written letters asking him for information, with a view of confronting and exposing any handcuff king. He said that if Houdini would help him he would not interfere with him. 'I wrote and told him,' said Houdini, 'that I would have nothing to do with a man who tried to take away the bread and butter from another man, I have letters from this man which I will fetch and read at the second house.' After a pause of a second or two, Houdini shouted excitedly, 'No, I shall fetch them now and you shall see.'

With this Houdini rushed off the stage and out into the street, hatless, just as he had appeared on the stage. During the time he was away there was an excited buzz of conversation all around the house and the orchestra began to play.

Then Houdini marched on the stage with a large pile of letters in a correspondence rack, and he and his wife and assistant began to look for the letters. Turning to Brown, Houdini said. 'Did you write these letters or did you not. If not, I'm a liar. If you did you're a ---' (but Houdini did not finish this part of the sentence). The man still denied it, but Houdini did the challenge and escaped from his cuffs anyhow.

At the next house that night there was not even standing room left. And there was even more trouble for Houdini, when another young man brought on unusual cuffs for Houdini to escape from. He was found to be the son of a man named Inspector Brookes, and the cuffs were non-regulation ones his father claimed he had invented, a style which Houdini came to call Scotland Yard Adjustables. But Houdini still opened them in less than three minutes, and young Brookes was booed. To get his own back, Houdini challenged Inspector Brooke to escape from the Sheffield police cells as he had done - and get £100 reward. Not surprisingly, Brookes did not take up the challenge.

Sheffield continued to attract some of the top acts in 1905. Chung Ling Soo was back in August, and at the city's other grand theatre, The Lyceum, the great Shakespearian actor Sir Henry Irving began his farewell tour in October.

Just a week after leaving Sheffield Irving was dead, collapsing at his hotel in Bradford two hours after stepping from the stage of the Theatre Royal.

Illness also stalked the Douglas household that year. Little Margaret was ill with rheumatic fever. It was a worrying time and though she survived, the fever left her too weak to ever go to school. Instead she was taught at home by a governess. No doubt her mother and her Aunt Katherine, who was sharing the family home, would have helped her with her education too. And perhaps her big brother Randolph entertained her with his dreams and tales of his future career in Houdini's footsteps.

Years later, Randolph's life would be touched by the effects of having had rheumatic fever himself, but whether he was ill with it at the same time as Margaret is hard to know. Certainly Greenhill School, which Randolph would more than likely have attended unless he too had a governess, was a place where fever was at times rife. The school opened just three months after Robert and Margaret married, with 16 male pupils and 14 females. Maybe Randolph was one of the boys who attended a few years later. If he was at the school he would have had arithmetic at 8.35am and drawing at 9.40am every thursday.

From the school it was a short walk around the corner back home to Yew House. If he had shouted from the yard his mother would have heard him from their little garden.

At the school there were periodic scarlet fever outbreaks. This illness often preceeds or is linked to rheumatic fever, so the school could have been a source of infection. Conditions at the school in cold weather were not too good for a child's health either, with room temperature down to just $42^{\circ}F$ ($5\ ^{\circ}C$). Whether Randolph attended the school or not, it was a major landmark in the village, and later in his role as an aspiring escapologist.

Greenhill School in 1910
Sheffield Local Studies Library

Randolph and his family in 1907. He wears a rose in his buttonhole

Private collection

6
The Great Randolph

The Living Mummy. The only act of its kind in the world. A great claim, but then Randolph didn't dream small dreams. It wasn't a bad idea, he mused as he put down his pencil and wiped the graphite from the side of his hand. He would be wrapped in bandages like the old Egyptian kings and padlocked into a painted mummy case. He could see the set in his mind's eye. The Death Chamber. Some old jars and bowls like the ones found in the tombs, a few columns for atmosphere and of course a skeleton to add a touch of danger.

When he escaped the crowd would go wild, the way they did for Houdini.

In 1906, back in New York, Houdini was thrilling those crowds with his latest stunts. Not content with just escaping from handcuffs on stage, he had progressed to jumping off a bridge into a swirling river locked in them.

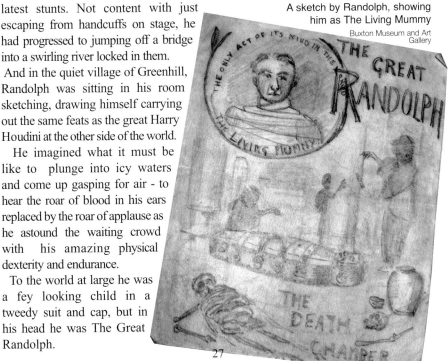

A sketch by Randolph, showing him as The Living Mummy

Buxton Museum and Art Gallery

And in the quiet village of Greenhill, Randolph was sitting in his room sketching, drawing himself carrying out the same feats as the great Harry Houdini at the other side of the world.

He imagined what it must be like to plunge into icy waters and come up gasping for air - to hear the roar of blood in his ears replaced by the roar of applause as he astound the waiting crowd with his amazing physical dexterity and endurance.

To the world at large he was a fey looking child in a tweedy suit and cap, but in his head he was The Great Randolph.

27

A drawing by Randolph, showing him in various scenes, carrying out feats based on those of Houdini Buxton Museum and Art Gallery

In this early career of dreams young Randolph did many fantastic escapes and came up with remarkable and sometimes gruesome ideas. As well as recreating Houdini's exploits he visualised himself doing the same amazing crowd pulling acts himself, as The Great Randolph. He sketched some of the most daring in a characterful composite painting, a theatrical style advertisement for his exploits. Carefully printing in his best handwriting, he wrote descriptions around each of the little scenes.

First he sketched his own version of a bridge jump, not in America but in the place of his family roots - Scotland. The Forth Railway Bridge.
His mind created the scene as he dipped his pen into the ink and neatly formed the words; crowds peered up as he plunged from the structure trussed, not in handcuffs, but a full length straitjacket secured with trailing chains. A newspaper reporter scribbled excitedly to catch the moment, just like when they wrote about Houdini; "Daring dive from the Forth Bridge. Fastened in a strait-jacket Randolph dived into the icy waters of the river Forth. Daily Mail- Jan 10th 1906".

Next was 'Randolph in Russia' a scene showing his escape, dated 29th March 1907, from a 'prison' van in Moscow, echoing Houdini's 1903 escape. He drew himself about to enter the van, shackled in locks and chains, with the uniformed guards standing escort.

Randolph warmed to his theme and added more scenes of his imagined successes. He painted himself enclosed within a glass case, bent over and manacled. It was 'The airtight glass box Pittsburgh' Getting out of this fix of course proved no problem for our daydreaming hero, who 'escaped in $3^{1/2}$ minutes without leaving a trace of his escape and without scratching the glass in any way...'

Next he pictured himself in America- with the USA mail pouch test. 'Randolph made his escape from our latest mail pouch fitted with our rotary lock. After being thoroughly searched Randolph escaped in less than 2 minutes. Police Gazette.'

By this he drew what looks like a version of the Mirror Cuffs.
Then, tracing over his earlier pencil lines with an ink pen, Randolph drew the largest central scene. He put a large and uncomfortable looking padlock around his throat and two locks holding heavy looking shackles around his ankles. In front of this self portrait of The Great Randolph is an evocative image of bare-chested workmen sealing the rather scared-looking escapologist, wearing a dinner suit and bow tie (as Houdini often did on stage) into a large boiler. The heat leaps off the page, conjured up by strokes of red watercolour reflecting off the metal.

'Riverside Boiler Co Boston Mass'. Rivetted in a hot water boiler by expearenced [sic] mechanic. This test took Randolph over 70 minutes to make his escape and to the astonishment of the mechanic and crowd Randolph...'

What it was that he decided had astonished them we'll never know. His ink ran out and he was off to some new pursuit, distracted by another idea, or perhaps it was just dinnertime.

A few of the
locks
Randolph
collected
Private collection

Birchinlee - 'Tin Town'.
Prof. Brian Robinson

Ashopton. The village now lies under the reservoir
Prof. Brian Robinson

7
A fondness for locks

The School of Art (now demolished)
Pawson and Brailsford's Guide to Sheffield

Robert Strachan Douglas had busy years too in 1906 and 1907. Not producing imaginary escape act plans, but works of art, with his silversmithing skills. He worked at a few different prestigious Sheffield firms, as well as Huttons. But wherever it was, he had plenty to do.

By November 13th 1906 he had quit from his role of librarian for the Artcrafts Guild 'due to pressure of work.' He still attended many meetings and gave lectures though, some of which were held at the School of Art on Arundel Street near Sheffield city centre. He also designed and made a badge for the Artcrafts Guild members to wear. The fine, delicate touch and attention to detail in his work would later be a key in his son's work too.

Though Robert's work was pressing, when he arrived at his job, he always made sure he posted his wife Margaret a love letter, which arrived home at Greenhill by lunchtime. If he ever went away for longer, he wrote tender letters back home. When he had to go back to Scotland for the funeral of a distant relative, he wrote, *"...I have found time to go shopping for our darlings. I have bought a doll for Marguerite and a crocodile for Randolph."*

It must have been a happy and loving home Randolph and Margaret were growing up in. And for Robert's delicate and artistic wife it was a secure environment too, with her parents living nearby and her sister Kitty to share the days and events, as well as the family home.

Time passed, and The Artcrafts Guild was blossoming. On July 6 1907 the members and some of their families, perhaps including Randolph, took a trip out to Birchinlee in Derbyshire. The village had been created to house the workers building a huge new dam and reservoir, together with their families. It was fondly nicknamed 'tin town.' The members went out there in 'dragonettes' from local coach firm Tomlinsons. It cost 3/- (around 15p) with tea at the Ashopton Inn for 1/- extra.

The Hippodrome in later years, as a cinema *Sheffield Newspapers*

Back in Sheffield city centre, a new theatre, the Hippodrome, opened on Cambridge Street that year. Yet another theatre didn't seem to diminish the draw of the Empire. Acts were still coming to the 'Palace of Varieties' in their many forms and guises.

In January 1908 Chung Ling Soo was back. His friend Harry Houdini, however was in St Louis USA, introducing a daring new act - the milk can escape. He had needed a new idea to revitalise his act and this was certainly impressive. The milk can was filled with water. Next Houdini squeezed down into it, then the lid was padlocked on. There was a real danger of drowning with this spectacular act and it was the sense of danger that added to its success. The crowd counted for what seemed an endless and impossible amount of time for anyone to hold their breath, before Houdini reappeared, dripping wet and triumphant.

1909 at the Empire Palace saw yet more entertaining and intriguing names treading the boards - probably very heavily in the case of De Gracias Elephants who appeared in March. They were billed as ' enthusiastic cricketers and footballers.'

And there was spectacle other than in the theatre when another Royal visit entertained the crowds in April. The Prince of Wales visited Sheffield with his Princess. They were driven around in a splendid carriage, again from Tomlinsons. Driving this was a man Randolph and his family would later meet, for he was the father of Harriet (Hetty) Bown, Randolph's future wife.

The Prince of Wales and his wife visit in 1909 and are driven in a Tomlinsons carriage by , the father of Hetty Bown, Randolph's future wife *Sheffield Newspapers*

Always looking for a new challenge, Harry Houdini had bought himself one of the new-fangled flying machines, a Voisin. In November 1909 he tested it out

The plane was little more than a glorified box kite with pram-like wheels. Taking to the air in such a flimsy creation required a lot of nerve, But Houdini was never short of that.

If Randolph could have got up close to Houdini's splendid new plaything he would have been fascinated by how a mass of wood and wire was coaxed into a shape capable of flight.

A torn drawing of Randolph's challenge
Buxton Museum and Art Gallery

THE GREAT RANDOLPH
PRESENTING HIS WONDERFULL ESCAPE FROM A IRON CADDY. ~~~~~~~~~~~~~~~~~~~~
RANDOLPH. OFFERS £1000 TO ANYONE WHO CAN PRODUCE PADLOCKS. THAT CAN KEEP HIM IN THE CADDY MORE THAN 3. MINUTES. THIS CHALLENGE IS OPEN TO ALL. ~ ~~ .~~~
ANYONE IS INVITED TO BRING THEIR OWN PAD
H. Randolph

He always loved working out how things were put together

He was especially fond of figuring out locks. Every lock that came into his hands he would take apart and reassemble, making sure he understood just what made it click. An escapologist would need such skills and he was still on track with his dream.

He drew himself performing an escape from an 'iron caddy', with the same declaration Houdini had in his act- that anyone could bring their own handcuffs and he would be able to free himself from them. He even signed it 'H.Randolph.' If he kept trying to understand his locks - he was sure that handcuffs would be just as easy.

He began to collect locks and keys of every description and even designed some of his own. One of his drawings, proudly captioned 'my own invention' shows a detailed lock mechanism sketched out in pencil.

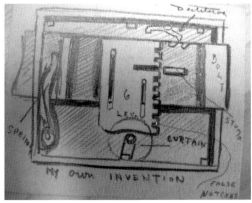

Randolph's drawing of a lock - his 'own invention'
Buxton Museum and Art Gallery

Another drawing shows a more precise representation of a locking mechanism for handcuffs, named after his imagined stage persona the 'Randin Double Action Cuff, 12 Lever.'

Locks became a great passion for the young Randolph, another sign of his determination to succeed as an escapologist, inspired by his hero Houdini.

Another thing a good escapologist had to know plenty about was tying knots and fixing ropes.

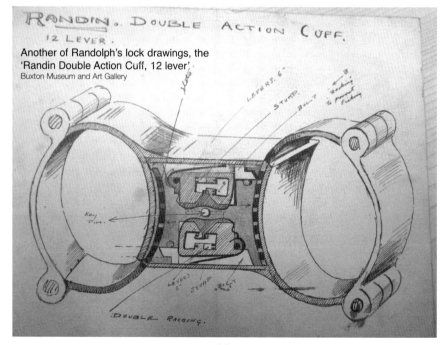

Little sister Margaret, whom the family fondly called Peggy, came in handy for that and his long suffering sibling was often bound up or tied to chairs in the name of research.

Randolph's bedroom at Yew House must have been full of the trappings of escapism, in more ways than one; there would be ideas and dreams in the form of sketches and press cuttings of Houdini, but also in a more literal sense in the form of locks, keys, ropes and handcuffs. He seems to have had the means to acquire all manner of locks, whether from indulgent relatives or from collecting his spending money. Sometimes they were quite expensive, but perhaps they were birthday presents and such as well. Robert always like to find appropriate and special gifts.

Two examples of Randolph's locks
Private collection

The fine silverwork Robert he doing would have earned him a good wage to support his wife and family, and his sister in law too. Peggy's governess, if it was not her Aunt Katherine, would also have had to be paid for. But the family still found money to feed their son's unusual passion.

Another of Randolph's lock drawings, the 'Randin Double Action Cuff, 12 lever'
Buxton Museum and Art Gallery

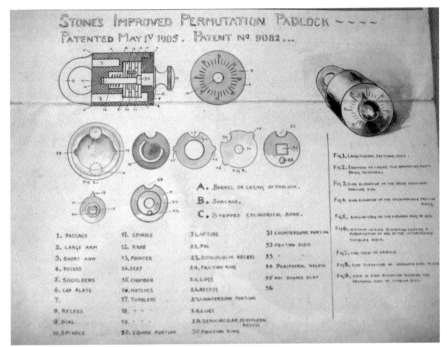

Randolph's drawing of The Stones Improved Permutation Padlock   Buxton Museum and Art Gallery

Margaret's parents, Randolph's grandparents, would more than likely have chipped in with governess fees if needed, to help educate the children. And it is quite likely they would also, like most grandparents, have indulged their little grandson, and aided him with his rather out of the ordinary interests. Though perhaps with all the publicity the enigmatic star Houdini was beginning to get, they could see the attraction for a young boy to emulate him. And getting to grips with intricate machinery, even in the form of locks and clocks, would be useful training for many trades.

Grandfather Henry George and grandmother Jane would have been in a good position to help out, with the family being such a wealthy one. The house they lived in at Woodside hamlet near the Chesterfield Road, reflected this. It was large, with the family having a servant and an apprentice living there too at one time. They had been successful and no doubt they wanted Randolph to be so too.

So perhaps they all settled down to be entertained after tea at Woodside a few times, by their talented grandson 'Randin' and his lovely assistant Miss Peggy.

Artistic people and entrepreneurs themselves, Randolph's family would perhaps enjoy the fact that their son was not hankering after the usual kind of profession. They would know and value the need for a dream in life, a need to rise above the mundane.

Watercolour paintings
by Randolph
The Magic Circle Archives

36

8
Unfinished portrait

It was a hard winter and 1910 got off to a bad beginning. January 28 saw eight inches of snow fall at Greenhill. It seemed an ill-starred year, as the school was hit with a major outbreak of scarlet fever which started on Valentine's Day and on February 24th the weather was still shocking, with impenetrable roads in an around the village.

Yew House was picture postcard pretty with the snowy trees and roads. But it was no happy fairy tale inside as the year unfolded in the Douglas household.

Randolph's mother Margaret was not well and the hard, cold winter was not helping. She always seemed so tired, and a bad cough was leaving her short of breath. She was never very hungry either.

Robert was worried, and when pneumonia was diagnosed he was afraid too. As if it was not bad enough, there was a complication. The illness had caused empyema, they said, which meant the lungs were full of discharge. Margaret would need an operation to relieve the problem by drainage.

Maybe Randolph and Peggy were told their mother was ill, at least Randolph, being an older 16 years. If not, they probably sensed there was something wrong. They would have seen that their mother was thinner and fatigued, less active and smiling than before. And when she went away for an operation they must have been sure she was ill.

An earlier photograph of Margaret
Private Collection

After the surgery, Margaret was back home and things seemed more hopeful. When she was a little more recovered from the operation, she carried on working on a self portrait she had been painting. It was of her standing by the piano, resting against a maroon chair near the window's drawn curtains. She was dressed in a white gown, and a golden yellow shawl, which showed off her reddish hair. Her delicate fingers were paused over the keys and she gazed down at the keyboard, as if contemplating the next tune.

They were all glad to see her happier in her work. But sadly it was to be only a short time of respite for poor Margaret.

Far away from snow and cold, at the other side of the world, Harry was flying again. In March the skies above Australia became another conquest for the irrepressible Houdini as he became the first man ever to fly there. He always liked to be first and best, his seemingly endless energy propelling him on to new and better feats, and more and more daring escapades. Aviation was a dangerous new pastime.

It was this determined spirit that shone through and inspired young Randolph as he practiced and practiced through the short winter and cold spring days.

And there were plenty of acts at the Empire if he needed any more inspiration for magical illusion. Chung Ling Soo was back for a run there on 25 April on one of his frequent visits. He probably didn't think much of the weather, as there were shocking amounts of rain that month.

Rain and cold. Back at Yew House, the damp weather was making Margaret's cough return with a vengeance. She seemed to be less herself and began to forget things. Randolph was worried. She was usually so happy about his birthday and this year she had not seemed so interested. Instead she seemed to be in a kind of dream. And she was still losing weight.

It must have been a hard time for Robert, trying to help Margaret, to keep working and providing, and also trying not to let his children be too worried about their mother. But by mid May, Margaret was no better. She had really been ailing since the operation. She had been flushed and tired, but more worryingly had been saying she felt responsible for the death of the King, and she feared she had lost her soul. She spent a lot of time standing by the window and seemed at a loss. The surgery seemed to have triggered off a breakdown, and as well as that, the doctors feared her weak state had led to tuberculosis. She needed to be taken into hospital.

So Margaret went through the door of Yew House with her doctor, away from Robert, Randolph, Peggy and Katherine. Robert feared she may be walking through it for the last time.

The place Margaret was taken was near Derby, at Mickleover, the most modern available. Robert wanted the best chance of any recovery for his wife, to help settle her thoughts again. But whilst there it was indeed found to be TB afflicting Margaret - and her mind was more disturbed too. Whose would not be, when they found they had the dreaded disease that people of all ages and class feared. The stealer of so many lives as *'day by day and grain by grain the mortal part withers away.'*

In the arts, such as the opera, TB was seen by some as a romantic affliction, an aesthetic fading of life to the infinite. But the reality was a sad and slow decline.

Robert and Katherine, looked after Randolph and Peggy, gently helping them adjust to their mother being away from the family home. Aunt Katherine was like a second mother, and with Margaret been so tired, ill and distracted for months, even before the hospital, the children may have started looking to her for support anyhow.

There were probably a few things going on to provide a distraction or two to take their minds off things a while. Maybe a trip to a show cheered Randolph a little. The theatre usually took him out of himself into a world of illusion and magic that was less harsh than the realities around.

On May 30th, it was 'The Great Vincent' who was drawing in the crowds at the Empire. He was billed as a man 'who performs wonderful feats with a table.' One can only muse on what they might have been.

And on August 15th Randolph could well have got a close look at a flying machine of sorts, when 'An airship under wireless control' was 'flown and manouvered in the auditorium of the theatre by the inventor Mr Raymond Phillips.'

He would have needed something rather wonderful to take his mind off the fact that his mother was away still in hospital. It seemed such a long time ago since she left.

Maybe, at home in his room, in the more controllable and happier world of Randin, he escaped to his escapes. His mother was somewhere she would probably like to escape from. Perhaps in some ways he felt like he was escaping for her too.

The place where Margaret was taken for treatment, near Derby
Peter Higginbotham

November was bitterly cold and there was snow. It didn't seem long since the snow in February had been covering the ground before at Greenhill. It had been a cold year in so many ways. The bitter month held bitter news for the Douglas household too. For they were told that Margaret, slowly fading for the past six months, had lost the battle against illness. She had died. It was the 27th, Peggy's ninth birthday. But there was no heart for celebration at Yew House.

Peggy found it hard that her mother had died, and hard too, that it had been on her special day, her birthday.

They were difficult things for a child to understand.

She looked at the painting, which her mother had been working on, now left idle and unfinished, depicting her delicate fingers paused forever over the keys.

Peggy picked it up, and slowly wrapped it in brown paper.

Then she put it to the back of her wardrobe, out of view. It was too painful to see.

Only when her own daughter unwrapped it, almost 80 years later, would it see the light of day again.

The painting Margaret was working on
Private collection

The funeral was at Norton, in the same church where the couple had made their wedding vows. On December 1st, Randolph, Peggy, Katherine and Robert, with other family and mourners, followed the carriage down Derbyshire Lane, to the church's graveyard.

Randolph looked at the tall trees on either side of the gate as they turned into the cemetery. They turned past the chapel of rest, with its little spired entrance tower, and came to rest by the piece of earth where his mother would lie. It was a grey day, with a cool breeze, and the hills of Derbyshire on the horizon were dulled and hazy.

They were only a short distance from Greenhill, the family home, and the place where his mother had spent her own childhood days. She wouldn't be too far away.

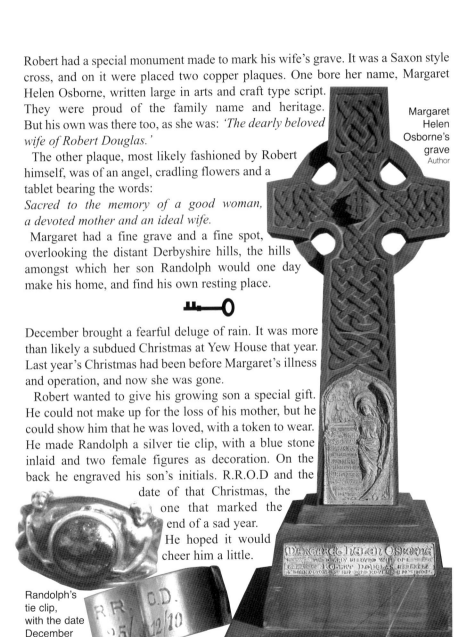

Robert had a special monument made to mark his wife's grave. It was a Saxon style cross, and on it were placed two copper plaques. One bore her name, Margaret Helen Osborne, written large in arts and craft type script. They were proud of the family name and heritage. But his own was there too, as she was: *'The dearly beloved wife of Robert Douglas.'*

The other plaque, most likely fashioned by Robert himself, was of an angel, cradling flowers and a tablet bearing the words:
Sacred to the memory of a good woman, a devoted mother and an ideal wife.

Margaret had a fine grave and a fine spot, overlooking the distant Derbyshire hills, the hills amongst which her son Randolph would one day make his home, and find his own resting place.

Margaret Helen Osborne's grave
Author

December brought a fearful deluge of rain. It was more than likely a subdued Christmas at Yew House that year. Last year's Christmas had been before Margaret's illness and operation, and now she was gone.

Robert wanted to give his growing son a special gift. He could not make up for the loss of his mother, but he could show him that he was loved, with a token to wear. He made Randolph a silver tie clip, with a blue stone inlaid and two female figures as decoration. On the back he engraved his son's initials. R.R.O.D and the date of that Christmas, the one that marked the end of a sad year. He hoped it would cheer him a little.

Randolph's tie clip, with the date December 25th, 1910
Private collection

41

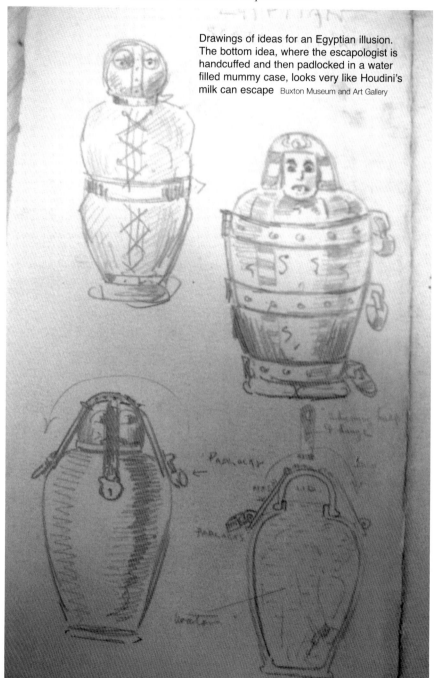

Drawings of ideas for an Egyptian illusion. The bottom idea, where the escapologist is handcuffed and then padlocked in a water filled mummy case, looks very like Houdini's milk can escape Buxton Museum and Art Gallery

9
Escaping the past

The furniture and all the trappings of the family were piled onto the wagon. The horse stomped its hoof impatiently outside Yew House as Robert slowly closed the door for the last time. Randolph gazed back at his childhood home, the place crowded with all the memories of his young life, all the sadness of the last few months flooding back into his mind.

It was a different kind of escape he was thinking of now. One that would take him away from the heartache of seeing his mother so ill and the pain of losing her forever. No magic trick could bring her back from beyond that final curtain.

It would be good for little Peggy to get away from the house too; she was taking it hard. He put his arm around her shoulders as they squashed into the seat with their belongings.

His father and Aunt Katherine climbed in next. She had been a stabilising influence on the family over the times of his mother's illness. And now she was to share in their new life, at Endcliffe, Sheffield.

Randolph was lost in thought as the cart trundled down from Greenhill, through the winding side streets and eventually onto the busy Ecclesall Road. Then with a left turn into the short hill, they pulled up outside their new home in Carrington Road.

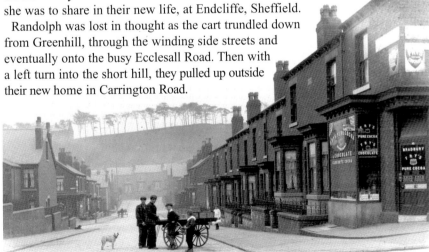

Carrington Road in 1910   Sheffield Local Studies Library

Randolph looked up at the tall end-terrace house. It was pleasant enough, though not in such rural surroundings as Greenhill. A bay window peeked out at one side and a curious offshoot was at the other side. The gable, topped with a wooden finial, seemed much higher than the little cottage he had known since he was born. But now, at fifteen, he was to start afresh.

They unloaded. Randolph struggled with his trunk of locks and keys as it rattled and slid about, falling from the cart with a metallic thump. He was to have the attic room. It seemed a long trail all the way up the three flights of stairs, but he managed and stood to gaze out of the window, which was just below the highest point of the gable. His breath misted the glass.

Wiping the moisture with his jacket sleeve, he surveyed their new domain. Opposite he could see the neat bays of the other houses, net curtained, with their lace edged, scalloped blinds lending an air of gentility. A corner shop advertising Fry's Cocoa and Rowntree's Chocolates had enticing glass sweet jars lined up in its window and a dog trotted down the cobbles with a purposeful air.

Below, he could hear the bangs and scrapes of furniture being unloaded and dragged. It was heaved through the gate in the lattice-topped garden wall, up the step to the front door. Randolph ran down the central attic stair, opened the panelled door at the bottom and wound down the rest of the way to help.

The kitchen was down yet another flight of stairs, in the basement, with a window looking out on to a small yard at the back. Aunt Katherine was already there, placing

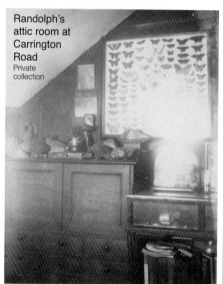

Randolph's attic room at Carrington Road
Private collection

pans and cups out on the large wooden table. She was going to help with all the housekeeping too. It was a busy and tiring day and they were all glad as the cart finally pulled away, empty, the clip clop of hooves fading as they closed the front door.

Over the next few weeks and months, the new house gradually became a home. Randolph made the attic space his own, carefully unpacking his treasures. His collection of keys and pistols were arranged carefully in the space above the zig-zag border on the walls. Framed photographs of his hero and inspiration Houdini were removed from their newspaper wraps and nailed up to gaze out from above the low metal bedhead. Little did he imagine that the enigmatic escapologist would one day gaze back at them.

Randolph's attic room showing his bed, with Houdini photographs and memorabilia framed above it. A collection of keys and pistols also line the walls, as well as what looks like some sort of pulley and handle above the bed head
Private collection

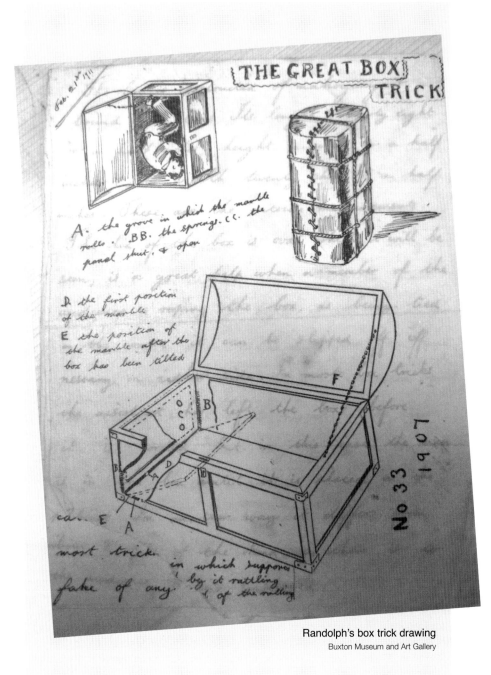

THE GREAT BOX TRICK

Feb. 21st 1911

A. the grove in which the marble rolls. BB. the springs. CC. the panel shut, & open

D the first position of the marble

E the position of the marble after the box has been tilted

most trick... in which suppose... fake of any ... by it rattling ... of the rattling

No 33 1907

Randolph's box trick drawing
Buxton Museum and Art Gallery

46

10
Magical inspirations

The new year, 1911, didn't seem to be starting out much better than the last. There was a fresh outbreak of scarlet fever at the school in Greenhill, where many Douglas family friends and relatives still lived, and there was a fearful gale in the night of February 17th. But in the attic at Carrington Road, Randolph Douglas and his fantasy life as Randin were both growing in stature.

On February 21st, the young boy was in an optimistic and forward looking mood, busily drawing out a diagram.

He called it "The Great Box Trick. No. 33 1907' and carefully labelled the sections, with instructions of how to work the illusion.

He was now more confident in his ability as an escapologist and had built up an even bigger collection of chains, locks, shackles and padlocks. He had even bought a 'straight jacket' for four shillings and six-pence. Certainly not the usual shopping wish-list for a fifteen year-old-boy.

But then he was not a usual fifteen-year-old. He was The Great Randin. And he was determined. Houdini had been a young boy too, when he decided his destiny. Randolph was just as set on how his life should unfold.

And the year ahead gave many chances for Randolph to see some of the great magicians of the time up close for inspiration. First to appear was his hero Houdini, at the Empire again.

47

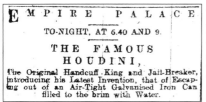

EMPIRE PALACE

TO-NIGHT, AT 6.40 AND 9.

THE FAMOUS
HOUDINI,

The Original Handcuff-King and Jail-Breaker, introducing his Latest Invention, that of Escaping out of an Air-Tight Galvanised Iron Can filled to the brim with Water.

Sheffield Daily Independent March 1911

The famous Houdini, 'The Original Handcuff King and Jail-Breaker' was there the first week of March, 1911. And it seems his young fan and imitator Randin was there too, as a programme for the show was proudly added to Randolph's growing collection of ephemera.

The show was to include an exciting 'new invention' by Houdini, 'Escaping out of an Air-Tight Galvanised Iron Can filled to the brim with water.' This is the famous 'Milk Can Escape' which Houdini did on many occasions after 1908, but no one in Sheffield was likely to have seen it before and it would have been a great new attraction.

The programme for the show proclaimed *'everybody invited to bring their own padlocks.'* Did Randolph take up the challenge? Who knows now - but he certainly had a few at home he could have taken along.

Programme for Sheffield Empire, March 6, 1911, owned by Randolph   Private Collection

Randolph could hardly wait, shuffling in his seat as strains of the 'Suite Romantic' filled the auditorium. His attention wandered as he waited and his gaze flitted around the theatre, taking in the gaudily magnificent gold-painted plaster-work, red plush seating, swirls and swags. It was like a jewel box, a magical palace indeed.

There were 3,000 seats, with room for more standing. The roof was a hexagonal dome shape, with plaster figures playing a variety of musical instruments gazing down. At the base of the dome, on balustrades, sat winged cherubs, with wreaths and sceptres. At the centre was an octagonal lantern roof which could slide open to let out tobacco smoke and give ventilation.

The stage was surrounded by a heavily decorated plaster, rope-like border. In the centre at the top was an egg-shaped panel with a painting of more cherubs, wielding musical instruments, frolicking about. On either side sat female statues, reclining on chairs and reading a book.

Frank Matcham, the architect, was a master of theatre design and the Sheffield Empire was up to his usual standard.

The final notes of the introductory music sounded and applause brought Randolph's gaze back to the stage in anticipation. And there, walking out into the glare of the lights, was the great Harry Houdini, in his trademark evening suit. The murmurings of the audience grew silent as he introduced himself in his accented tones, his steel - blue eyes looking out and surveying the crowd as he gave them a charismatic smile.

It was a magical moment for Randolph, seeing his idol before him and watching the tricks and escapes with a keen eye for detail. As well as enjoying the show he could get a valuable insight into ways to improve his own. One day, he mused, it would be he who drew the applause and disbelieving gasps, who baffled the audience with seemingly impossible feats that seemed to border on the supernatural. But for now he was in the hands of Houdini, who charmed and astounded the people of Sheffield.

He also shared his latest daring, out of theatre exploits, showing films of his manacled bridge jumps in New York and Paris and also his first flight in Australia. It must have been an incredibly exciting treat for the spectators, watching the latest and dangerous miracle of man in flight from their safe seats.

Houdini also 'broke free of a strait jacket in full view of the audience' and then it was time for his new showpiece, a 'characteristically startling trick.'

Randolph watched closely as a zinc vessel was brought to the centre of the stage and placed on a canvas groundsheet. The vessel was then filled to the brim with water as Houdini disappeared off stage, returning in a bathing suit. It seemed impossibly small to hold a man, yet Houdini managed to squeeze into it, getting into a crouching position inside.

As he bobbed down into the water, rivulets poured down and splashed onto the stage. Fitting in such a tight space seemed enough of a feat in itself, but getting out, after the lid was quickly placed on, and secured with six padlocks, would be amazing. But he did - in an incredibly short time, appearing behind the screen dripping and smiling as the audience clapped and wondered.

Randolph thought about how it could be done. Perhaps the top of the can had false rivets that could be undone from the inside? Maybe he worked it out, or maybe he too was baffled. But whichever way, he would have been inspired.

Perhaps he met Houdini that day, and went backstage - or maybe even onstage - with those handcuffs. But we will never know now. It was to be later that their friendship grew.

Above: Programme for Sheffield Empire, March 6, 1911, owned by Randolph. A cross marks Houdini and also an act called Lola Patey 'The Dutch Colleen' Private Collection

Sheffield Daily Independent, Thursday, March 9, 1911

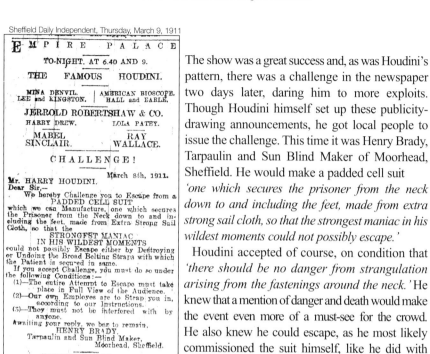

EMPIRE PALACE

TO-NIGHT. AT 6.40 AND 9.

THE FAMOUS HOUDINI.

MINA DENVIL. | AMERICAN BIOSCOPE.
LEE and KINGSTON. | HALL and EARLE.

JERROLD ROBERTSHAW & CO.

HARRY DREW. LOLA PATEY.

MABEL RAY
SINCLAIR. WALLACE.

CHALLENGE!

March 8th, 1911.
Mr. HARRY HOUDINI.
Dear Sir,—
We hereby Challenge you to Escape from a
PADDED CELL SUIT
which we can Manufacture, one which secures
the Prisoner from the Neck down to and including the feet, made from Extra Strong Sail
Cloth, so that the
STRONGEST MANIAC
IN HIS WILDEST MOMENTS
could not possibly Escape either by Destroying
or Undoing the Broad Belting Straps with which
the Patient is secured in same.
If you accept Challenge, you must do so under
the following Conditions:—
(1)—The entire Attempt to Escape must take
place in Full View of the Audience.
(2)—Our own Employes are to Strap you in,
according to our Instructions.
(3)—They must not be interfered with by
anyone.
Awaiting your reply, we beg to remain,
HENRY BRADY,
Tarpaulin and Sun Blind Maker,
Moorhead. Sheffield.

HOUDINI ACCEPTS!
On Condition that there should be No Danger
from Strangulation, arising from the
Fastenings round the Neck.
TEST TAKES PLACE AT THE SECOND
PERFORMANCE ON
FRIDAY NIGHT, MARCH 10th.

The show was a great success and, as was Houdini's pattern, there was a challenge in the newspaper two days later, daring him to more exploits. Though Houdini himself set up these publicity-drawing announcements, he got local people to issue the challenge. This time it was Henry Brady, Tarpaulin and Sun Blind Maker of Moorhead, Sheffield. He would make a padded cell suit *'one which secures the prisoner from the neck down to and including the feet, made from extra strong sail cloth, so that the strongest maniac in his wildest moments could not possibly escape.'*

Houdini accepted of course, on condition that *'there should be no danger from strangulation arising from the fastenings around the neck.'* He knew that a mention of danger and death would make the event even more of a must-see for the crowd. He also knew he could escape, as he most likely commissioned the suit himself, like he did with other challenge items such as packing cases.

Maybe Randolph went back to the Empire on friday night to see this challenge. And maybe he took his trusty notebook this time, to write and sketch. Sketches he drew of a man wriggling to escape a full length strait-jacket certainly resemble the description of Houdini as he carried out his challenge in the newspaper review the next day:

'wriggling and twisting like a human snake in full view of the audience for 30 minutes, he escaped...and staggered from the stage amid deafening applause from the audience.'

If Randolph was watching he would have been entranced as Houdini allowed himself to be placed in a sack-like arrangement with only one aperture for the head and be bound up with numerous straps as effectively as a fowl is trussed. Fastened around the chest, the waist, the thighs, the knees and the ankles, the straps all met behind.

Left: Sketches of an escape from full length straitjacket. From Randolph's notebook
Buxton Museum and Art Gallery

But the bonds were no match for Houdini. Freeing his legs from the straps after 21 minutes had passed, Houdini thrust his right arm through the head aperture and then tugged with his feet until his shoulders and arms emerged. To free himself entirely was then the work of moments, and at three minutes past eleven o'clock, after half-an-hour's struggling, he unsteadily regained his feet.

Applause erupted and filled the auditorium. The exhausted master showman knew he had triumphed again.

Away from the Empire footlights, there was another type of show in town that March, which must have provided some exciting and inspirational sights for Randolph too.

The Bostock Jungle was a popular show near the centre of town. It was a kind of circus and was known locally as just 'The Jungle'. The original Bostock Jungle was in Coney Island, New York. A touring version went around the UK.

The advertisement in the newspaper for the elephant act certainly sounded exciting enough to tempt many a punter through the gates: *'A revelation in the annals of elephant training'... 'Begins about where other trained elephants finish'... 'Has forgotten MORE than other performing elephants ever knew.'*
What the elephants thought about it is another matter.
What Randolph thought about it, who knows, but he was impressed enough to buy a pack of twelve postcards for 2d (1p) as a souvenir.

And The Jungle had a show in September too: The Royal Italian Circus: 'The Greatest and Grandest Circus Entertainment ever Seen in This Country.' 'Over 200 performing animals. Truly a sight of a lifetime.'

It sounds like something Randolph would find hard to resist.

Far right: Souvenir from The Bostock Jungle, Sheffield, in Randolph's collection. Buxton Museum and Art Gallery

Right: Newspaper ad for The Jungle

Sheffield Daily Independent, Tuesday March 2, 1911

An early advertisement for The Empire   Sheffield Newspapers Library Archives

On Saturday May 6 it was another inspiring visit to the Empire for Randolph, this time to see Chung Ling Soo 'The World's Greatest Illusionist and Master of Mystery." He had opened at the Empire on May 1st the week after W.C. Fields and was 'an enormous attraction'. The review in the Sheffield Independent the next day described *'no vulgar ostentation but a graceful performance of mystifying feats. Miss Suee Seen was made to appear from all sorts of places...'*
There is no mention of Soo's most dangerous illusion, the bullet catch, the one that would later end his life.

Sheffield Daily Independent, May 1, 1911

The Sheffield Daily Telegraph reviewer enjoyed Soo's show but seemed a little less impressed by the supposed nationality of one of the performers...
'there are mysterious tricks which baffle the closest observer. They are associated with much Eastern splendour but perhaps lose something from the fact that none of the tricks is given with a word of comment. There are numerous Chinese assistants as well as a young lady called Miss Suee Seen who looks more English than Oriental.'
He was right of course. The 'famous Chinese conjuror' was in fact an American named William Robinson, and Suee Seen was really his American wife, Olive, known as Dot because she was so small. People in showbusiness knew the deception, but the audience were willing and ready to be convinced by Robinson's Oriental stage persona.
The lack of comment was so Robinson would not reveal his true American voice and also because he was not very good at the necessary stage patter. He hid this fact behind the enigmatic silence of his stage creation Chung Ling Soo. If Soo ever talked to reporters, he spoke in a made up gobbledy-gook, which was then 'translated' by his assistant.

There were ten other acts on the programme with Soo including The Delevines described by the same reviewer as *'very clever in their spectacular scene. Transformation of an ugly witch into a beautiful girl gives the Satanic creatures scope for gymnastic gyrations.'*
Also on were *'entertaining comedians'* Rich and Rich and Walter Aubrey, who *'delights people who favour noisy wooden shoe dances* and J P Carroll, a *'soldier tambourinist'*.
The newspaper also advertised a special saturday matinee, when Chung Ling Soo's act would fill the whole bill. Randolph must have been eagerly counting the days to this 2.30pm spectacular. Matinees were done by stars like Houdini and Soo for a more family orientated show. Because of this family feel, it is not likely that Soo would do the bullet catch, at this show either. But even when he did, he never advertised it on the programme.

Right: William Robinson's creation,
Chung Ling Soo Magic Circle Archives

Like the rest of the audience Randolph would probably have assumed Soo was indeed a Chinaman, silent during his act because he knew no English. It all added to the exotic and mysterious appeal of the fabulous conjuror from a far off land - but not the land most people expected.

'The Demon Smoke' opened the act, as Randolph shuffled forward and leaned on the back of the seat in front. The stage looked magnificent. Soo was famous for his elegant and exotic stage settings and artistic publicity posters as well as his magic. The conjuror was dressed in a colourful silk costume and the tiny Suee Seen looked like a doll as she trotted about the stage.

Randolph sat enthralled as Soo did illusion after illusion, all with wonderfully evocative names; enchanted knots and rope, the charmed dove and bouquet, the rice of the Mandarin, sun and moon, misfortunes of a watch and more.

He did his famous 'catching of gold fish' too. As the audience watched, Soo picked up a bamboo fishing pole, with about five feet of line on the end. He reached into his pocket and pulled out some bait, which he attached to the end of the string. Then he swung out the line over the heads of the audience.

Randolph followed the strings movements expectantly. Soo was staring out into the audience, peering above their heads as if he could see a shoal of fish that was invisible to everyone else. Slowly he followed the phantom fishes, waiting for the right moment. Then he struck- flicking his wrist to jerk the rod - and a small gold fish appeared dangling from the end of the line. He pulled the rod back to the stage, grabbed the line, unhooked the fish and dropped it into a glass bowl, swimming around as the incredulous audience applauded. But this was not the finish - Soo caught two more of the magical gold fish to place in his bowl before he put down his rod, clasped his hands together and took a bow.

Another highlight act came just before the interval; The Girl Who Changes to an Orange Tree. Randolph watched closely as a table was brought on-stage. Above it was lowered a large metal tube, slightly conical in shape. The tube was swung upwards towards the audience and he saw that it was empty. Then the tube was lifted up again.

Suee Seen got up onto the table. As she stood there the tube was quickly lowered again, this time over her. One handclap from Soo and the tube was lifted once more. But the little lady was gone, transformed into a big orange tree in a pot. As the tube was fully raised, the branches of the tree seemed to grow in size. It even had oranges on it.

Soo went up to the tree and picked some of the oranges, putting them in a basket and walking to the edge of the stage. He threw oranges into the audience. They were real. It was a stunning trick and Randolph watched as the lucky man near him reached up and caught one. Attached to it was a a paper tag printed with a picture of Chung Ling Soo. A novel piece of showmanship.

Voices rose in excited conversation during the interval, as the crowd talked of the marvels they had witnessed. Then, after just 10 minutes break, Soo and his company were back on stage. It was another whirlwind display of skill, each trick better than the last. The Human Volcano, a fire eating trick, even had streamers and fireworks much to the audience's delight. Next, Soo seemed to shoot an arrow attached to a long rope straight through his diminutive assistant, as she stood in front of a target which the arrow pierced after apparently passing through her body.

Another wonder then filled the stage- a giant oyster shell, supported by three carved dolphins. It was a very pretty effect, with coloured lights and a small waterfall. The audience watched as the shell was opened to reveal first nothing but its silky pink lining, then a pearl and finally Suee Seen reclining inside it.

The last two illusions were even more spectacular. The Crystal Lamp of Enchantment (wrongly spelled in the newspaper ad as the less aesthetic sounding Crystal 'Lump' of Enchantment) featured a six-sided glass cabinet, like a giant lantern, which was hoisted into the air. Randolph was dazzled by the glass as it spun in the stage lights.

Soo took a pistol from his belt and shot at the spinning cabinet, which became filled with colour - colour which turned into Suee Seen, who stepped out as the lantern was lowered to the stage once more. Enchantment it was indeed- the audience loved it and were still clapping wildly as the finale was put in place - The Mystic Cauldron. A fittingly fantastic finish, the cauldron, about two feet in diameter and surrounded by flames, was filled with water and began to steam. Comically tatty stuffed animals were dropped into it. Soo stirred the cauldron with a large stick, dipped his hand in and pulled out in turn live versions of the stuffed ones he had put in. Ducks, doves and chickens wandered around the stage as Soo extinguished the flames - and pulled out of the cauldron his brightly clad assistant Suee Seen- dry and smiling.

It was certainly a magical night for young Randolph, who left the Empire in a dream, his head bursting with wonders.

Programme for the Empire Chung Ling Soo matinee   Buxton Museum and Art Gallery

One of the earliest photographs
of Randolph, around the time
of Randin's first show
Buxton Museum and Art Gallery

11
Randin's First Show

Randolph sat proudly in the chair, with a slightly cocky, knowing look on his face as he posed for the camera. He felt ready now to face the public for the first time as his alter ego. Randin had got a booking.

He thought about how it would be in front of the crowd, and smiled, anticipating applause. All morning he had been going through his act again, making sure of his moves, working on his patter. He had seen Houdini work the Empire crowd and knew that what you said was just as important to woo an audience as what you did.

If he had known that even the great Chung Ling Soo he had seen five months before was really a man who couldn't manage the patter, and had decided to be a silent chinaman to get around the problem, he would perhaps have felt better.

But he felt he was doing well. He was decked out in all his chains, shackles, padlocks and cuffs, accumulated over the last few years. They were heavy. The great padlock around his neck pulled down on a metal collar. He knew Houdini used big padlocks to hide a lock-breaking mini toolkit. He knew a lot of things about his hero. If only he could share his dreams and ideas with the Great Self-Liberator, the man whose feats he emulated. What talks they could have, of locks and chains, tips and secrets.

He looked down at the restraints on his arms. They were a tight fit and the metal was squashing the skin around his elbows badly. Six sets of cuffs held his wrists and he cupped his hands around the thick chains leading to his metal-cuffed ankles. It was a jumble of metalwork that looked quite alarming - but he knew he could escape from it all.

The big day had come. It was Tuesday, September 26th, 1911. In a few hours he was to perform in a smoking concert at the Catholic Young Men's Society club rooms. They were on Solly Street, the middle of the Irish quarter in the centre of Sheffield, next to the Catholic church of St. Vincent's. The church was being fitted with a fine new Norman style tower and funds were badly needed. Proceeds from the concerts would help provide extra cash. And Randin would be on the bill.

It was also the day that Houdini took up one of his most peculiar challenges; escaping from the belly of a 'sea monster' which had been washed up in Boston Harbour. He was almost overcome with the stench of the carcass and the chemicals used to preserve it. But he emerged, pale and triumphant from the creature.

And back in Sheffield, Randolph Douglas was taming his own monster; the fear and excitement of his first public show.

He grew more excited as they came closer to the venue. They wound up the cobbles of Hollis Croft, with the almost completed tower of St Vincent's beckoning them on, as it peered over the rooftops of the little workshops and run-down houses huddled in the courts. The area was changing rapidly, with crowded back-to-back houses being cleared and new tenements being built in the area, including some on nearby Hawley Street, not far from the site of The Jungle.

They came out on Solly Street and turned down to the church, past the Catholic Boys School. Randolph imagined he could smell the ghost of incense on the air. A glow faintly lit the church windows as they reached the entrance to the club rooms.

The gates swung open with a metallic squeak and he went through the large stone gateposts. Up a step and then he was at the threshold of his dream - he would perform to an audience as The Great Randin at last.

As he pushed open the door he could smell the cigarette and cigar smoke. Inside was the hum of conversation, dipping slightly as people turned to see who had come in. Randolph had a quick glance around at his waiting audience before he was ushered off to prepare himself by Mr O'Hara the steward.

There was a good crowd; and amongst them was Commander Scott, the man whom Houdini had presented himself to on January 19 1902 at the Water Lane police cells. It was Scott who had signed and presented Houdini with his certificate of escape from the Charlie Peace cell.

Scott had challenged Randin to escape from shackles that he would bind him in. The challenge was probably set up by Randolph himself, taking tips on publicity from the ace showman and attention grabber Harry Houdini.

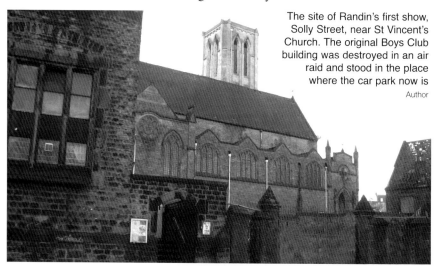

The site of Randin's first show, Solly Street, near St Vincent's Church. The original Boys Club building was destroyed in an air raid and stood in the place where the car park now is

Author

It was time. Shy young Randolph had disappeared - and out in front of the audience stepped Randin, the escapologist, ready to take up his challenge.

Commander Scott stepped forward too. Randolph stood firm as Scott fitted on shackles and cuffs, clicking closed the padlocks and arranging the chains. Then he sat down and waited for the young lad to escape as promised.

Now he had to prove himself. Like Houdini, Randolph wriggled and tugged, freeing his hands, scraping his skin on cuff and metal as he rushed to free his feet. Metal bonds fell to the ground with a rattle He had done it.

Stepping forward, he took a bow as the crowd applauded.

Randolph was thrilled. Now he had even more in common with Houdini. He smiled as Commander Scott shook his hand then wrote his signature on a handy ticket as a souvenir for Randin's debut evening.

Randolph looked down at the ticket. There it was - a note to say he had done his first show. And with it was the signature of the very same man who had signed Houdini's letter in 1904... another echo of his hero had touched his life. .

His mother would have been proud. And was his father there to watch his son's triumph? Was he smoking his pipe with a wry and proud smile on his lips as he watched his son air his creation Randin for the first time?

Whoever was watching, they would probably have seen a delighted young man packing away his shackles and cuffs that night, as he looked back over the evening and smiled to himself. Randin had finally escaped the attic dreamworld and launched himself in to the real one.

He proudly put the autographed ticket onto his pocket, picked up his heavy bag and walked out of the door, his mind on ways to better his act for the next time.

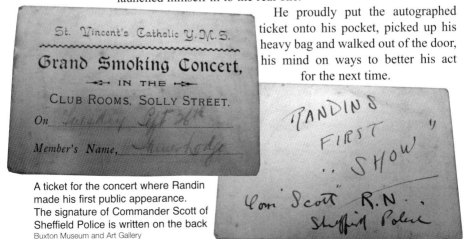

A ticket for the concert where Randin made his first public appearance. The signature of Commander Scott of Sheffield Police is written on the back
Buxton Museum and Art Gallery

Aunt Katherine was perhaps waiting with Peggy at home, to congratulate the conquering hero. But Randolph wouldn't be calling her Aunt for long; he would soon be calling her step-mother.

Katherine, 'Kitty' had been like a mother to Randolph for a long while already in many ways. She had always been there in his childhood; and there were then two loving female faces he had grown to love. She had helped more as Margaret grew ill and tired. When death took his poor mother, her sister was still there to help heal his and Peggy's hearts...and that of his father too. She had kept house and home together.

Over the past year Robert and Katherine had grown closer as they grieved and tended to Randolph and his little sister. It was a natural step that they should marry and seal the family together.

So, just four days after Randolph's exciting evening at Solly Street, he found himself at another big event - a wedding.

Robert Strachan Douglas and Katherine Osborne faced each other as they took their vows at the District Register Office on Union Road, Sheffield, a grand, double fronted house with a fine staircase.

It was a new start. The pain of remembering that first wedding day in Norton church with Margaret was softened by the smile of his new bride. They signed the register, and a new chapter began in the life of Randolph Douglas. He had a new step-mother - and a new determination, for Randin had finally taken a bow.

The house on Union Road, once a Register Office, where Robert and Katherine took their vows

Author

It was a bad winter in 1912. Blizzards came in January, with thick fog and more snow in February. But in April it was an iceberg that made the news as the 'unsinkable' Titanic went down with terrible loss of life on the 16th.

Hearing of the disaster brought back memories of the poor Douglas family who had suffered the same fate in merciless waters. There was a great wave of public emotion after the Titanic's sinking. Songs were written about the disaster and it was hard not to hear the popular 'Stand to Your Post' on a gramophone somewhere that June. The mournful words of the chorus wafted out from many a parlour *"In the darkness of the night there came a crash, a crash of doom, And the gallant crew soon realised the sea would be their tomb."*

The year unfolded. Randolph spent more money on chains, locks and keys, including an old bank key and a night latch. He also fiddled around with old clocks. He knew that any knowledge he could cram in his dream-filled head about cogs and shafts, mechanisms and barrels would be invaluable to Randin.

Chung Ling Soo was at the Empire again in June with more magical mysteries and the exotic enticement of his stage illusions. And Randolph was more than likely there too, to be amazed once more by the art of the great magician.

Randolph worked worked harder at his own art as well, thinking of new ways that Randin could amaze the public.

Man in chains by Randolph
Buxton Museum and Art Gallery

Harry Houdini had got a new way to amaze the public too. It was called The Water Torture Cell, or the Upside Down and it had been built for him in England the year before. He had licensed it as a stage play instead of a magical effect, to prevent anyone trying to copy it. It was in his autumn tour of 1912 that Houdini first performed it, in Berlin.

But Randolph would have to wait a while longer before he could witness this impressive new feat for himself. For it was not until January of 1913 that Houdini brought his Water Torture Cell to England, and not until April of that year that he performed it in Sheffield. As he toured, Houdini sent advance promotion letters by registered post to tell theatre managers of his *'sensation...which is the greatest feat I have ever attempted in my strenuous career.'* It was a great piece of theatre. It was dangerous.

And Randolph couldn't wait to see it.

A signed publicity postcard of Harry Houdini, to Randolph Douglas. It was signed in 1920 but is an old photo, showing Houdini as he looked around 1913 *Buxton Museum and Art Gallery*

12
Face to face

R andolph's keen eye and delicate workmanship, developed from taking apart and mending locks and clocks, were ideal skills for a silversmith. He had a gift for very fine detail and watching his talented father had given him a good grounding too. Robert Strachan's work was becoming renowned and he had many prestigious commissions.

To help his young son out into the world, Robert got him an unpaid apprenticeship at a silversmiths - maybe John Round and Son at Tudor Street where he had worked a while himself. Round and Son had begun in 1847 as suppliers to Huttons, the firm where Randolph's spoon was made. Their trade mark was 'all the world Round.' The firm grew in size and had become famous for high quality silver plated hollowware, flatware and cutlery.

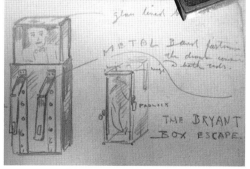

Near Tudor Street stood another fine Sheffield theatre, the Theatre Royal. The lure of the footlights was never to be far away. Later, Rounds moved to a site on Arundel Street, and that was near the Empire. He would always be able to nip up for the evening show.

Randolph did try to please his father and do his apprenticeship. He certainly had great flair and

A padlock and key made by Randolph (actual size) and one of his escape ideas *Private collection*

promise, but he just didn't like the work. His head was full of other ideas and it wasn't what he wanted to do. He knew that even the great Harry Houdini had begun life as a tie cutter before his handcuffs skills rescued him and enabled him to take another path. But he didn't want to wait. So his understanding father let him indulge in his dream still, the silver designing intended to be a filler until he could forge his own path in that more unusual career, as Randin.

But Randolph made rather a good silversmith too, and his talents in that area grew, along with his talent in escapology, his knowledge of locks and his collection of curiosities.

He dragged the trunk into place, put on the cuffs and climbed in. It was a tight squeeze and he was curled up in an awkward fetal position, but Randolph was determined to last it out.

He was getting hot, it was dark and his feet were going numb. Sucking air through the hinge gaps of the stuffy, steel lined trunk he stayed put and tried not to panic. The cuffs were hurting his cramped arms and he felt a little light-headed, but he thought of Houdini and how he endured discomfort and danger. He could do it too.

Three hours and ten minutes later he pushed his way out. Hot and dishevelled. He threw off the cuffs and then smoothed back his hair with a satisfied grin. He had survived his self-inflicted test.

With a Houdiniesque eye for self promotion, Randolph had a publicity photo taken before the trunk lid was closed on his squashed form. It was a good image. He scribbled a note on the back of it: *"Endurance test 1913. Remained in steel trunk in upside down position 3 hours & ten minutes. The only means of getting air; through the hinge gaps in the trunk! Rather cramped but no worse for my 'siege'."*

He showed the photo to his father and Kitty. They were duly impressed, but he really needed to talk with a person who understood his drive and passion, Someone who could share his ideas and sense of achievement. He needed to talk to Houdini.

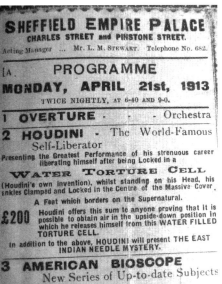

In April 1913, the man in question, the World Famous Self-Liberator Houdini, was back in Sheffield at the Empire. He had seen his props hauled properly into the wings, rested in the dressing room and was ready for the first show.

One of the props was his Water Torture Cell, the new, sensational feat he was promoting this UK tour. Houdini was familiar with the Empire in Sheffield by now, and knew there would be an appreciative audience for his new and dangerous spectacle.

He had sorted out an idea for setting up a local challenge and made sure leaflets advertising it would be ready in time for the Friday night slot reserved for his challenge. Now all he had to do was amaze as usual. Not hard for the seasoned and dedicated trooper Harry Houdini.

Meanwhile, his equally dedicated fan Randolph was taking his seat in the auditorium. He had read all about the Water Torture Cell, 'a feat which borders on the supernatural.' Now he could see it for himself. It was time. The orchestra struck up the Overture as the last few stragglers took their seats, hastened on by the music, and Randolph glanced through his programme, settling down for the show.

Houdini was as fascinating and in command as usual, his small and stocky frame spruced up in an evening suit, his larger than life manner totally absorbing his audience. He did his famous East Indian Needle Mystery. Volunteers from the audience were invited on stage. Houdini showed them a large number of needles, then promptly chewed and swallowed them as a few people winced in disbelief.

Next he produced a thread and swallowed that too. Beckoning to the amazed volunteers, he asked them to look inside his mouth. It was empty. But then he put his fingers inside and drew out the end of the thread, slowly pulling it between his lips. The needles were threaded on it at intervals, popping out one by one and swinging glinting by his chin. Randolph and the rest clapped loudly as Houdini took a bow, and left the stage. Next was the thing Randolph had been waiting for.

Curtains opened to reveal the Water Torture Cell, set in the centre of the stage, on a large square tarpaulin. It indeed looked just like a torture device waiting for a victim. It was a mahogany box, with a glass front, the whole thing encased in a metal frame - and it wasn't very big, just about five feet tall and two feet wide. It would be a tight squeeze. Houdini's assistants, dressed in waterproofs, took hoses and began to fill the cell with water. They mixed hot water in too, from buckets. He didn't want to be too uncomfortable after all...

As they filled it, Houdini came back on stage, circling the cell slowly as he described it to the crowd a declamatory voice: *"Ladies and Gentleman, introducing my original invention the Water Torture Cell. Although there is nothing supernatural about it I am willing to forfeit the sum of £200 to anyone who can prove it is possible to obtain air inside of the Torture Cell when I am locked up in it in the regulation manner after it has been filled with water. Should anything go wrong when I am locked up one of my assistants watches through the curtain, ready to rush in demolishing the glass allowing the water to flow out in order to save my life."*

Houdini then invited members of the audience to come and take a close look to satisfy themselves about the cell's construction and lack of air holes. As they did so he walked off-stage, returning in a bath robe. He nodded to say he was ready, took the robe off to reveal a bathing suit, and lay on the floor. The volunteers were asked to help secure Houdini's ankles in a set of stocks, which doubled as the lid of the tank and were attached to a rope. This done, Houdini was hoisted into the air, dangling like a hooked fish as his assistants pulled on the rope. Houdini's other name for his Torture Cell was the USD- The Upside Down. It was easy to see why- he was going into it head first.

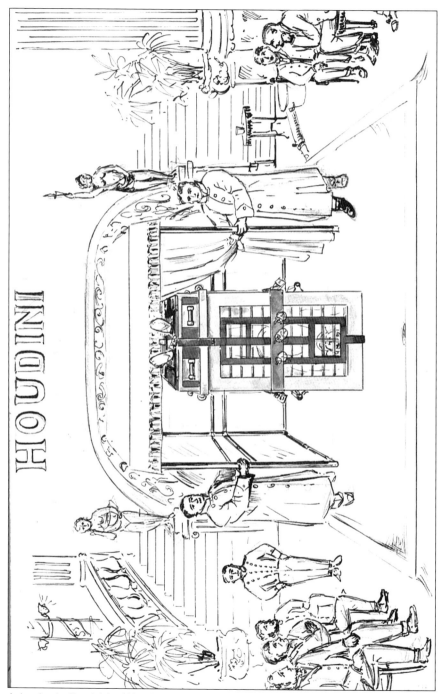

A drawing by Randolph of Houdini's Water Torture Cell escape

The Magic Circle Archives

The assistants positioned Houdini directly over the top of the cell. There was a pause as he took a few deep breaths and nodded to give the go-ahead. The rope was quickly lowered, dropping Houdini into the small water-filled space. He could feel the water seeping fast into his coarse curly hair, over his forehead and enclosing his body. Water poured out onto the tarpaulin as assistants rushed forward to lock the stocks to the top of the tank. Houdini's feet were sticking out of the top. He seemed helpless.

The audience could see him through the glass, his head at the bottom and his body trapped, with no space to turn. It was a dangerous stunt and he could easily drown. But it was the danger that made it so exciting.

A curtain was pulled quickly around the cell and a man with an axe stood by, ready to smash the glass if anything went wrong.

The audience watched in tense silence. Then the curtain twitched, and Houdini burst through, dripping and smiling as the audience applauded wildly.

EMPIRE PALACE
6.40. TO-NIGHT. 9.0.
HOUDINI. SOLO,
And Strong Variety Co.
CHALLENGE:
HOUDINI has accepted a Challenge for Second House TO-NIGHT from the employees of Sales & Teather, Eyre street Saw Mills, to attempt an escape from a box which they will construct, nail down, and cord in full view of the audience.
Box Office 10 to 4. Ring up 682 for Seats.

Ad for the challenge from the Sheffield Daily Independent, Friday 25th April 1913

Randolph was in awe. It was such a showy, physically demanding escape - and he thought he just might know how it was done.

As ever he had his sketch book in his pocket, and quickly he took a few notes.

As if this watery feat wasn't enough, there were flyers advertising the second house challenge on the friday night - an escape from a packing case - and Randolph would be there. He wanted another look at that torture chamber water cell too.

A leaflet for the challenge. *Buxton Museum and Art Gallery*

On friday night, the challenge was taken up. Men from Sales and Teather's Eyre Street Saw Mills brought wood, rope and nails on stage and constructed a 'strong heavy box.' Then Houdini climbed inside it and they nailed down the lid, bound the box with ropes as an extra precaution and pulled a curtained screen around it. The audience sat waiting, and Randolph kept pondering, he was always trying to figure out how Houdini did it.

Thirteen minutes later the curtains were drawn back to reveal Houdini, dishevelled, perspiring, coatless and collarless. The packing case was undamaged, but when the men dramatically smashed it by *'belabouring with heavy hammers and hatchets'*, inside were Houdini's coat and collar. Houdini had won his challenge as usual. And of course no one claimed the £200 for proving he could get air from his water torture cell either.

When he got back that night, Randolph was excited. He knew how to make rigged boxes already and had drawn them, but was sure he had the secret to the Water Torture Cell too. He quickly did a drawing of how he thought it worked.

Perhaps Randolph met Houdini backstage after earlier shows, but they certainly did meet at the end of this run at the Empire on 27th April, 1913.

It must have been a great thrill for Randolph, meeting his idol, the one who would understand and share his love of locks and escapes. Two pairs of piercing eyes, Randolph's brown and Houdini's steel blue, regarded each other as they met, talked - and recognised a kinship.

Randolph was two inches taller than Houdini, as well as younger. Houdini's sharp cheekbones were shadowed by the light from the stage door as the young man walked towards him. He welcomed his fan with a warm, charismatic smile, leaning forward to take the extended autograph book.

On the page was a pen and ink drawing of Houdini, ready for him to write his name under. He duly obliged, writing a little message - and his home address too.

Randolph's autograph book, with Houdini's signature and message
The Magic Circle Archives

What the young and enthusiastic imitator Randolph said and did to impress the great Houdini is lost through the years, but impress him he did. Houdini knew this was a special young man. It probably wasn't every fan that he gave his home address to. They talked enough to make a connection that led to a correspondence. The great Houdini began sending his fan, and then friend, Randolph, letters from at least September of 1913. Whatever had taken place it was enough to begin a friendship with Harry Houdini that lasted his lifetime.

Randolph could well have hinted that he knew how the Torture Cell worked. Houdini would more than likely have found it hard to resist a chance to check that out, to see if he this perceptive young man had got it right.

Perhaps too, Randolph showed Houdini his Box Endurance Test photograph to prove his talent and dedication, talked knowledgeably of locks and escape techniques.

And maybe this was the meeting when dreams met reality and Houdini decided to make a special effort for this special fan, and visit him at his home.

When Randolph extended an invitation for Houdini to visit the Douglas household, he could hardly believe it when the great Houdini accepted. He and Bess were actually going to come into his life, it was like royalty visiting and a little unreal. It was a dream come true, to share his ideas and time with the man who had inspired him for so long.

It was a flurry of activity at Carrington Road, Robert and Kitty were bemused that such a great star as Mr. Houdini was visiting their son and wanted to make a good impression.

So, Houdini and his wife Bess made a first visit of many - and probably set a few curtains twitching along Carrington Road as they arrived at Randolph's door.

Randolph opened the door with a tentative and excited air, He still couldn't believe it.

There was a polite introduction as Mr. and Mrs Houdini were ushered in, though of course they didn't really need any introductions. Everyone knew Houdini.

Tea and cakes were brought in by Peggy, which she politely and shyly offered their star guests. If the couple were shown around this creative household, with Robert Strachan's wonderful studio room crammed full of silverware designs and tools, the little models and trophies lining the shelves, they would see where Randolph had got his artistic and creative flair from.

During the visit, Randolph took Houdini up to his own little world of escapology, in the attic. Houdini was amused to see a painting of a mummy on the wall at the top of the stairs as he climbed up. The stairway came up through the middle of Randolph's room. Houdini glanced around. On one side was a small bed and he noticed with a smile the portraits of himself on the wall above it. He must remember to send the kid a few photos.

On the other side of the room was a collection of oddments and a bookcase, a case of butterflies and some geological specimens.

They had lots to talk about. Conversations Randolph had rehearsed dozens of times in his head. He had ideas and drawings of escapes he wanted to show Houdini. And there was his collection of locks to show off too. He had recently bought more, plus thumbscrews and padlocks and the best man to share his excitement was with him.

Houdini encouraged the man who perhaps reminded him of his younger self and he more than likely heard all about Randolph's first show at the CYMS. He knew the thrills of wanting to succeed and be the best.

Then Randolph unfolded the drawing he had been itching to show; the Water

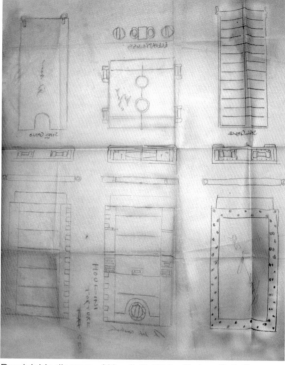

Randolph's diagram of Houdini's Water Torture Cell. Some bits are reversed, as he folded it and traced through to get the different sections . Maybe Houdini was given a more finished version *Buxton Museum and Art Gallery*

Torture Cell, with his careful details of how he thought it worked. Houdini was duly astounded. Randolph had worked it out, just by watching from the audience. Houdini begged the drawing as a memento - and also maybe to make sure no one else saw it.

Too soon the couple had to leave and get back to the theatre. They were moving on to the next booking, at Birmingham, Maybe Randolph was invited. He knew that now they would be friends. They had too many shared interests not to be. And Houdini knew too. He could well have been aware that this talented young man, with his inventive mind, may come up with a few ideas he could use. He understood locks so well he would be a good man to have backstage when he visited theatres in the area again. He would easily spot any cuffs that were tampered with and help keep an eye on things.

So after an afternoon of cakes and cuffs, shared ideas and shared pleasantries, the Douglas family waved their famous guests off. Tea cups were collected along with thoughts, as they all sat down to chatter about the visit. Robert and Kitty were so pleased Randolph had at last met the one who could share his dreams, and understand his drives, the one and only Mr. Harry Houdini.

13
Perfecting a craft

Randolph put more time and thought into his chosen career, searching for locks, keys and curiosities wherever he could. Houdini had been an inspiration and made him more determined. The collection grew and his attic bedroom was filled with all sorts of objects that had taken his eye or snagged his imagination. A bigger assortment of wonders was beginning to pile up on the shelves and bookcases and more keys were pinned on his wall.

It was his own little world of wonder, where he had spoken with the great Houdini. Here he was the Great Randolph. But not so great that he didn't do his own cleaning and keep his curious family from disturbing his precious collection.

And not so great that he didn't have to work.

In July 1913 Randolph was working, at J Round and Son.

Sitting in the workshop he turned around in his hands a shiny key, the bright gleam of it contrasting with the dust and oily machinery.

This key was a special one. Not one he had collected on one of his browsing trips around the 'Rag Market' in Sheffield, but one made by his own hands, of silver.

Round and Son had been commissioned to make it and Randolph got the job. It was soon sent to do its task, to open a padlock in Boston, Lincolnshire.

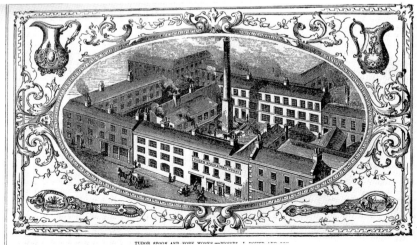

TUDOR SPOON AND FORK WORKS.—MESSRS. J. ROUND AND SON.

Drawing of J. Round and Son   *Pawson & Brailsford Guide to Sheffield, Sheffield Local Studies Library*

Ad for J Round and Son *Pawson & Brailsford Guide*

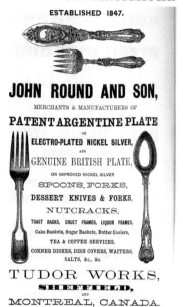

There, in the centre of Boston, was the just completed New Town Bridge, and across the roadway stretched a rope, joined in the centre with a tripod and the padlock, and awaiting a key.

A procession through the bunting-decked town on 18th July ended at the new bridge, where there were speeches and prayers. The deputy Mayor and Mayoress were there, and the Alderman too. Randolph's silver key was given to the Alderman by the engineer of the bridge.

The key was turned, the padlock opened and the rope released. The new bridge was open. Schoolchildren and a band blasted out the national anthem and somewhere back in Sheffield was Randolph, who had just opened yet another padlock, this time with a little help from the Alderman of Boston..

As ever, Randolph browsed the newspapers and magazines for news of Houdini, or any other acts he would enjoy at the theatre.

And taking in the other stories. Suffragettes were in the news a lot that year. They had destroyed letters in postboxes at Nether Edge in Sheffield and on the 4th of June there was a tragedy when Emily Davison threw herself in front of the King's horse as it ran in the Epsom Derby..

The Bostock Jungle, which Randolph enjoyed to visit, also made the papers in February, regarding the suffragist movement, when a suffragette took up a challenge to speak whilst in the lions den. She did ask for three keepers to be present but it was still a dangerous gesture. She must have decided that it was a little too dangerous, as she pulled out before the challenge date.

In August, a man called Harry Brearley working at Firth Brown's steel works, invented a new type of steel. The story being told was that he was trying to make an erosion-resistant steel and thinking a test piece no good had thrown it in the rubbish pile. Later he noticed that the steel had not rusted. He had inadvertently found out how to make Stainless Steel.

Magical discoveries came in all sorts of places and guises, thought Randolph as he scanned the newspaper for other stories, and of course to see who was on at the Empire.

14
A most terrible thing

In July of 1913, just three months after talking with Randolph at the Empire, Harry Houdini had a blow that hurt him much more than the bruises, cuts and knocks of his many escapes. His beloved mother died. He was on tour when he was given a letter telling him the news. It was so distressing for him that he collapsed with shock. All engagements were cancelled as he went back home to sort out a funeral and try and manage his grief.

He didn't work again until September 1913, when he had a booking at the Apollo Theatre in Nuremberg.

When he was there, he was fascinated by a torture room which was on show in the castle. Anyone so used to putting himself willingly into painful contraptions was bound (in more ways than one) to be curious. In the gruesome collection was an Iron Maiden. This cruel invention was an iron cabinet, made to look like a cloaked figure by being given a face. It was a claustrophobic place for anyone to be kept in, but as well as this, it had a terrible addition. Double doors at the front opened to reveal dozens of sharp spikes, designed to pierce the body and vital organs of any poor soul put inside it as the doors were closed. It would be a slow and horrific torture.

Maybe Houdini was in a more macabre state than normal in his grief, but he was very taken with the device. It was also giving him ideas for a spectacular escape act or two. He made a few notes about for a Spanish Maiden escape, with spikes holding him fast. Rigging the hinges could be the way out of that one. And maybe he could have some kind of rack too- an entire torture gallery theme.

He warmed to the idea and he knew that his friend Randolph, back in Sheffield, would also be interested in any new escape ideas. Maybe he could come up with a few suggestions of his own.

He also remembered that, like he, the young man knew the pain of losing a mother. It was like a spike through the heart.

Houdini had a photographer take some pictures of the Maiden, and also of some of the more unusual locks that were on display. Randolph would definitely be interested in those. He also purchased a postcard. Back at his hotel he picked up his pen, sat down and penned a note to his friend Randolph on it:

"Just saw the original 'Iron Maiden'. a most terrible thing.
a great collection of locks at the museum here.
Regards, H Houdini apollo theatre Nuremberg"

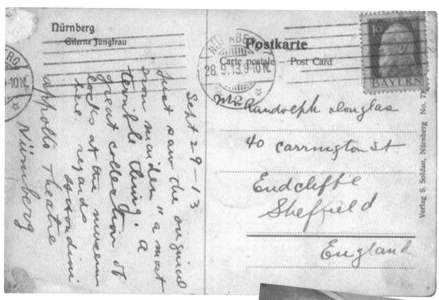

In Sheffield, Randolph hastily picked up the postcard from the mat. He knew it was from Houdini. It was a great thrill having a personal card from the man he had admired from afar for so long. And about such fascinating things too.

He still couldn't quite believe it, that the great mystifier would take time to write to him, especially when he had only just returned to work after his mother's death..

But they had so much to share that the need and desire to do this had made them friends, instead of a mere fan and his idol. Houdini knew he would find a keen and receptive reader in his young friend Randolph.

The picture on the card was of the Iron Maiden and it reminded Randolph of sketches of a mummy escape he had designed in his sketchbook. He would love to see the real thing and all those locks too!

Above and right: The Iron Maiden postcard to Randolph from Houdini

Buxton Museum and Art Gallery

Less than a month later, a package arrived. His mother shouted up to the attic. Randolph always called his step-mother Kitty mother now, as she had filled that role for so long in so many ways. She told him there was a package from Nuremberg. Randolph bounded excitedly down the stairs to retrieve it, taking it back to his attic sanctuary to open. Inside was a letter from Houdini and a small parcel wrapped in paper. He carefully opened the paper to reveal a tiny model of the Iron Maiden.

What a cruel and ingenious thing, thought Randolph. But this maiden was less of a terror. It was made to hold toothpicks. Setting his little gift down, he picked up the letter. There were a few spelling mistakes, but it conveyed Houdini's enthusiasm perfectly:

"My Dear Mr Douglas, Have sent you an exact model of the Iron Maiden from Nirnberg and as it was made by a Nurnberger, you can rest assured that it is exact.

The two spike in the head, were used to penetrate the victims eyes.

They were not crushed to death at once, but with the aid of a windlass, the doors were forced together about an inch ever half hour or hour.

Then when Death relieved the poor suffering form, the Jailers would open trap door, the body would fall on a cutting machine which would cut the body into thousands of pieces and the Pegnitz River would carry away the remains.

I have been very fortunate in obtaining a lock of the 15 Cent. One of the Rare ROUND locks, which are only to be seen in museums, and I doubt if there is an example in the British Museum.

Regards, H.H.

Until Oct 28th. Circus Corty Althoff Stuttgart Nuremberg (Germany) Month of November Alhambra Theatre Paris France."

A round lock, Randolph was impressed. It was good to know Houdini was as passionate as ever about collecting locks. More trips around the Sheffield Rag Market and other places had certainly added to his own collection.

The Iron Maiden would be a wonderful addition too. He placed it carefully on his shelf, next to his other treasures, just under the framed photos of his generous, globe-trotting friend.

The toothpick holder Iron Maiden sent by Houdini
Buxton Museum and Art Gallery

RANDINI THE SELF LIBARATER.

A publicity shot of 'Randini'. Notice the similarity of pose and attire with the one of Houdini from Randolph's scrapbook *Buxton Museum and Art Gallery*

15

The Self Liberator

The new publicity photos were ready. He thought he looked very dapper. If he could have but known back then, he may also have thought that he looked for all the world like a 1950s rocker, with a quiff of hair falling over his eyes and drainpipe type black trousers.

What he did know, and what he was aiming for, was that he looked a lot like Houdini's publicity photograph, with his evening suit, rolled back sleeves and cuffs, dress shirt and shiny boots.

He thought this change of image was a good idea. He didn't notice the spelling mistake 'Libarater' He was too busy writing an 'i' on the end of 'Randin' to see how it looked. Perhaps Houdini had suggested it as a gesture to show how he held Randolph in high regard - it made the name sound more like his own.

He had a booking too, to show off the new photo, at the cricket club at Greenhill, his childhood haunt. The club had won the Norton and District League. There was to be a Grand Concert on Thursday, November 20th, in the Greenhill Council School, where the winners shield and medals were to be presented.

Randolph knew Greenhill and the school well of course. It would be odd returning to the place of his first early dreams, now officially 'Randini'- The Self Liberator. Posters were already up around the village to advertise the evening.

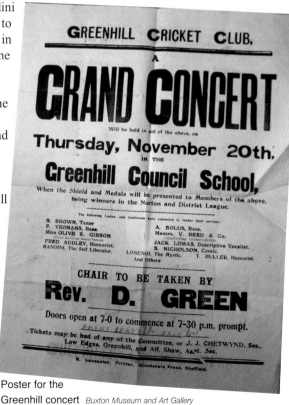

Poster for the Greenhill concert *Buxton Museum and Art Gallery*

Randolph had seen one and taken a look. The acts were all advertised, so he scanned the list. There was Fred Audley and T. Buller, 'humorist' Jack Lomas, a 'Descriptive Vocalist', S. Nicholson, Comic, Lonengi, The Mystic, as well as some singers and concertina players. And there too, in capital letters, was himself: RANDINI, The Self Liberator.

Randolph was there early to prepare, and enjoyed meeting the other acts. Maybe he knew them already if they were locals.

Doors opened at 7, and the concert began at 7.30. Randolph took his place with the others. He looked every inch the smart and confident showman in his best new suit, ready to wow the crowd.

These little shows were a big step, but they were still only like the 'dime' shows that Houdini did before he got famous. Maybe one day he could play The Empire, and get to travel the world like Houdini himself.

He sat patiently through the prizegiving and through Reverend Green's speeches and watched the other acts with interest, trying not to get too nervous, and going through his stage patter in his head. Then it was his turn.

He strolled to the front and took a bow. Then he told the audience he would escape from any locks he was bound with, for he was the great Randini. He rolled his jacket sleeves up to prepare for the handcuffs and shackles.

He was ready.

Greenhill School. where the concert was held
Author

Members of the audience were invited to click the padlocks, thread the chains, clasp on the handcuffs. The heavy links and locks seemed even more bulky on his delicate-looking young frame. Then the bemused crowd watched as he challenged the constraints and won. But of course he did. For wasn't he the young man who had shared tea, cakes and ideas with the great Houdini?

Maybe Robert and Kitty were there cheering Randolph on again, enjoying seeing their usually reserved young Randolph in his more outgoing show persona. If they were, Peggy most likely came along to the show too - maybe it was an early birthday treat. It would have been fun seeing all the other acts and she was always interested in her big brother's rather unusual hobby.

They would more than likely have gone to congratulate a smiling Randolph afterwards, putting away his locks and shackles as he packed up after the show, rolling down his sleeves and notching up another performance on his chosen career path.

These drawings by Randolph seem to be for additions or changes to Houdini's Water Torture Cell escape. Perhaps Randolph and Houdini talked them through together one day as Randolph sketched out new ideas and twists on the escape   *Buxton Museum And Art Gallery*

Randolph in 1914 *Buxton Museum and Art Gallery*

16
Faithfully yours

Randolph stood and faced the camera, looking surprisingly comfortable in his array of chains, padlocked hasps and cuffs. Shifting his weight idly onto his right leg, he waited for the shutter to blink. Young and confident, he felt he had the world to conquer. His concert at Greenhill School was successfully under his belt, and the poster for it proudly folded away in his scrapbook.

The cuttings and photos in there were growing nicely, with Mr. Houdini sending cards and newspaper articles for him to paste in. Now he would have another of himself to keep alongside those of Houdini. Up there in his attic Randolph followed Houdini's travels and triumphs. It was like a window onto the world, as if his future life were lived a little through Houdini, with himself just a few steps behind and trying to catch up. He knew he could do escapes, he knew about locks. He knew about stage illusions. And he knew he could help Houdini. He had already in some ways, with his ideas, sketches and enthusiasm.

Taking off the ironwork after his photo session, Randolph thought about the letters they had shared since that meeting in 1913. He looked across at the little iron maiden Houdini had sent him as he put the locks and cuffs back into the trunk he kept them in. It gave him another idea.

Fetching paper, pen, ink and paints he set about his task. He drew a human shaped case, with a face, but a mummy not maiden, harking back to his 'Great Randolph, 'living mummy' theme, but now drawn with more details and colour, and including a cabinet to use for doing it.

He labelled it carefully, wondering if Houdini would like the idea.

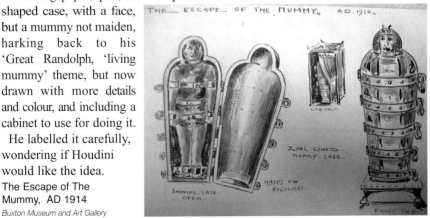

The Escape of The Mummy, AD 1914
Buxton Museum and Art Gallery

Randolph's scrapbook, with an ad
for Sheffield Empire, Feb 2 1914
and a picture of Houdini
Buxton Museum and Art Gallery

As well as coming up with novel escape ideas, Randolph had also been busy in his fathers workshop in January 1914, making a special gift. It was a jewel box. His mother had one and Randolph decided that the wife of his friend and fellow lock expert should have one too. Of course it had a padlock and key. He knew that Houdini was back in Sheffield next week and he was determined to have it finished in time. Now it was done. He polished it and set it aside.

Houdini visited England quite a lot during 1913 and 1914, amidst the rumours and beginnings of war. Whether, as has been proposed by some, that he was spying on factories and such, is open to conjecture. The truth may remain another of his secrets.

The week he visited Sheffield in February 1914, the local papers were full of tales of a possible merger between the German Krupps firm and the Sheffield firm of Vickers Ltd, who had also just got a large million pound order from a Russian gunworks. America were probably not too happy about a British firm getting too cosy with a German one; neither would the British Navy be, as Vickers held plans for British warships. So it didn't seem likely. But perhaps if Houdini was doing such undercover work, Vickers would have been a good place to have a snoop in. The challenge that Houdini took up on this visit was of a plank escape, to be done after being tied up by riggers - from Vickers. If he went to meet the riggers to set it up himself, it would have been a good way of getting that snoop.

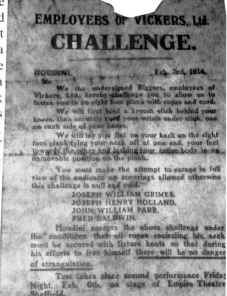

EMPLOYEES OF VICKERS, Ltd.

CHALLENGE.

HOUDINI.   Feb. 3rd, 1914.

Sir,

We the undersigned Riggers, employees of Vickers, Ltd., hereby challenge you to allow us to fasten you to an eight foot plank with ropes and cord.

We will first bind a broom stick behind your knees, then securely cord your wrists under stick, one on each side of your knees.

We will lay you flat on your back on the eight foot plank tying your neck off at one end, your feet towards the other and lashing your entire body in an immovable position on the plank.

You must make the attempt to escape in full view of the audience no coverings allowed otherwise this challenge is null and void.

JOSEPH WILLIAM GRIMES.
JOSEPH HENRY HOLLAND.
JOHN WILLIAM PARR.
FRED BALDWIN.

Houdini accepts the above challenge under the conditions that all ropes encircling his neck must be secured with fixture knots so that during his efforts to free himself there will be no danger of strangulation.

Test takes place second performance Friday Night, Feb. 6th, on stage of Empire Theatre Sheffield.

Randolph scanned the Empire advertisement. His escapologist pen pal was billed as 'The World Famous Houdini.' Indeed he had been to many countries by now and was a household name. He was certainly talked about a lot in the Douglas household. And he would be coming to see them again at least once now he was back in Sheffield and they had become friends.

Houdini had invited Randolph to go back stage and help at the Empire, checking that any handcuffs were not plugged, or any other stunts were pulled. If anyone would spot a problem his friend and lock expert Randolph would.

So, on the first night, Randolph was likely to have been there, helping out backstage, or maybe even on it. It was the first time since they had met in person since Houdini's mother had died, unless Randolph had gone to see him in London, so there would probably be time to express sympathies, time to talk family as well as business.

Friday night came and the challenge was met. Vickers Ltd employees had told Houdini they would fasten him *'to an eight foot plank with ropes and cord.*

We will first bind a broom stick behind your knees, then securely cord your wrists under stick, one on each side of your knees. We will lay you flat on your back on the plank, tying your neck off at one end, your feet towards the other'

As they did this, Randolph watching out front, did a quick sketch of the prone and trussed Houdini, before he made his escape in full view. Which he did of course, with much wriggling and writing... What a showman.

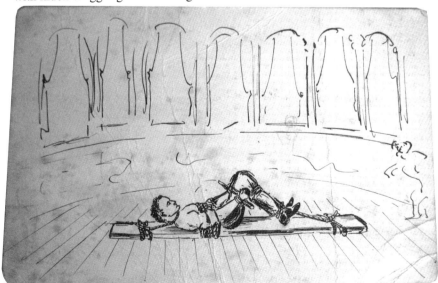

A drawing by Randolph of Houdini during the Vickers Ltd challenge   *Buxton Museum and Art Gallery*

Mr and Mrs Houdini popped in on the Douglas household for tea, perhaps more than once, during their stay at the Sheffield Empire this tour and others.

Randolph was keen to show Houdini his new photos and escape ideas, whilst Bess, his sister and his parents chatted downstairs. Peggy was delighted to see Mrs Houdini again and serve up more fancy cakes- they were a treat for her too. And Bess Houdini had another treat for them- she gave Peggy's mother a big china doll in a fine dress. Bess was rather like a doll herself, so petite and dainty, thought Peggy.

Randolph, however had a surprise for Mrs Houdini too - he brought down from the attic the jewellery box he had made and gave it to the delighted Bess.

On February 19th, whilst her husband and herself were at the Leeds Empire, Bess looked at the beautiful jewellery box. Their friend Randolph was so talented. Not only was he a lock expert and escapologist like her husband, he was a wonderful silversmith and craftsman too. The box was exquisite. She had to write a letter to thank him properly, and set about the task
"Dear Mr. Douglas,
Kindly pardon my delay in writing, thanking you for your very lovely present, which I admire for the craftsmanship displayed by you in mounting it and assure you it will be one of my prize recollections and shall keep it for the rest of my life.
I have put all my jewellery in same and it looks lovely. You do not know what a source of pleasure your kind gift has been to me. Give my kindest love to your Mother, Thank her for the lovely tea and accept kindest regards for your father and yourself. From Thankfully Yours.
(Mrs.) Beatrice Houdini.
Next Week:- The Palace Theatre, Manchester"

⊫━O

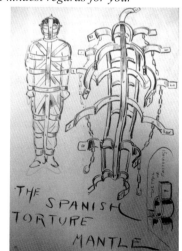

In March, Randolph looked again at his Vickers challenge sketch and copied it onto a postcard. He popped this into an envelope along with the page about Mongolian Tortures he had found. He was an avid collector of magazines and journals and had piles of them around his room, an eclectic mix bursting from the bookshelves.

Houdini was still on tour in the UK and Randolph knew his whereabouts, writing out his theatre address for this week, ready for posting

He had done a couple more sketches of his own on the torture theme too.

Escape idea, From Randolph's notes
Buxton Museum and Art Gallery

MONGOLIAN TORTURE CHEST ESCAPE.

He supposed some people may find it odd, thinking up these gruesome looking escapes. But Houdini would understand. Their escapes were all things to pit your strength and wits against, something to be conquered and controlled in an unpredictable world. They were also illusions - less impossible than they appeared to be with their hidden secrets, short screws, openable hinges, false lids. But they all still needed daring and stamina, endurance and patience.

They made a man feel reborn maybe, as he cast off the restraints of the ordinary to become the extraordinary, the eccentric, the enigma.

And there was always the search for something new, more daring, Houdini was like that too. He was famous, but still he was remaking himself as he went along. He had to keep the crowd on its toes.

The review in the papers after the Vickers challenge didn't give as many column inches as it used to give Houdini, Randolph had noted, just a brief paragraph: *"Houdini held the audience spellbound with his 'water torture cell' feat and there was a good deal of interest in the Indian Needle Trick"*.

The media and crowds needed yet more to keep them interested. And he thought he had just the thing. But the letter Randolph had just received from Houdini said he and Bess would soon be gone for some considerable time. If he was going to tell Houdini his latest idea, he had better do it soon.

"This week Empire Bristol
Next week Empire Newcastle on Tyne
Bristol, March 25th 1914
My Dear R.O.D.-
 Thanks very much for that page re Mongolian Tortures, I had not seen it.
It is about the limit for 1914.
The post card drawing of the Vickers Challenge is good.
 We do not get to Nottingham until June 8th.
Which will be our last week in England for we sail for America June 18th and will be gone some considerable time.
 Am rather rushed this week, kindest regards to your parents in which Mrs Houdini joins, I remain as ever faithfully yours
 H Houdini"

The man who helped Houdini, Randolph Osborne Douglas
Buxton Museum and Art Gallery

17
Suspended

By 1914. Houdini was a name that was synonymous with amazing stamina, baffling escapes and feats 'bordering on the supernatural.' He was the ultimate escapologist. But he also wanted to be known as a great magician. Houdini's bold and larger-than-life persona well suited the grand scale escapes and spectacles that he had won over the the public with. But he wanted to try his hand at the type of stage magic that he had admired in others, such as the famous magician De Kolta, and he set up a show in 1914 to do so. The 'World Famous Self Liberator' was now 'The Supreme Ruler of Mystery' and presenting a 'Grand Magical Revue,' that would 'prove himself to be the Greatest Mystifier that History Chronicles.' Houdini never was short on hyberbole and it seems he always wanted to be the best, most famous at everything.

In May, he was billed as the star turn to celebrate the reopening of the newly renovated Palace Theatre in Manchester. And in June he was at the Nottingham Empire. He probably invited Randolph over as Randolph often travelled to other cities to see his friend and more than likely help out backstage to oversee the latest challenge. But this time was different, with the second part of the week, after the Water Torture Cell, being his Magical Revue, featuring many new magic tricks that Randolph had not seen. He was looking forward to it.

Monday June 8 was the start of the Nottingham run for Houdini, and 'Positively the Last Appearance in England prior to making his Second Tour of the World.' Randolph it seems had indeed been to the show in Manchester in May and had pasted the review in his scrapbook, but it would be good to get another look at it.

As ever with the Empire chain, the Nottingham theatre was a splendid venue. Randolph watched closely as Houdini walked on to loud applause and began his show. He opened with The Crystal Casket, where a pretty glass box hung above the stage as Houdini threw coins, which mysteriously disppeared from his hands and appeared inside the box. Though Randolph was near the front it was a little hard to see the effect properly.

Other magic followed on, including Good-Bye Winter, where he made a lady disappear, Money For Nothing, where coins were conjured up, Arrival of Summer, in which a lady was made to appear from a pyramid, Calico Conjuring, Lady Godiva, in which he made a pony and rider disappear and then De Kolta's Marvellous Cube, which started out small then amazingly kept growing until it was big enough to open to open and reveal a woman sitting inside.

The revue closed with Metamorphosis, one of Houdini's earlier showstoppers. Wearing an overcoat, he was handcuffed and put in a sack, then climbed into a trunk, which was locked. Curtains were drawn around it. A trice later Houdini appeared through the curtain, out of the box, free of handcuffs and without his overcoat. When the still-locked trunk was opened, it was now Bess who was inside it. That was the finale. Bows, house lights up, exit.

Sometime after the show, Randolph and Houdini talked. Maybe Houdini could feel that the audience were not as taken with his magic as they were with his escapes. It wasn't what they expected from the showy American. Maybe he decided he would therefore have to keep on with the type of thing they expected.

But it would need a new take on things to keep the escapes interesting. And maybe that is when Randolph told Houdini his latest idea to do just that. Whenever it was, it was enough to entice Houdini back to the Douglas household in Sheffield again.

Houdini pushed open the little gate to the house at Carrington Road. He was curious to see what his friend and fellow escapologist Randolph had come up with now. The quietly spoken and reserved young man was always so full of enthusiasm and new ideas.

Knocking on the door he was met by Randolph and ushered inside, given tea and warmly welcomed by Robert, Kitty and Peggy. It was still exciting, having such a big celebrity call, though Randolph seemed to take it all in his stride, being more interested in sharing ideas with the great mystifier on a level, than sitting in awe.

After a meal and some pleasant conversation, the impatient Randolph led Mr. Houdini up the small staircase

Left: Flyer for the Nottingham Empire Magical Revue show, from Randolph's scrapbook
Buxton Museum and Art Gallery

88

to his attic room. Houdini was quite familiar with the place now, the dimly lit stairway and its banisters up to the first floor, then a dog leg up to the door which opened onto a final few steps into Randolph's domain. He rested his hand on the round finial as he glanced around again at the portraits of himself, the books, the geological specimens, all the trappings of his friend's ever searching and curious mind.

Then he noticed the rope. It was attached to a winch on the wall, and also to a beam in the high, gable ceiling.

The stairs leading up to Randolph's room *Author*

Randolph was enjoying the moment, the great Houdini now his audience, instead of the usual way around. The mystifier was mystified, wondering what his friend was up to.

What Randolph did next would change the course of magic's history.

He asked for Houdini's assistance to don a straitjacket, as his mother Kitty, who had joined them, stood and watched. She was used to his carryings on by now. He always used the all-in-one type jacket, with the sleeves stitched together.

And now he was ready. Nodding to Kitty, Randolph lay down as she tied the rope around his feet, and walked over to the winch. After asking Mr Houdini to give her a helping hand, they slowly hauled Randolph up into the air, until he was dangling from the beam.

Then, as the bemused Houdini watched, Randolph proceeded to shed the straitjacket, looking like some kind of emerging butterfly. The jacket fell to the floor with a dull thud, and the released Randolph swung slightly to and fro, his arms opened out in a gesture of accomplishment, his face in a wide, upside down grin. An iconic image was born.

It was a simple idea, a type of escape Houdini was known for, but with a whole new twist, literally, as this time the action was done upside down, with the body bending upwards to release itself.. Houdini was impressed. It was just what he needed - a new way to gather a large crowd - and out in the open it would be spectacular.

Carefully he helped lower his young friend down. He had come up with a winner.

Randolph around 1914/15
Private Collection

18
War and wonders

Houdini, armed with his new idea, set off back to the USA aboard the S. S. Imperator, a huge vessel on which he and Bess travelled first class to celebrate their twentieth wedding anniversary on June 22. Whilst on board he entertained Theodore Roosevelt and was proudly photographed standing next to him in a group shot.. Later he had the others airbrushed out to leave just himself and Roosevelt. The Imperator was crowded and many people were glad to be returning home to the States, as rumours of unrest and war were rife. Three days after the vessel arrived in New York, rumour turned more towards reality as Archduke Ferdinand was assasinated

Goldin, in Randolph's autograph book *Magic Circle Archives*

It must have been a worrying time for everyone, Randolph included, as the storm clouds gathered. Maybe trips to the Sheffield Empire took his mind off things. In July he was there seeing Horace Goldin, an American illusionist famous for his rapid presentation. Randolph managed to meet him, getting a sketch of the magician signed in his autograph book.

But things outside the magical world of the theatre got worse. On Wednesday August 5, Randolph's father arrived home from work. He was by now working as a silver designer and craftsman at the firm of Cooper Brothers, on Arundel Street, just around the corner from the Empire. As he came in he handed his son the day's newspaper. It was a headline they had been dreading. Randolph looked at the story:
"England has declared war on Germany. And from today a state of siege will exist in this country." It was probably an evening filled with worry about the future at Carrington Road that night. Randolph was unmarried and at the right age to have to fight. Perhaps he went up to his room and tried out an escape from a pair of his newest handcuffs. At least he could determine the outcome of that.

91

Front of the Sheffield Independent on Wednesday August 5,1914   *Sheffield Local Studies Library*

On August 5th, Kitchener took over as Minister for War and issued orders to expand the army. A campaign for recruits began in earnest, with 'Your King and Country Needs You' posters calling men to enlist. 100,000 men did so within two weeks. Randolph was not one of them. It seems that he either didn't agree with the war, didn't want to get taken in by the wave of war fever, or most likely that he had a protected job that was important for him to remain in.

Sheffield had armament factories: Vickers, Hadfield's, Cammell Laird and Firth's. As many people as possible needed to stay behind to keep the much wanted steel coming. Some silversmiths and cutlers took on jobs to aid the war effort. Steel helmets were made at Hadfields, but also many were made by the firms of silversmiths and cutlers to help meet demand. Randolph could have been involved in these jobs and so have a protected occupation. like so many Sheffield men who were in the steel trade.

Even so, many skilled men went off to fight and there was a labour shortage. Women took up jobs such as that of tram conductress. It was a new life of liberation for many women that fuelled the fight for emancipation.

On 28th August, Kitchener asked for another 100,000 volunteers. Enough and more signed up. Sheffield sent many young men, and on September 10th hundreds

enlisted at the Corn Exchange in the city centre. Placards saying 'To Berlin - Via Corn Exchange' were on display as a Sheffield battalion of university and professional men was formed, the Sheffield City Battalion, the 12th (service) Battalion York & Lancaster Regiment. It was known as the 'Sheffield Pals' as most of them knew each other, were from the same place, or were even the same families. Randolph's family most likely knew people in the battalion.

The Corn Exchange *Sheffield Newspapers archives*

Almost 1000 men were recruited in just two days. Some men may even have volunteered for a square meal and to make one less mouth to feed at home. Many had such hard jobs and long hours of hot, dusty, tedious and body-draining work in the mills and foundries that army life and a smart uniform may have seemed more exciting. The rush to sign up probably didn't give much time to think they may instead by going to a life of terror, mud and blood.

The war took on a terrible reality as Sheffield became full of soldiers. Hundreds of young men paraded at the Norfolk Barracks on Edmund Road, trained at Bramall Lane, home of Sheffield United Football Club, then moved to a camp further out in Redmires. on the edge of the city for more training and trench building.

It must have been a welcome relief to enter the cosy auditorium of the Empire, and be taken away to a world of magic and wonder.

In early October Randolph went there to see Herbert Brooks. Brooks was known for his manipulations with a deck of cards. He was also known for escaping from a small trunk. Randolph watched carefully. He of course had his book with him and did a sketch of the act, drawing Brooks holding cards. Behind him, he drew the trunk and cabinet, waiting for the escape routine.

When it came, the performer had to be squashed into the trunk, which then had a canvas cover laced over it. It was even rolled over and upside down as ropes were put around it. Maybe Randolph didn't show Houdini this drawing - his friend wasn't too happy with other people doing trunk escapes.

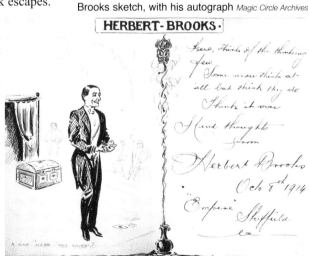

Brooks sketch, with his autograph *Magic Circle Archives*

Houdini would always be Randolph's main inspiration, but perhaps it could have been Brooks who inspired his own 'box endurance test' in 1913, and not Houdini.

He was happy to take inspiration from any good performer and a photo of Brooks in his trunk, in a fetal position, looks a little like the one of Randolph. And Brooks had been to the Sheffield Empire in 1913 too.

Signed Brooks photo
Buxton Museum and Art Gallery

Randolph met Brooks, who gave him a signed photograph. Randolph also got his drawing signed as was his usual way and added it to his collection. He was getting quite a few now. He had also got a good collection of leaflets, cuttings and articles about magic and magicians, He put them all in a scrapbook, 'Magical Matters' which he had done a cover for, with sketches of escapes on it. Any magician was fascinating to Randolph and he saw as many as he could.

The next one was the famous David Devant. He was at the Sheffield Hippodrome a couple of weeks later, with a special matinee.

It was a change to be at the Hippodrome. The frontage wasn't quite as elaborate as the Empire but it was still fine. Inside, Randolph climbed the marble stairs which led to the foyer. It was designed to look like a Venetian palace, with mirrors, colonades. and alcoves. He got his ticket and took a seat.

The auditorium was gold and white, with crimson plush seats and green and grey carpets. The proscenium arch had marble pillars at either side. and the stage was huge and could revolve if needed. One of the other novel features of the theatre was a sliding roof, which opened at the interval or if it was a hot night.

David Devant came on stage to a rush of applause. He was known for his friendly, humorous patter.

He did some small effects, such as multipying billiard balls at his fingertips, but also some more elaborate and romantic ones, such as 'The Artist's Dream'. Randolph had been looking forward to this one.

Devant appeared in the guise of an artist painting a large portrait of his dead wife. A cloth was placed over the finished painting and the weary artist falls asleep, dreaming of his wife.

As Devant sat there dreaming, Randolph watched as a woman, representing a spirit of mercy, entered and drew back the cloth.

Randolph's magic scrapbook
Buxton Museum and Art Gallery

94

The image of his wife was not in the painting anymore, but standing there, real, on stage. The artist jumped up, awake and reached towards her but she disappeared, back into the canvas, two dimensional again. Devant as the artist reached towards the spirit, as she disappeared in a flash. Then he collapsed in sorrow as the music swelled. It was a clever and very moving illusion. A great piece of theatre. Maybe Randolph mused how wonderful it would be if the illusion were real, and he could conjure life from the portrait of his mother. which was still hidden away in the back of Peggy's wardrobe. Even for an instant it would be good to see her again, well and smiling.

Randolph's programme
for the Devant matinee   *Buxton Museum and Art Gallery*

Another highlight of the Devant show was 'Biff' or the 'DD Rays.' The curtains opened to reveal a large packing case. It was raised off the stage by blocks and a short ramp led into it from the stage.

Randolph heard the roar of an engine starting in the wings and suddenly a motor-bike burst on stage. The rider was wearing full leather boots, cap and goggles and rode the bike around and around the stage. Then he quickly zoomed up the ramp and into the packing case.

The end of the crate was then closed, trapping in the bike and rider. Randolph could hear the engine throbbing inside, and shaking the crate. A haze of exhaust fumes were leaking out.

Ropes hauled the crate high into the air as Randolph held his breath, waiting for the climax of the illusion. Devant, waiting at the side of the stage as the box lifted, held a lamp. He told the audience it produced a mysterious variation of X Rays, called 'D.D Rays.' He aimed his lamp at the crate and switched it on.

A green beam shone out across the stage, and the noisy, throbbing crate was lit by an eerie glow.

Suddenly the noise of the engine stopped. The audience jumped as the crate seemed to explode, causing the planks of wood it had been made from to fall to the stage, clunk after clunk. Randolph looked up to where the crate and contents had hung. There was just an empty framework left, swinging slowly in the lights. The bike and rider had disappeared into thin air.

The Disappearing Donkey was another Devant favourite. This time the curtains opened to reveal not a crate, but a donkey, standing there with a bemused air. Behind it was a stable on legs, painted in bright colours. Devant told the audience the donkey was called Magic, because it could disappear.

A clown was on hand to persuade Magic to climb into the stable. Once the donkey was in there, the clown quickly shut the stable doors. When they were opened again the baffled audience were shown an empty stable, the donkey was gone.

But it was 'Biff' The Vanishing Motor Cycle that Randolph drew in his autograph book and which David Devant signed after the show. He drew the crate as it was breaking into pieces, the zooming bike and Devant holding up his lamp, powered by a battery and with a little gauge next to it. And above this a pensive Devant. Randolph was certainly seeing, and meeting, most of the best magicians of the day.

Devant 'Biff' drawing
from Randolph's
autograph book
Magic Circle Archives

Troops in Surrey Street, 1914 Sheffield *Sheffield Newspapers*

On Wednesday 4 November 1914, the front page of the Sheffield Independent had a large photograph of troops from another Sheffield regiment, the Hallamshires. Randolph stared at it. Rows of pensive faces looked back. Underneath was another photo, a young soldier with an optimistic smile betrayed by his worried eyes. He was holding a pipe and tobacco which he had just been given. Randolph thought it could almost be him. But so far he had escaped this fate.

Randolph had been in the centre of Sheffield that day, as a sea of men in uniforms, with bristling guns resting on young shoulders, had flooded around Surrey Street. The thousand or so men had marched from their camp to the Town Hall. Some faces were smiling, some were looking full of dread. The Lord Mayor had addressed them all and given them the pipe and tobacco each. It would be the last sight of home for many of them.

In December, the famous Chung Ling Soo was back at the Sheffield Empire, *'In a performance of Oriental Splendour and Weird Mysticism introducing in Rapid Succession a Beautiful series of BAFFLING NEW MYSTERIES Bewildering the most Astute Minds'*

Soo had revamped his act to be more patriotic too. In one illusion, 'The World and Its People,' he used soldiers and a large Union Jack flag, which drew cheers from the audience. The war was hard to escape from, even in the magical music halls.

Pages from Randolph's autograph book, with signed drawings of many famous magical acts he saw. They include Karenzo, De Biere, Oswald Williams, Frederic Culpitt, Nazare the Miracle Maid and Van Bern. *Magic Circle archives*

19
Houdini hung

More magic shows filled Randolph's life in between work in the silver-smithing trade. In 1915, through the worry and fear of the war, music halls and theatres kept up morale with entertaining distractions. The Empire had Walton's Musical Dogs on offer on January 18th to distract people. It would perhaps lighten his mind as the headlines were full of gloom. On January 18th, when the dogs were performing, the front page headline ominously stated 'Zeppelins sighted over East Coast.' They raided Britain for the first time the day after. And on the 25th it was more scares for readers with 'German fleet heading for England.' It was a frightening time.

The war and air raids didn't stop performers getting to Randolph's area though. Some of the ones touring had clearly been influenced by Houdini. On January 11th John Clempert was on in nearby Rotherham and on February 22 Karenzo was at the probably germ-free Sheffield Empire - *'in the interests of public health this building is disinfected throughout with Jeyes Fluid.'*

Clempert was Russian born, a former professional wrestler. He did an act where he was hung, but one night it went wrong and almost killed him. Needing a new persona, he imitated the successful Houdini, billing himself as 'The Napoleon of mystery' and 'The Handcuff and Siberian Gaol Breaker.' He copied Houdini's publicity stunts - and a lot of his act. He even did an escape from a glass and galvanised steel tank

Randolph saw Clempert's act, and did a water colour of it - the Russian style backdrop, a curtained cabinet and the water-filled tank, complete with the tin baths and buckets used for filling it. It must have been odd for Randolph, seeing someone steal his friend's act.

'The Great Karenzo' too, imitated Houdini and escaped from a 'Death Defying Water Torture Cell.' It seemed everyone wanted to be like Houdini, not just Randolph.

Karenzo also had a 'Siberian Jacket of Torture', the 'East Indian Needle Mystery', and 'The German Torture Board' billed topically and with a great bit of wartime propaganda as 'illustrating German methods of treating prisoners.'

Below: One of Randolph's more gruesome ideas perhaps inspired by Karenzo's Siberian Jacket of Torture He has signed it 'Robert Randini.' *Buxton Museum and Art Gallery*

In February Randolph took his mind off the war by watching a magician called De Biere. The same day the newspaper had a large photo of 'Gunner Alcock' being buried at Norton church, his coffin covered in a Union Jack. Maybe Randolph knew him. The papers were pull of young and haunting faces lost after 'doing their bit.'

Another famous American magic act appeared in Sheffield in May. The Leons, billed as 'The Wonder Workers.' An act named 'Fire and Water,' described on posters as 'A Modern Miracle' was their top illusion at the time and it was this that Randolph chose to sketch.

A young lady stood in an iron cage above the stage. At the other side of the stage, a glass tank suspended by chains, was filled up with water. The tank was than locked and covered. Next the lady in the cage was covered, a torch set to her, and she vanished in the flames.

Randolph's drawing of Leon's Fire and Water illusion
Magic Circle Archives

The Leons
Private collection

When the tank full of water was uncovered. There she was, resting underwater. Randolph got his drawing signed of course, and another photo for his collection.

⊪━O

In July Randolph was posing for some photographs of himself again. But for once there was no sight of a cuff or a shackle, no defiant gaze of a trussed up Randini. These were tender portraits of a handsome young man, pensive and gentle looking. Maybe he had thoughts of having to go to war and had the portraits taken as a keepsake, just in case. One, taken on July 10th, he signed, *'Your affectionate son Randolph'*.

But Randini was still very much a focus and dream for Randolph, He was still buying locks, and still hoping to follow Houdini's example into showbusiness.
But the war was holding up everyone's life - and ending it for many.

Randolph in 1915. In these photographs he wears the tie clip that his father gave him for Christmas in 1910.
Private collection

In October 1915, an event that made many more sign up for war and duty was the execution of nurse Edith Cavell. She was working at a nurse training school in Brussels when she was arrested under accusation of harbouring enemy soldiers and helping them escape. She was shot on the 13th, promoting an outcry and rush of enlistments. It seemed the war just got worse, with more deaths and more lining up to be next.

And the press were helping the drive with the demonisation of the enemy. On Thursday 4th October, a headline of the Sheffield Independent said *'Another visit from the baby killers. Incendiary bombs in London area. 42 casualties'*.

The same newspaper's front page of October 23rd had 'King George's inspiring message to the nation' too, another way of making young men feel they should be signing up- *'I ask you men of all classes to come forward voluntarily and take your share in the fight.'*

Back in America, Houdini was busy entertaining as usual. He was 'Walking Through A Wall,' and even working on a diving suit to aid the US government. The war had put a stop on his tour of Europe and he had been busy moving into a new house at Flatbush and had taken a few months off in the spring of 1915

When he was back working again in November, he grabbed headlines again by trying to make the world champion heavyweight boxer Jess Willard come on stage in in Los Angeles. Willard refused to join in on the act and insulted Houdini. Newspapers reported it and recorded Houdini's reaction: *'I will still be Harry Houdini a gentleman when you are no longer champion of the world.' The crowd backed Houdini and Willard left the theatre. Obviously Houdini came out on top with a bit to spare'* said the newspaper.

Los Angeles paper from December 1st, 1915, in Randolph's scrapbook
Buxton Museum and Art Gallery

Houdini sent clippings of the event and his other exploits to Randolph. He knew his friend would want to know all that was happening. He sent posters, leaflets and newspapers. Some articles would have meant even more to Randolph - they were of Houdini doing the very thing he had showed him up in his little attic in Sheffield, half a world away. His own idea made famous.

One of the bigger spreads was from the 'Los Angeles Express,' on December 4th, 1915. He stared at the photo of his own escape idea, the one born in his room with an audience of two. Now it was being done in front of a huge crowd and making headlines. Perhaps he felt a twinge of envy, a sense of lost opportunity. Or perhaps he felt a wave of pride knowing that it was he that had helped Houdini boost his public image with the spectacular stunt, the stunt that would become one of the most iconic and enduring images of his career.

Randolph read through the article before carefully pasting it into his scrapbook.

The escape was in front of the Tribune newspaper building- guaranteed easy publicity with the press on the doorstep. And the crowd was the 'greatest in the city's history'. Houdini addressed the huge crowd with a megaphone and told them the daring feat he was again going to do. Then he took off his hat and coat, loosened his tie and stood firm as two burly men strapped him into a straitjacket. They pulled the ties so hard he was shunted about and almost fell over.

This done he sat down. As his ankles were tied he surveyed the scene. Thousands of people were mobbing around for a closer look. It had been a great idea of Randolph's this and perfect for an outdoor spectacle. A theatre would never have got him such a crowd or so much publicity at one go. And there was lots of time for a dramatic build up as he was being hoisted up.

It was actually a little easier than escaping from a straitjacket standing up, but it looked so much more sensational and dangerous - just what he needed to give his escapes a new lease of life.

Cutting from the Los Angeles Express, December 4th, 1915, in Randolph's scrapbook
Buxton Museum & Art Gallery

Houdini smiles whilst hanging, ready to escape a straitjacket
The original photograph, in the Dr. Bruce J. Averbook Collection, shows an umbrella just by Houdini's head.
This has been digitally removed here by the author to make his figure clearer

The block and tackle was attached to his bound feet and Houdini felt the blood rush to his head as he was pulled up slowly, high into the air. He could see a sea of faces below him topped with hats and caps, all tilted skywards to see his dangling form.

The odd drift of smoke and waving arms reached upwards as they waited. Houdini took a deep breath and began. Writhing about on the rope like a trapped animal he swayed back and forth like a human pendulum, shaking until his arms came free. Then he bent his fit body upwards, and undid the buckles on the jacket, the back of it opening like beetle wings to reveal his bright white shirt underneath. Then the jacket was shed and fell down to the feet of the people below. He opened his arms out wide in a gesture of triumph and as the crowd cheered and waved their hats, perhaps he smiled a silent thanks to his young friend in Sheffield.

It was a very different kind of straitjacket that was looming in Randolph's life - that of the regimented army routine. The war was chewing up young men at an alarming rate and there was a desperate need for more soldiers. Randolph was young and unmarried, a prime candidate that had so far not been swept into the fray. But the possibility was getting more likely.

Another type of routine was also stopping young Randolph achieve his Houdini style dreams - that of having to earn a living, which he was still doing, at Cooper Brothers in 1915. But working there did have some compensations.

A girl who was in charge of staff in the silver warehouse had taken his eye.

Hetty Bown was a lively girl, with shiny hair and bright eyes. She laughted a lot, and was as determined to get the most out of life as Randolph was. They had a great rapport, with him winding her up constantly with his good natured banter.

Randolph was a fascinating man with his craftsman's skill, his gentle wit and his artistic nature. He was handsome too. And no doubt his tales of escapology and his dreams and hopes to go on stage would make him even more attractive and interesting. He had already done some shows and was on friendly terms with the great Houdini. With all this talent and a famous friend, it really seemed he could one day become the Great Randini. But it was who he was now that interested Hetty and they developed a close friendship. Friendship which would grow into love.

Hetty Bown
Private collection

Randolph was enjoying life and this relationship with his 'little pal' so it must have been hard to think that they may soon be parted like so many other sweethearts. But the enlistment drive for the war was relentless and it seemed only a matter of time.

Just a week later after Houdini's Los Angeles escape, dreams of being a famous escapologist himself seemed even further out of reach for Randolph. The recruitment drive was no longer resisted. Randolph signed up.

Randolph in a new
persona. This time
as soldier, in 1915
Private Collection

20
'Am now a Soldier'

There was still voluntary enlistment in December 1915 and the idea of conscription was not yet forced. Instead there was a sort of 'halfway house' idea introduced by Chief of Recruiting Lord Derby, The Derby Scheme. Men could enlist at once, or attest with an obligation to come if called up. The public were told that voluntary enlistment would soon cease.

On the 11th of December, Randolph, aged 20 years and 9 months, went to join the other young men heeding the call from Lord Derby. There were recruiting stations at the Town Hall, The Corn Exchange and even The Jungle where he had spent happy hours before the war began. Some firms had stations too, to enroll their staff, so he could have signed up at Cooper's.

On Randolph's attestation form it states that it was Cooper Bros & Sons who gave him notice. His father Robert, still working there too, must have been full of apprehension seeing his young son go to join up. He must also have been worried by the state of the world for little Peggy and now for his unborn child, for his wife Kitty was pregnant. But it was the fate of Randolph that was foremost at the time. He was the one to maybe go to war.

Wherever Randolph attended he would have been in a crowd. The newspapers reported a great turnout that weekend, with thousands of men signing up to go on the reserve battalion list. Saturday the 11th saw a 'great rush of recruits' with 500 people waiting at the Corn Exchange when it opened at 9.30.

The weather was atrocious but the queues waited patiently. The Jungle was just as busy and recruits were 'attested' promising to serve for the duration of the war, at an average rate of 200 an hour.

BRAVO, SHEFFIELD !

Magnificent Close to the Recruiting Rally.

FINAL SCENES.

Recruiting under Lord Derby's scheme concluded in Sheffield at 11 o'clock last night, and there is no doubt that when the figures come to be known it will be seen that the men of Sheffield have responded nobly to the call of duty. The great bulk of the work, of course, had been got through before the recruiting stations closed on Saturday, but that the extension of time for another day was well advised was proved by the fact that there was a fairly steady flow of attestants at the Corn Exchange yesterday, which increased in volume in the early afternoon, and again in the evening; when, for a time, the staff found their hands quite full. In fact, the total for the day was only a few hundred short of that for Saturday, and brought up the grand total for the two days at all stations to a figure running into many thousands.

Saturday's Rush.

Saturday opened, as was expected, with a great rush of recruits. The staff at the Corn Exchange found about 500 waiting at 9.30, and there was a similar state of affairs at the Jungle, but preparations in the provision of ample assistance, and the devising of a new system of working, had been made overnight, with the result that all applicants were dealt with in a very short time, and by about 11 o'clock men were attested as soon as they arrived. There was another big rush of time, but the stuffs were equal to all emergencies, and the work was got through with perfect ease.

At the Jungle, where Mr. J. C. Skinner was in charge, everything went on with admirable smoothness, and it is calculated that during Friday and Saturday attestants were dealt with at the average rate of 200 an hour.

Mostly Married Men.

It was noticed with regret that the proportion of single men was small. Much the larger proportion were married men, and generally speaking, they appeared to be actuated by a patriotic feeling rather than by the sense of being driven by the tide. Many of the men appeared to be very near the age limit, and one man who gave 39 as his age was obviously much nearer 50. When questioned closely in regard to the matter, he said that neither he knew his age, but he had a son in the Army, and he thought he had done his bit at the time.

Sheffield Daily Independent
Monday 13 December 1915

After attesting, these 'Derby Men' as they became known, were sent back to their homes and jobs until they were called up. They were given a khaki armband, with a red crown on it, to show they were willing to serve when needed.

Randolph, back in the grind of his silversmithing job, looked down at his armband. Maybe it felt like the first step to his doom, maybe it felt like an exciting new opportunity to serve his country. Maybe it was a symbol of the death of his dreams.

He waited and perhaps hoped against, the call to arms. Much as he could escape irons, padlocks and ropes, it didn't seem that he could escape war.

The papers he had expected, but maybe dreaded, arrived. Randolph was no longer waiting in a reserve battalion - he was now mobilised, and called to war.

He was recruited into the 3rd Yorkshire and Lancaster Regiment on January 27th 1916, the day the Military Service Act came into force, so the army had probably held back till everyone was called up together. The Military Service Act was nick-named 'the bachelor's bill' as to start with conscription only included unmarried men between 18 and 41. By May it included married men as well and by April 1918 men up to 51 would be called.

The day after being mobilised he was posted, leaving Sheffield with other young recruits for an army training camp, then moved to Sunderland. Now Randolph had another new persona. Not Randini, but Private Douglas, number 24446.

Cocken Hall, Fence Houses, County Durham
Reproduced by permission of Durham County Record Office and the trustees of the former DLI

Randolph and the others arrived at Fence Houses, the nearest rail station to Cocken Hall. He looked around him at the signal box and the unfamiliar surroundings as they were ushered off to the hall, where their training camp was based.

The camp was the headquarters of the local reserve battalion, the Durham Light Infantry and it was where they were to be moulded into military material. At least it looked a pleasant place to be posted. The old hall was covered in ivy, with leaded light windows and a large conservatory. Almost a year before it had a narrow escape when it was attacked by

Fence Houses signal box *John Hinson*

militant Suffragettes. They had poured petrol on the staircase and set it alight but it was saved by a quick thinking caretaker. All the smoke damage and the slogans 'Votes for Women' had by now been washed away.

Newly-shorn hair hair flattened down and parted down the middle, his left hand clenched a little, Randolph had a photo taken in his new uniform. Maybe he was thinking it could be his last pose, standing there looking a little less at ease then when wearing shackles and padlocks.

At Cocken Hall, Randolph and his fellow soldiers settled into their hut, and began their new routine. Hair cuts were one change, but Randolph managed to retain a little more than the others. He wrote about it on February 2nd, when he sent a letter to Hetty back in Sheffield, a world away. Sitting down at the wooden table when they got a break, he thought about the girl he was missing and began to write:

"We've had a pretty hard day of it to day but Randolph is feeling fit and that's the

main thing. Up for 6 you know is different to Coopers @ 9.30"

It seems Randolph's health was not to strong, and he felt fresh air and army life may do him good, even with the earlier mornings. But it was all too clear what the future was set to hold:

"We've been dished out with our kit and trenching tools so you'll have to guess what we're going in for."

Durham Light Infantry at Cocken Hall.
Randolph's mess was probably much the same
Reproduced by permission of Durham County Record Office and the trustees of the former DLI

The envelope Randolph sent to
Hetty from Cocken Hall camp
Private Collection

But Randolph must have packed his bags with a few unusual personal belongings,
and his dreams of Randini went with him too:

*"Today I have been asked to give a show tomorrow in the concert room & so I've
thrown a challenge out for them to fasten me in a strait jacket & me to release
myself in full view. Shall I do it, well we shall see"*

It must have been fun telling the others about his exploits and his friend Houdini.
Did he give other soldiers a few tips on how to escape if they were captured, like
Houdini was doing back in the States? Who knows, but it would have been an
entertaining night in that concert room. It is more than likely that Randolph met
his challenge, though he didn't write about it in any letters that survive.

Part of a list
Randolph made
in 1918 of
when he
bought his
collection of
locks etc. A
section for
1916 just
says
'Gap?
Army
Life'
*Private
Collection*

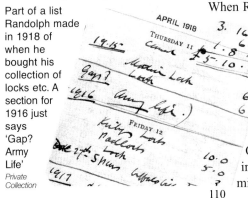

When Randolph had finished his letter, he
went outside and did a sketch of
their hut on the envelope,
writing Hetty's address along
the roof. Then he put it in the
post. These painted envelopes
would become a regular delight
for Hetty, another wonderful aspect
to her multi-talented Randolph.
Opening his artistic mail back
in Sheffield must have made her
miss him.

110

On March 12th, Randolph decided to catch up with his fellow escape artist. Houdini had sent Randolph papers and such before he left for camp and he had never thanked him. Houdini also didn't know how his life had changed and that any civilian 'inclinations' of this particular escape artist were on hold:

"Dear Mr Houdini,

I must offer you my sincere apologies for not writing before this to you, & especially to acknowledge the Papers & Post cards you sent me, but there has been such changes squeezed into a few brief months lately that as you may imagine, one has hardly been living the same life. You will know of course that we have all been called up in my group, & am now a soldier".

Randolph's letter to Houdini   *Magic Circle Archives*

He told Houdini he was *'liking the life very well. I think it will be beneficial to my health"* and that he hoped he would soon be back to *'civilian life & my loved inclinations'.* Houdini would know very well what kind of inclinations he meant.

It was good to think about getting back to his old life and it was good being able to keep in touch with Houdini. It reminded him of the life he had left behind in the attic, with the trunk of locks, and photographs lining the walls.

He signed off with a pleasant thought, of soon seeing his friend again at the Empire, *"With all good wishes professionally. Hoping to see you in Sheffield in the near future. I remain yours sincerely, Pte R. Douglas."*

Soon after, Randolph got news that he now had a brother, for on April 10th 1916, Ambrose Strachan Douglas was born; though he would have to wait a while to meet him. There seemed no chance of the war ending and Randolph was transferred to a different regiment just five days later, The Scottish Rifles.

Four days after Randolph's transfer, on April 19th, Houdini was wowing the crowds back in the USA with the upside down straitjacket escape, showed to him by Randolph back in his little Sheffield attic.

By now, Houdini probably new that the talented young man, with dreams of the stage, was wearing a uniform instead of chains. Perhaps he was pleased to hear that Randolph was entertaining the troops with a straitjacket escape of his own. Randolph's escape was for a roomful of soldiers; Houdini's inverted version was in front of a crowd of thousands. And it was a roaring success.

The throng of spectators were filling every available space, waiting to see Houdini 'hanged' in front of The Munsey Building, Washington DC. They watched expectantly as he was strapped into a straitjacket by two attendants from the local psychiatric hospital, tied with a rope and hoisted, by his legs, one hundred feet into the air. There he twisted and jerked, with the crowd cheering as he released each strap. When he was free he threw the shed straitjacket to the ground. The sea of people watching erupted into applause. He had done it again.

Randolph's attic escape trick had grown to be one of Houdini's greatest publicity stunts. It had given a whole new lease of life to his crowd pulling ability and fame. But the young man who had inspired it was an unknown, a soldier, and perhaps wondering if he would even survive, let alone be famous.

April 20th,1916 Munsey Building. Newspaper cutting in Randolph's collection *Buxton Museum and Art Gallery*

Randolph, at his training at Cocken Hall, seemed to be enjoying the life. His new regiment, the Scottish Rifles, was quite an appropriate one for Randolph, as it had connections with the old Scottish Douglas family.

Also called The Cameronians, it was an infantry regiment of the British Army, the only Rifle Regiment amongst the Scottish regiments of infantry.

The original Cameronians were Covenanters. As the threat from government forces increased the Covenanters began to carry weapons. The Regiment was formed in one day, 14 May 1689, on the banks of the Douglas Water in South Lanarkshire.

The badge of the Cameronians incorporates one of the oldest insignia in Scottish Heraldry, the Douglas star, with a bugle below and thistles surrounding it. The regiment also wore the Douglas tartan, as Randolph had as a child in his little kilt. He was probably was proud of this connection by family name and maybe even chose to transfer.

Randolph's new number was 3893. In July, he and a friend had a photograph taken in their Scottish Rifles uniforms, sporting the Glengarry headdress with the white metal badge of the Cameronians. Sitting on a fence, they look relaxed and proud. Randolph holds a cigarette and seems about to say something to the photographer. His friend was perhaps a piper as he wears a piper's dress belt.

Randolph wrote on the photograph, *'Aircraft scatter'* signed it *'your affectionate son'* and sent it home to Robert and Kitty. Judging by his unconcerned demeanour, they were probably reasurred about their son's welfare.

The Sheffield Pals, however, were not so relaxed, or safe, They were in France. Their main objective was to re-capture the small hamlet of Serre, which was in German hands.

On July 1, 1916, first day of the Battle of The Somme, they fought there alongside the Accrington Pals. It was a slaughter, with hundreds of them being killed or going missing.

Randolph and friend in their Cameronian uniforms, July 16th, 1916   *Private collection*

How Randolph and his fellow soldiers felt hearing these awful losses is hard to know, but they must have been wondering if they were next. And maybe Robert, back in Sheffield, feared more for Randolph as he heard how the soldiers at the front were killed and more were sent to take their place.

But at Cocken Hall, things were not going too well with Randolph's army training. He had hammer toes and marching around, being turned into a soldier, had aggravated the problem. As well as that, he was finding it hard to breathe sometimes and had aching joints and a slight fever. The long route marches for training were tiring him out. He seems to have been to see the army doctor as early as August 1916 according to a note on one of his army forms.

In October 1916, just nine months after joining up, Randolph was sent to the army doctor to be looked over again. On the doctor's report it states that Randolph was diagnosed with rheumatic endocarditis, *'origin unknown'* and that he *'says he had rheumatic fever two years ago.'* It would have been in October 1914 that he had this illness; if that is so, it was the year he made Bess her jewellery box and saw Devant and others at the Empire. But maybe an earlier childhood bout of rheumatic fever, around the same time his sister was ill, was the culprit. There were frequent problems with scarlet fever outbreaks in Greenhill then and scarlet fever bacteria could cause an allergic reaction which resulted in rheumatic fever. Rheumatic fever was also much more common in children than adults and leaves a lifetime's weakness, as with Randolph's sister Peggy. Symptoms of any resulting heart damage may not show up for years.

Having had rheumatic fever earlier in his life would explain why Randolph would develop the symptoms that worsened in the army. One result of the illness is that it damages the endocardium, the inner lining of the heart which also covers the heart valves. When this is damaged, an infection, known as endocarditis, can easily develop, as it did in Randolph's case. He seems to have been a little concerned about his health when he joined up, judging by the comments in his letters to Hetty and Houdini.

It seem hard to imagine that the young man also known as Randini had a damaged heart. Wrestling with locks and chains and wriggling upside down in a straitjacket must have been very tiring but he had managed admirably. Now maybe he was paying for it. Not everyone had Houdini's super fit constitution.

On 12 October, Private Randolph Douglas of the Scottish Rifles 2/6 Battalion was discharged under paragraph 392XVI KR, medically unfit for further military service. He looked well enough, and was described as 'well nourished' on his discharge papers. But his weakened heart meant he was no longer fit for war. The illness that threatened his life once, may just have saved it.

21
A new direction

Randolph must have had mixed feelings about being discharged from the army. His friends and fellow soldiers were still at Cocken Hall and would be sent to fight, but now he would be sent home, a soldier no more.
He may have felt his other persona was no more too. Randini would need to be fit and able, and a weakened heart was no good for a career in the physically demanding world of escapology. Houdini was older, but he was tremendously fit. Randolph was not.

Arriving back at Carrington Road in October 1916, when the war was still raging, must have been odd for Randolph. He was free of the bonds of the army, bonds that could have sent him to his death like so many of the young men of Sheffield listed as dead or missing every night in the newspaper. But now it seemed he was also to be freed forever from the literal bonds, and cuffs, that were his dream.

But Randolph was a determined and optimistic young man. His mother's early death perhaps gave him the focus to make the most of every moment. He was welcomed home heartily by Robert. Kitty, Peggy and met his new little brother Ambrose. And there was another person waiting to give Randolph a big welcome - Hetty.

Hetty must have been delighted to have Randolph back safe. He resumed working, perhaps at Cooper Brothers, where she still worked. The mornings there didn't seem quite as early now, after the army routine. But it was still hard work and by the end of his shift at 6 o'clock, he was 'covered in brass dust'.

But after work he and Hetty made the most of their time. They met often at the junction of Cambridge Street and Division Street, near the City Hall, ready for an evening's outing to the Hippodrome or the Empire.

As he was writing to invite Hetty out again in December 1916, Randolph couldn't resist a joke...'*Glad to hear you've tried for the Empire (the Germans have been trying for it for some time now). Never mind, if we can't have the Empire we'll have the 'Hippodreuim' first house, somebody's got ta ha' us.*'
He signed it Randin. The dream was still in his heart.

And he was still collecting locks. He now had one he had made whilst in the army to add to his collection too, fashioned from cap badges and oddments he had found.

And now he was home he had more chance to help Houdini with his own lock collection. It was perhaps some kind of compensation if his own career was shortened, that he could still take part in that of his friend.

Even amid war and uncertainty, Randolph and his family kept in touch with Houdini and sent him locks, some that Randolph or his father may have made themselves. One invoice from Cooper Bros, made out for Randolph's father Robert, is for a lock costing 1/6 to be sent to New York; and other parcels were sent to Harry Houdini Esq.

Houdini in turn still sent Randolph photos, magazines and cuttings and he and Bess had always sent a Christmas card. December 1916 was probably no different. Randolph was busy buying presents and also needed to get one for his uncle from Canada who was shortly to come and stay before going out for the 'Big Push.'

He penned a letter to Hetty on December 22nd bemoaning the icy road he had to brave to go shopping, hanging on a lamp-post to steady himself.

He also bemoaned the overtime he was having to do at the 'Simple X.' Maybe this was Randolph's joke name for the Simplex car. The car was Sheffield made, at Tinsley and was set to be a rival to Rolls Royce.

Perhaps he was working somewhere other than Cooper Brothers after all. A firm called William Brothers, on Green Lane, were making parts for the Simplex. They did the brass brushing and castings for it. This could explain the brass dust.

Or maybe this intruiging reference is to something else entirely, an in-joke between the two of them.

When he had finished writing, Randolph put his letter into his carefully drawn envelope. This time it was a painting of a 'tank'. The name was given to the new innovation in warfare, armoured vehicles with a new kind of track for moving. They were given the nickname as, when they were being moved to the front, they were covered in canvas to disguise them and marked as 'water tanks'.

Randolph had opened his letter *'Just sending you one of the 'tanks that broke the ranks,'* - a reference to a popular song of the same name they would no doubt be hearing from many a gramophone.

The tune was the same as that for 'The Man that broke the bank at Monte Carlo.'

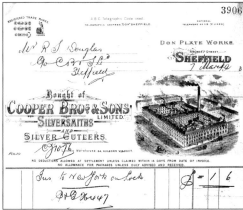

Cooper Bros and Sons invoice of Robert Strachan Douglas, for a lock to be sent to New York
Magic Circle Archives

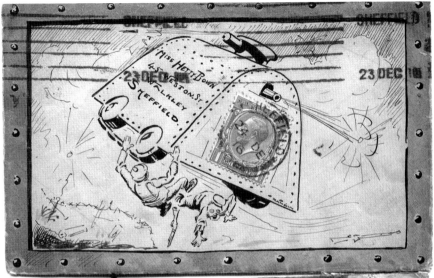

Randolph's 'tank that broke the ranks' envelope to Hetty   *Private collection*

'And the tanks went on, and they strolled along with an independent air
And their guns began to blare, and the Huns began to swear
For they pulled the trees up by the roots, and they made the Huns look like galoots
Did the tanks that broke the ranks out in Pic-ardy....
And the tanks went on, and they strolled along with an independent air
Said the Huns, "It isn't fair! You're not fighting on the square!"
At the fortress then they made a call and started walking through the wall
Did the tanks that broke the ranks out in Pic-ardy.'

Tanks were created as a means was needed to get across No Man's Land to the German trenches. Other types of vehicles had become stuck in all the mud. The idea was to use a 'caterpillar track' instead of wheels. An early prototype called 'Little Willie' was made, then improved and renamed 'Big Willie'.

The tanks were hard to drive. Inside, the noise was so great that soldiers couldn't communicate. Turning was difficult and if a tank got hit on a joint or rivet, splinters flew about inside, so drivers had to wear thick jackets and chain mail masks.

These lumbering, thunderous and innovative new war machines attacked the German front line on 15th September 1916, no doubt Randolph, then still a soldier, had taken great note of this success. The Germans had fled in terror - the tanks had broke the ranks. A report was in the Manchester Guardian on 18th September, 1916 said:

'Armoured cars working with the infantry were the great surprise of this attack. Sinister, formidable and industrious, these novel machines pushed boldly into 'No Man's Land' astonishing our soldiers no less than they frightened the enemy.

Tanks were the hot topic of the war. and still would have been when Randolph wrote his letter. It was a fitting subject for his envelope. Maybe he played the song as he drew it. ...
'In No Man's Land one early morn at sixty in the shade
From out the British lines there came the famous Tank Brigade
The Huns began to strafe 'em, couldn't make it out at all
Especially when the tanks began the Caterpillar crawl.
  His drawing though, is not much like a tank of the time. Perhaps by then he had not even seen a photograph of one of the great new inventions as they were developed in such secrecy before being sent off in their deceptive canvas coverings.
  But a year later he could have got a really close look. In 1917 a tank was parked in Fitzalan Square in Sheffield City Centre, to promote the sale of war bonds. Perhaps he and Hetty went to take a look and are somewhere amongst the crowd of curious onlookers.

A tank on display in Fitzalan Square, Sheffield, in 1917   *Sheffield Newspapers*

In March of 1917, Randolph had trouble with toothache. On Monday the 19th, a very wet night, he stoked up a roaring fire to warm the house, wrapped himself in blankets, 'until just a tuft of his hair was sticking out of the top', and hugged a hot water bottle. He wrote almost daily letters to Hetty, enclosed within his beautifully illustrated envelopes and on the 19th he wrote bemoaning his aching jaw and face, swollen 'like the dome of St Paul's.' The envelope had a sketch of him buried in his blankets, with that tuft of hair sticking out and a wisp of cigarette smoke trailing upwards.

Envelopes painted by Randolph, sent to Hetty in 1917. Left is him with toothache
Private collection

He and Hetty had been out together for a long walk the day before. They both loved the outdoors and Sundays, when they wandered all day in the countryside and away from work, seemed a year apart.

On the 22nd he wrote to her again, painting searchlights on the envelope this time. He could probably see the lights from his little attic world, peering out of the same window he misted with his breath as a child. How the world had changed. Now the country was at war and the lights were a reminder of constant danger even so many miles from the front, in Sheffield. On 26th September in 1916 a German Zeppelin had dropped a bomb in the Attercliffe area of the city killing ten women and ten children. Searchlights around the city, including Norton, near his old home of Greenhill, swept the skies to seek out any new attack.

It was a worrying time and he didn't like his job much either. It was a mundane routine for someone so creative and artistic. His father was making some exquisite works of art at Cooper's - cups, caskets and trophies, yet he seemed to be doing long hours without any great job satisfaction.

But Hetty made life seem much better. She was a regular visitor at Carrington Road. Robert and Kitty were fond of her; Robert teased her terribly, making her blush. Randolph no doubt proudly showed her his collection of locks and Houdini photos

119

and those of himself in his Randini mode. He must have been a breath of fresh air, dreaming and finding such pleasure in all the things he collected: the geological specimens, the keys, the curiosities picked up from junk shops and markets.

And he made her feel so special with all the lovely letters, notes and envelopes he sent. He did some written backwards, or done with little pictures instead of words. Such a creative man. Being with Randolph must have made the daily job in the silver warehouse seem a world away. It was such a sad thing that now his dream of being Randini was halted by a body that was weak when his mind and spirit were so full of energy and idealism. But he was home and safe and now. And he always found something to wonder at.

Randolph was still busy collecting. In 1917 he bought the key to Tickhill Castle for 3 shillings, as well as around 40 locks and more keys. He was a foremost authority on locks by now and Houdini would often ask his friend's advice in letters, or ask him to look out for a certain type of lock and send it.

He may not have been doing any physical escape tricks, but he was doing them in his mind and heart.

Left: A note from Randolph to Hetty, written in picture symbols.
'My dear Hetty
Just a line to see if you wood like a stroll to morrow about 3 o clock if the weather is fine as etty hodgson wood say. It would do you good also me as well, what thinkest thou. I'll be ready for that above time if you care to have a stroll up to no. 40, and if not well I will see you at no 45 47 as arranged.. best love and kisses Randolph"
Private collection

Around this time Randolph gave his notice in at work. He wanted to try and get a job with better hours. He wrote to tell Hetty of course, this time in a tiny letter only around six times bigger than the stamp. ('s.s'. is perhaps short for 'silversmiths'):

The tiny letter to Hetty, actual size.
Private collection

"I didn't manage s.s. for monday and I doubt whether I will manage it again at s.s. in other words I have just given my notice in so there is just going to be no more s.s in future for Randin."

It must have been a relief to leave the work he was not enjoying, but Randolph still needed a day job. He was not very good at the conventional 9 - 5 and still had hopes of a more unusual career. Now he had a new dream and enthusiasm. If fate meant that he couldn't be a master escapologist, he decided he would change direction - he was going to be a master modelmaker instead. He had the skills, and talent too, to make intricate models. He could use the same painstaking dedication he had for intricate work like making and unpicking locks, and making jewellery boxes and keys. He had made a few small buildings already and when he was ill at Cocken Hall, waiting to be sent home and thinking what to do next, he had resolved to develop this skill. Maybe he could eventually make a living doing it - lots of places wanted models for advertising displays and such.

Perhaps he wrote and told Houdini his new plans. Houdini would understand this new passion. Both men were determined to make the most of their gifts in life, to push the boundaries of their talents. Houdini was always looking for a new direction to pursue himself and seemed to want to be the best at everything, the greatest escaper, the greatest magician, the greatest performer. And now, just recently, he had discovered a new passion - a film development corporation. Scripts that never quite came off the ground about secret agents filled his mind and he was full of enthusiasm, but it was not going too well. Maybe his friend Randolph would fare better with his new career hopes.

But Houdini would know it was hard to keep dreams and creativity alive in wartime. The war seemed to be just getting worse, and on April 6, 1917, America joined in.

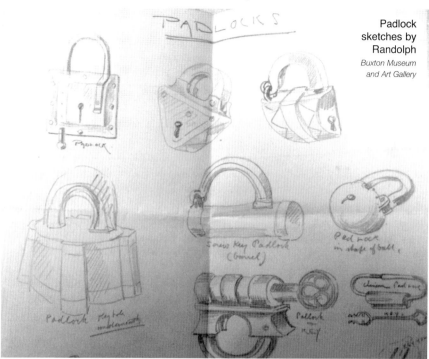

Padlock
sketches by
Randolph
*Buxton Museum
and Art Gallery*

A photograph of Randolph's 'little pal' and sweetheart Hetty Bown   *Private collection*

22
Sticking it

A merica had entered the war on Houdini's adopted birthday of April 6, 1917, when he was forty-three. He was determined to make a public show of his patriotism and was doing his bit for the war. Too old to sign up, he contributed by entertaining or instructing troops, advising them on how to escape ropes, German handcuffs and locked cells. It must have been a strange feeling using his skills, usually kept for entertainment and risking only his own life, for very real life and death situations the soldiers could face.

In January 1918, the war that people said would be over by Christmas 1914 was still not over and Houdini also starred in an uplifting, patriotic show called 'Cheer Up' at the Hippodrome in New York. Here he did one of his most famous stage illusions, 'The Vanishing Elephant.'

On the huge Hippodrome stage was a big, long cabinet, painted to look like a circus wagon. The ends of it were opened to show it was empty. Jennie the elephant was ushered up a ramp and into the cabinet, which was then closed with doors and curtains. After an instant the cabinet was opened again and Jennie had seemingly vanished. No one could figure out how he did it.

It was a fabulous publicity stunt. The 'New York Times' of January 13, 1918, told how people were baffled:

"Not even the keeper, who disappears with the elephant, declares Houdini, knows how it is done. The keeper and the elephant are done away with by different methods, both of which are so complicated - still according to Houdini- that the elephant has just as good a chance of understanding it as the keeper.'

No doubt back in Sheffield Randolph was fascinated too. He knew his friend wanted to be a success with illusions as well as escapes. He had certainly made an impression this time.

Thinking of how it must feel to have a crowd so puzzled and probably trying to work the illusion out for himself, Randolph idly piled up his latest purchases, 36 locks and two pairs of handcuffs, into his trunk. Still collecting, it was getting rather full. He was thinking of having a place to one day display all his treasures and bought a showcase too. He would like people to come and be awed by what he collected. If he couldn't perform wonders, maybe he could show people wonders instead.

In wartime there was a need for hope and wonder, a sense that the world could be a better and more magical place again. But it was hard to feel optimistic sometimes in the dark times of conflict. There had been more zeppelin raids, and on March 15 there was a public meeting to discuss plans for a memorial to remember Serre, where so many Sheffield lads had been slaughtered.

Houses were feeling the pinch too because of a gas strike in nearby Doncaster, meaning gas was in danger of being rationed, darkness of a different kind loomed.

The music halls were a place to go to try and forget the realities and killing, or maybe be fired up again with patriotism by the performers. But on March 23, 1918, death came very publically to the music hall too.

William Robinson, aka Chung Ling Soo *Magic Circle Archives*

At the Wood Green Empire in London, the famous conjuror Chung Ling Soo was performing. He had changed his act to capture the mood of the time and often had a huge Union Jack flag waving in one of his tricks. At the evening show of March 23, he was performing his famous Defying the Bullets act. Standing, armed only with a porcelain plate as a shield, Soo stood ready to deflect the bullets from the rifles aimed at him by his assistants.

It was a clever trick of course, no one could deflect real bullets like that. Soo's version involved specially adapted guns, where the real bullet was still safely kept in the rifle, whilst a blank bullet fired out from the tube used to insert the ramrod instead. But it was still dangerous and could go wrong...which it did.

As Soo stood erect and waiting, the rifle shots rang out, the plate shattered and the enigmatic magician fell. A real bullet had been fired by mistake - one of the adapted rifles had developed a fault - and it had hit Soo.

Chung Ling Soo was rushed to hospital, but nothing could save him. No magical twist and puff of smoke could make it alright again, and mend his broken body. Without a drumroll, or any applause, he made his final exit the following day. His life ebbed away.

Amidst the sadness and disbelief about his death, Soo had one last illusion to astound his public with. Everyone found out that he was not really a Chinese man named Chung Ling Soo, after all, but William E Robinson, from America.

If Randolph hadn't already known this deception, he did now and thought about how the magical world would be shocked by the accident. Houdini knew Robinson well, he would be shocked too.

Randolph's sketches of his imagined escapes

Buxton Museum and Art Gallery

An idea for a chest escape, by Randolph

Buxton Museum and Art Gallery

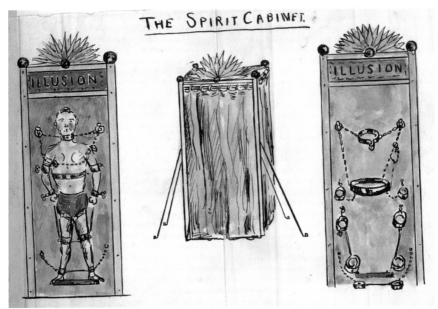

Spirit Cabinet escape idea drawn by Randolph

The Magic Circle Archives

A drawing of a stage set by Randolph

The Magic Circle Archives

Colour plates

A stage set for two escapologists- Mokana and Randolph *The Magic Circle Archives*

Randolph's painting of Clempert's stage setting *The Magic Circle Archives*

Cossak firearms expert Zakaree Ermakov's signature in Randolph's boo *The Magic Circle Archives*

Randolphs autograph book with Karenzo signature   *The Magic Circle Archives*

Colour plates

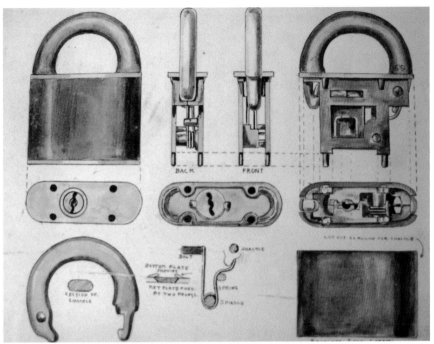

Drawings of locks from Randolph's collection

Buxton Museum and Art Gallery

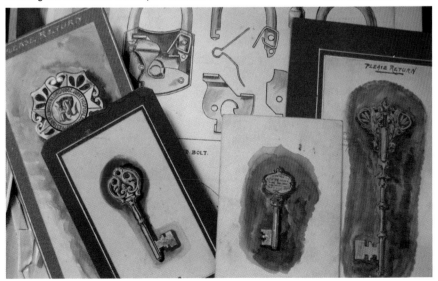

Puttrell and co, with Randolph going down the pothole   *Private collection*

Envelope to the letter about working on the flypress   *Private collection*

Colour plates

Envelope celebrating the coronation of King George VI on May 12th, 1937   *Private collection*

One from Scotland and a Scottish thistle posted in Sheffield   *Private collection*

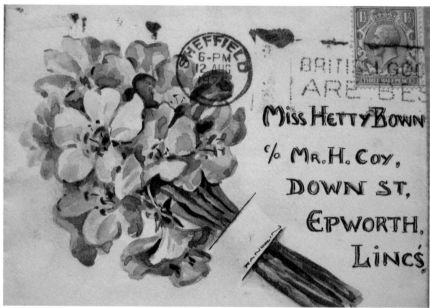

A posy for Hetty, whilst she was away in Epworth

Private collection

Windmills at Epworth for Hetty

Private collection

Colour plates

The clockwork House of Wonders sign, made by Randolph   *Buxton Museum and Art Gallery*

The entrance to Peak Cavern and another view of Castleton, by the river   *Author*

Models of the Wheatbridge and Walton Dam sites of Robinsons *Chesterfield Bor ough Council Museum Service*

The Wheatbridge site of Robinsons (top), a close up of the little van, and a close up of one of the buildings on the Portland site model

Chesterfield Borough Council MuseumService

Matchbox cottages that Randolph gave to his nieces

Private collection

Inside the entrance to Peak Cavern, with ropemaking equipment. Rope was made there and people lived inside the cavern. Randolph's sister, in later years, said that Randolph and Hetty had climbed the rockface outside the cavern *Private collection*

Douglas House, once home to Randolph's museum and now a private residence *Author*

Speedwell Cavern, Castleton *Author*

One of Randolph's models of Speedwell Cavern *Private collection*

A view up Winnat's Pass, Castleton *Author*

A view over Castleton, from Peveril Castle   *Author*

Randolph and Hetty, re-united, in Castleton churchyard   *Author*

Whilst Houdini was doing his bit for the war and wondering about Soo's death, Randolph was still working, and not just on his modelmaking, but at another firm. He was 'sticking it' at a job he didn't like. Wherever it was, it didn't seem any better than the other job he had given up. It wasn't as dangerous or wearing as being an escapologist and certainly not as dangerous as doing 'defying the bullet.' ...he hoped Houdini never tried that one... and it was a world better than many young men at the front were having to endure. But still it was heavy steel work that was making his hands as marked with lines as a jigsaw. He worried about that, as he needed dextrous hands for his model work.

It had been hard to go in again on Monday, especially after a lovely Sunday out walking with Hetty. What a contrast. Instead of beautiful scenery he was stuck in a dingy, ill-lit old workshop, with a smoky old gas stove burning away and the flapping noise of machine belts filling his ears instead of bird song.

Randolph sat in the corner and had a break, picking up his pipe. The beastly thing wouldn't light. His dad had given it to him, but he still preferred his Woodbines.

A young lad in knee breeches, with his hair flopping over his eyes and a bright red muffler tied like a hangman's rope around his neck walked past. He was the general shop runabout. Yes, thought Randolph, he did always run about; usually so far and fast that you couldn't find him when you wanted anything doing.

Back to work then, Randolph sighed, turning to pull the bar of a fly press, bringing down the heavy punch with a metallic 'plonk' onto the 'hairyplane' blanks he was working at. By tea time he had punched 4970 holes.

As he punched, he daydreamed. At least soon he would have a few hours relaxation from this carry on. He and Hetty had a night out at the Hippodrome to look forward to on Wednesday. He had got tickets for the second house.

After work Randolph got home to Carrington Road tired and dirty, but stayed up to write to Hetty again.

She was staying at Cemetery Road, for her birthday. On the envelope he drew the countryside they had walked in on Sunday and on the right the smoky chimneys of the city. He sketched his tools, scattered around a box bearing the address, locked with a 'Randin' inscribed padlock. Above the box he drew a plane and to the right,

Letter to Hetty in April 1918   *Private collection*

125

a little sketch of the spotlit stage of the Hippodrome where they would soon be sitting. He reminded Hetty of their Hippodrome date. The tickets were safely tucked in his pocket, for the 8.30 show.

Everyone else was in bed, so he didn't stay up too late burning the sitting room lights, they had to save gas, after all. Maybe life would be better if they could one day go and live in America, like Houdini. So with his thoughts full of America, Hetty and pleasant things, he turned into his 'fleabox' (his pet name for his bed), pulled up the blankets and nodded off.

Hetty met Randolph at their usual spot and they wandered down to the Hippodrome. It was a birthday treat for Hetty and they were looking forward to the show, Phyllis Dare. Dare was a well known musical comedy act, treading the boards since she was just sixteen. Though she was older, she was still an attractive and amusing act to see, with a sweet voice.

A few years ago she had been a hit in the London West End playing a factory girl in a show called 'The Sunshine Girl' written about the village of Port Sunlight, famous for its soap factory. No doubt Miss Dare entertained Hetty, Randolph and the rest of the audience with a rendition of one of the show's hit songs:

An early publicity postcard of
Phyllis Dare *Private Collection*

'We do the toilin' work, Boilin' work, oilin' work, we do the soilin' work all the 'ole day through...'

In between the weekend rambles with Hetty and the shows, the collecting and the early attempts at model making, Randolph carried on 'sticking it' at work, using the machines which hurt his craftsman's hands.

Meanwhile, in America, Houdini was concerned with a destructive machine of his own - The Automaton.

It was a robot, the sinister creation of Dr Q in Houdini's latest screen venture, The Houdini Serial, also known as The Master Mystery. He filmed it in the summer and autumn of 1918, but it would be a good while before Randolph would be able to see it. Maybe he could get to watch it after the war, he thought. The war seemed like some unstoppable mechanical monster too, with guns and tanks, shells and grenades all relentlessly crushing out young lives. And even Quentin Locke, Houdini's filmstar hero, could not stop that monster.

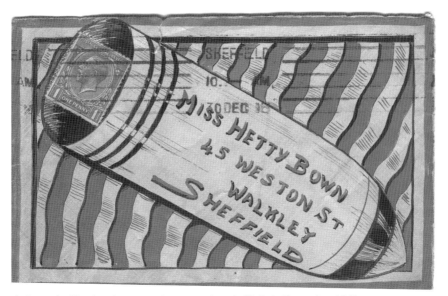

A cheery looking bomb on a post war envelope to Hetty in December 1918. *Private Collection*

As the war and the work wore on, Randolph was still collecting. It was what he spent any spare cash on. His father Robert may have been a little annoyed when in September, the £5 he had given his son to buy a new suit was instead spent on a grandfather clock to add to the collection.

The month also saw more locks, an antique vase, one gypsum and two blue john 'eggs', a sundial and two 'Alladin' lamps joining the growing pile of curiosities in Randolph's little attic museum.

Then in November, the news people were beginning to think they would never hear came. On the 11th, Germany signed an armistice with the Allies. The war was over.

A generation of young men were devastated, and the world would never be the same for many. In Sheffield, every house had an empty chair, or knew of one.

But Randolph had survived. In his ill-lit little workshop job, monotonously doing his bit for the war effort with his punching. He had hurt his hands, but he had been safe.

Now Randolph, Robert, Kitty, Peggy and little Ambrose no longer had to look out at the searchlights, wondering every night whether the zeppelins would come and blow their world apart.

That night at Carrington Road, as darkness settled, it would have been with a less troubled mind that Robert thoughtfully sucked his pipe, perusing the newspaper and glancing over at his son Randolph, sketching in the corner.

Randolph and Houdini outside the Sheffield Empire in March 1920
Buxton Museum and Art Gallery

23
Side by side

Randolph settled down into his cinema seat as the light flickered on the heads of the people in front. The music began playing and the credits rolled. It was The Houdini Serial, The Master Mystery, and he had got to watch it at last. He couldn't wait to see the amazing 'Automaton.'

Houdini was the star of course, as Quentin Locke, laboratory manager. He looked very different, Randolph thought, with his eye make up and touched up lips. His hair shade seemed to vary in colour between scenes too.

It was odd seeing his friend up on the big screen. Though Houdini had used some footage of escapes in his shows, he was here in huge close up, exaggerating looks and giving meaningful stares with raised, pencilled-in eyebrows.

The robot too, was a big star, and it wasn't long before there was a glimpse of it, hiding behind a half open door. But the first real look was a little surprising. Instead of an avenging monster, it seemed to be getting ready for a dinner party, striding jerkily through the bad guys' secret passage...holding a candelabra. But these were no ordinary candles, they released a gas that caused the dreaded 'Madagascar Madness' - so he was a bit of a monster after all.

The Automaton, with its rather smiley face, big eyes, jerky walk and huge, cylindrical hips, waved and plodded, as the somewhat slow moving and just as plodding story-line unfolded over fifteen episodes.

Of course Quentin got the girl.

Right: The Master Mystery robot and the 'Houdini Herald', advertising the film
Buxton Museum and Art Gallery

129

After his movie success and the filming of his latest venture 'Terror Island' in 1919, Houdini was back on tour in January 1920. His publicity poster for the Alhambra in Bradford proclaimed 'First appearance in England after his world's tour. It was a nice piece and Randolph was glad Houdini had posted it to him for his collection.

Houdini was touring his Torture Cell again, yet more hard physical work for the ageing performer, but he had just been swimming by Niagara Falls and rescuing yet another damsel in distress on film, so it was all in a day's work.

Randolph was regularly in touch with his friend by letter, so he knew all about the tour and how it was going. After he had watched The Master Mystery, he decided to send an envelope with a scene from the serial on it to entertain Houdini, after the serial had entertained him.

On January 18th, Houdini sent Randolph a reply from the Empire in Birmingham, letting him know he would soon be in Sheffield, so they could meet up again:

My Dear ROD -
Glad to hear from you - and that alls well. from all inclinations? -
we may be in Sheffield March 15. our time over here is limited.
Never rec'd any letter from you in america. This one just rec'd shows me you
have been to see my Serial. Regards to your folks sincerely yours Houdini.
...we're only doing the torture cell!

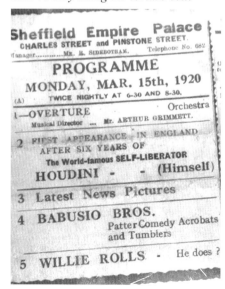

From The Sheffield Daily Independent

It was in March 1920, a month holding both their birthdays, that Houdini and Randolph met again, after six long years. The world was wearier with war and they were both older, with new experiences under their belt.

At the Empire Palace the two got together as Houdini's booking began. They had much to talk about and Houdini and Bess probably had an invite to Carrington Road again to catch up and find out the latest news in each other's lives.

It was the first time they had been together since Houdini began the upside down straitjacket escape, the one he had seen first in the attic room above, in the

130

long ago days before the war. No doubt Randolph was keen to know how it felt to do it out in the open, with thousands of pairs of eyes watching every move.

Randolph knew now that he would not be doing the escape for himself. His escapology days were over. It must have been with a tinge of envy or regret that he heard his famous friend tell of the success of the idea, to think how it would forever be associated with the great Harry Houdini. No one would remember the name of Randini, the one who had inspired it and passed it on to him.

But Randolph happily worked behind the scenes for his friend still, helping backstage again at the Empire, and also watching out front as Houdini the World Famous Self Liberator once more diced with death underwater in his Torture Cell.

Between shows they caught up on ideas for locks and escapes, talked over anecdotes from the Houdini Serial and the films his now 'movie star' friend had made. They would have talked over many other things too, probably including Houdini's latest ideas about spiritualism.

Houdini was now even more interested in life after death. He had always been fascinated, since his early days as a fake medium; and since his mother's death he was always wondering if a real medium would be able to let them communicate once more.

The subject of spiritualism was much in the news at the time and the famous author Arthur Conan Doyle was helping publicise the cause. Houdini had lately been in contact with Doyle, hoping to meet him. Knowing of this interest, Randolph probably showed Houdini the local newspaper on Tuesday March 16th.

On the front page of the express edition, was a story about a rigged seance, headed 'Ghost blinked in the light'-

'Amusing evidence was given yesterday when the hearing was continued by Mr Justice Darling of the action in which Mr.PT Selbit, theatrical agent sued Messrs Grossmith and Laurillard, the theatrical producers, for 'the medium in the mask'. A Sunday Express correspondent at the seance said the medium described with great detail what was happening in the hall'.

Arthur Conan Doyle was there then too. Objects, including a ring which had belonged to Doyle's dead son, were put into a box. The medium was able to read the initials on the ring even though she could not see it. The whole thing though, was less than convincing. When one of the people attending shone a flashlamp on it the 'ghost' winced in the light and blinked. No doubt Houdini was not surprised.

The day after the 'Sheffield Daily Independent' published drawings by a 'psychic artist' Mr C Horsfall, one of which showed 'the soul in its progress from darkness into light.' The subject would have given plenty of food for thought and discussion for the two friends. Randolph also collected cuttings and magazines about such matters. The two men shared a fascination with escaping of the final kind too.

Houdini was very conscious of the fact that all things pass and he was determined not to be forgotten after his own death. His film career would see to that. In the 'Houdini Herald' advertising the Master Mystery he made his determination clear in his usual, grand style: *'I am the hero of a romance that is replete with thrills, suspense and love. But with it all I am preserving for posterity an authentic record of my accomplishments. I believe that I am known in every hamlet of the world.'*

It was true. Houdini had become a byword for escape and mystery, He was a household name. Randolph was part of the story too, though no one knew it.

During the Sheffield Empire run of March 1920, Houdini signed Randolph's autograph book again. Never wishing to miss an opportunity for self promotion, he wrote a reminder of his former exploits, including his Sheffield jail cell escape.

Randolph's autograph book *Magic Circle Archives*

He also wrote out one of the well known sayings he used. *'Stone walls do not a prison make, nor iron bars a cage.'* and took the chance to state the place and date of his birth he wanted people to remember, even if they were not true. His public persona was his own invention. Harry Houdini was much more real to people and maybe to him too, than Ehrich Weiss. It was as if he was writing a reminder of who and what he was; re-affirming the myth, always an eye on his own immortality. As he grew older and more aware of the mortality of Ehrich the man, he grew yet more conscious of how Houdini the icon could perhaps live on forever. His friend Randolph would never forget him, that was for sure.

Randolph went down to meet Houdini again, before the show moved on to the next booking. He had papers under his arm; ideas for escapes, lock information maybe, a wad of things he was eager to share with his friend. Maybe he had some photos of little models he was working on too, his new career in the making.

The two men stood talking by the stage door. In almost identical, double breasted overcoats, their eyes shaded by hat and cap, they posed for a photograph as Randolph stopped for a cigarette. Maybe Bess took the photograph, or Hetty, one of the two women who loved these driven dreamers. The great Houdini, destined to be remembered and Randini, destined to be almost forgotten. He could easily have been, but he had drawn and pasted his dreams onto pages, marked the life of his friend in scrapbooks, a labour of love fostered by friendship.

Randolph persisted in the remarkable, treasuring wonders as well as creating them. And Houdini was a wonder.

It was a dream to be beyond the ordinary that had united the two men in friendship, a wish to bring thrills and magic to everyday lives, to be larger than life, and in doing, so growing into the created myths of themselves.

As the men stopped talking to gaze at the camera, it was a moment that held within it long years of friendship, marking a bond born of shared enthusiasms and talent. It was a moment that maybe held a sense of something passing too. It would be the last time they would ever meet.

Letters passed between Houdini and Randolph often as he toured that March. In April he wrote asking Randolph for *'One dozen and half...Double blade knives. One dozen and half...Single blade do. and dozen & half...Scissors'.* to send to his friends in America, He also asked Randolph to help him find information on various locksmiths. In return he sent Randolph some photographs:

'My Dear R.O.Douglas
When I was in Nuremberg in 1913, I had a photographer take a picture of some of the peculiar locks there. Enclosed you will find same. My assistant, whom, as you know, lives in London, happened to have the negatives - and I had forgotten all about them. Also enclosed - 'A Crash in Mid-Air' - from the GRIM GAME.'
They are marked; 1, 2 and 3. These photographs are taken direct from the moving Picture. Regards and best wishes. Sincerely yours HH

A letter in June was a last one from England, as his friend left the shores for home:
"Dear Douglas....We leave for Paris Sunday June 27th, (I go via Aeroplane) and we catch the Imperator in Cherbourg Jul 3rd. This is a rush letter, pardon brevity, even though it is the soul of wit.
Regards, best wishes to you all, sincerely yours, Houdini."

Out exploring in the 1920s. Hetty sits at the top, J.W. Puttrell is on the left and Randolph, cap on backwards, strikes a pose on the right *Derbyshire Pennine Club*

24
New Challenges

Randolph clutched the rope. He was familiar with ropes of course, but this time he wasn't escaping bonds, he was taking part in a very different sort of challenge. Now he was Randolph the intrepid explorer.

At the end of the rope was Hetty, his best pal and sweetheart and he was slowly lowering her down into darkness. She was clutching a candle and as she disappeared into the hole he could see the glow reflecting on her pretty face. Her head, topped with a little woolly tommy-shanter hat, was getting smaller as she descended. Randolph watched, smiling. She was quite a girl. Not many would be willing to be covered in mud, wade through water and scrape their knuckles and knees. Overalls and heavy boots were not the usual attire for a day out with your beau, but Randolph was not your average sort of man and Hetty was not your average sort of sort of girl, she was as daring as Randolph, full of life and energy and he loved her for it.

They were out cave exploring again, in search of adventure, and a few specimens maybe, to add to Randolph's collection, or that of their friend and fellow explorer, Jim.

During the 1920s, Randolph and Hetty had gone from walking the Derbyshire hills to wandering under them, and sharing most of their adventures was a man called James William Puttrell; Jim, or JWP to his friends. Older than Randolph, he provided another role model perhaps, like Houdini, an expert in his field, daring and bold. He pushed himself to physical limits too, like Houdini.

Puttrell was a pioneer of cave exploration, famous for climbing High Tor Gully in Matlock. The Derbyshire Pennine Club had been formed in November 1906 by Puttrell and friends and after the war they got back into exploring again.

Whether Randolph and Jim met whilst caving, or elsewhere, they quickly realised their interests matched and became good pals.

Photos of Hetty and Puttrell, by Randolph
Derbyshire Pennine Club

135

Hetty usually went too, as they squeezed and crawled, waded and scrambled their way though caves and caverns. Speedwell, at Castleton in Derbyshire, was a favourite, with the friends exploring the Bottomless Pit and beyond. Puttrell wrote about his explorations. Randolph did occasional maps of the systems they explored and together they worked their way through the fascinating underground world. They shared a love of collecting geological specimens and brought back many finds to add to their collections, some with considerable risk, as they hung and scrabbled and balanced, to get the perfect piece. They were happy and challenging times, with the friends pushing themselves, mentally and literally, through tiny gaps, down deep drops and up steep rockfaces. And the social life was good too, sitting by waterfalls, sharing a flask of tea and a spot of lunch, or wandering the hills, stopping for the many photographs Randolph and his friends took.

Randolph and Hetty in their caving gear
Private collection

Above, Randolph and Hetty in the centre, and Puttrell in the foreground, with another friend resting by a waterfall. Right: Hetty and Puttrell *Derbyshire Pennine Club*

The gang having a rest, with a rope ladder coiled and
ready, possibly at Gaping Ghyll in North Yorkshire.
Derbyshire Pennine Club

Hetty's turn to hold the
rope for Randolph
Derbyshire Pennine Club

Randolph still used some of his escapology tricks, amazing his fellows by having the knack of winding the rope around his arm, shaking it in a particular way and it coming out knotted, at the correct distances. He couldn't resist a little performance, or striking a theatrical pose now and then.

And maybe Randolph entertained with tales of his friend Houdini's escaping exploits, and of his own, as he pulled his large cap down over his eyes, wrapped his coat around against the wind and sipped from his flask.

It was strenuous exercise and exciting too, being a cave explorer. Just the ideal things to appeal to Randini. No padlocks, but still needing plenty of ropes and daring.

His health certainly seemed better with the outdoor life. The weakness that had seen him signed out of the army must have still been there, and he still had trouble from his hammer toes, with walking boots rubbing and hurting, but he was determined to live life to the full, ever searching for adventure.

Maybe he sent Houdini a picture or two, of himself adventuring in the depths, in return for those which Houdini had sent of himself adventuring in the air, in The Grim Game shots.

Left: Randolph and Hetty in a lovely shot by a waterfall, possibly Gaping Ghyll. Randolph has his big cap on backwards again and Hetty wears her favourite tommy shanter hat. Randolph was said to have piercing eyes and that is certainly the case on this photograph, as he gazes into a compass with a mesmeric look to rival that of master mystifier Houdini!. Right: Hetty and Puttrell in Speedwell Cavern, Castelton *Derbyshire Pennine Club*

Hetty and Randolph loved exploring together, There were few women cavers then, so Hetty was one of the forerunners, perhaps even the first woman down some of the caves they explored in Derbyshire and further afield.

Sometimes though, Randolph and Jim went off together and Hetty stayed behind. He missed her when she wasn't there to share in his adventures, but he was always sure to send her one of his artistic envelopes and a letter to tell her what he was up to.

In July 1920, Randolph and Jim Puttrell were off on one of their jaunts together, staying at a place called The Beeches, in the village of Clapham, North Yorkshire. Randolph had been up early and out for a brisk walk. Back at The Beeches, he sat down to a second breakfast, listening to the faint thunder of the falls sparkling in the sunlight outside.. What a morning to be alive. He wished Hetty were there to see how lovely it all was. She had stayed at The Beeches before, but not this time.

After breakfast he went off to the harness room. Mr Brown, who lived at The Beeches, was helping him make a waterproof covering for his camera, so he was missing out on the exploring for a day.

The Beeches. Arnold Brown's house is the centre one *Courtesy of Ken Pearce, Clapham*

He was determined to get some more good shots of the underground caverns they ventured into, the darkness pierced by their candles, reflecting on wet rock and flowstone, so it would be worth his efforts. He worked at it until early evening, when Puttrell came back and they all tucked into a hearty feast.

The next day they were out straight after breakfast. Randolph looked around him at the hills stretching out in the distance. It was a long walk up past Gaping Ghyll, but he was looking forward to the days adventures and feeling fresh as a daisy.

When they got to their chosen spot, Long Kiln East, Randolph sat down for a smoke as Jim unpacked his bag. Randolph leaned over to his own bag and pulled out his overalls Slipping then up over his trousers, he heard Jim muttering in annoyance - he had forgotten the candles. That ended it, no exploring today for Randin. But the day was still a pleasant one, with an impromptu ramble over the top at Ingleborough.

What a view! Sunny slopes, and large patches of limestone. Randolph took the chance of taking photographs before they worked their way down. They found a few good specimens too. By the time they got back to the Brown's they were tired out.

After tea, Randolph relaxed as Puttrell wrote up notes of the day's events. He was missing Hetty. She would have been asking lots of questions as usual. So he took out his pens and inks and set to, taking an envelope and drawing a cartoon of their caving exploits. He drew himself, a huge 'R' on his back, falling down a hole. A pie and a pile of bottles gave a clue to some of their indulgences.

Randolph stayed up late writing his letter to Hetty. He often wrote or drew late into the night. He could concentrate better. And he liked to put his best into everything he did.

139

A painted envelope by Randolph, to Hetty. On it is Snitterton Manor Farm Cottage,
where he stayed in July 1921. In front he has drawn some of the specimens he collected
Private collection

A photograph of the same cottage, with an earlier caving group outside, taken in 1908
Derbyshire Pennine Club

25
More adventures

In January 1921, Randolph got to see the aeroplane disaster Houdini had told him about. Houdini's first full length film, The Grim Game, was playing at the Cinema House in Fargate, Sheffield, and of course Randolph was there. He had got the photographs Houdini had sent him pinned on his bedroom wall, but seeing the moving image was much more exciting. What an adventure!

Two bi-planes were flying high, heading for the ocean. It was a climactic scene of the story. Houdini's character is aboard the highest plane, at around 3,000 feet. A rope drops down - he has to get into the cockpit of the plane below to rescue the damsel in distress. Next is a daring stunt. Our hero begins to climb down the rope, but the wind blows the planes into each other. Propellers mesh together; the two craft spiral to earth.

It wasn't supposed to happen that way. It was a real accident. The skill of the pilots managed to glide them to land, but there was still a huge smash. The director had kept the camera running. and the unexpected drama became a spectacular publicity stunt for the film. Stills of the collision and crash were used in advertisements and Houdini had some printed to send to friends like Randolph..

It was a death-defying feat. Randolph was amazed no one had been hurt. Did he worry for his friend, or did he know that Houdini was using a stunt double and that whilst the event was unfolding, Houdini was safely on the ground watching?

In The Grim Game, Houdini does an upside down strait jacket escape, a big screen showing of the escape that had first been done in the small attic a couple of miles away. Randolph, watching, and maybe imagining himself into Houdini's role again as he did so many times as a boy, might well have felt like shouting to the fellow cinemagoers - that was my idea! If fate had been different he could be up there doing it too. Now he just was a spectator.

An advert for The Grim Game at The Cinema House, Fargate, Sheffield, in 1921 *Sheffield Newspapers*

141

Randolph's sense of wonder and passion for collecting had not diminished though, even if his career as an escapologist had. Lately he had purchased a hand grenade, a case of beetles, a Turkish lock and shackles, fossils, sea shells an American revolver, more locks, a lock chest, stamps, 'crystalline forms,' two Davy lamps and a bird's nest. His room was getting a little crowded to say the least, but he still found space to make models. He was getting even better at it now, practising making tiny cottages, and collecting magazine cuttings and postcards for inspiration.

Robert Strachan had also been making a miniature model. Like his son he wanted every detail to be correct. But he wasn't making cottages - he made a tank, out of silver. The ten inch long model of a Mark VIII tank had been commissioned as a presentation gift to a Mr. F. J West, chairman of the Manchester Tanks Association, and the gift was from the firms associated with him making the actual tank, *'as a token of their appreciation of the zeal and success achieved by him and the committee during a period of grave national peril.'*

The Mark VIII was a joint British and American project, but after the Armistice was signed, the grand project was never carried out. But the model was a wonderful reminder and *'exacted the highest enthusiasm and praise from the experts to whose order it was executed'.*

In July 1921, Randolph was off adventuring with Jim Puttrell again. This time they were staying near Matlock. It was a well known-place for the explorers and cavers. Manor Farm Cottage, where they were staying, had long been used by climbers.

It had been an early start and the bus arrived at Carrington Road as Randolph was just staggering out with the large box he used to collect stalactites. It was hard getting it strapped onto the roof, but after a lot of hammering and other things beside, they set off. It was a hot day and they got to Matlock about twelve, then carried on up to the village of Snitterton. Randolph drank it all in as he stepped off the bus and looked around. It's a fine little spot, he thought to himself, one of those old world places it's jolly hard to find these days. Manor Farm Cottage itself was picture postcard pretty. Embedded in the thick clusters of ivy were quaint old mullioned windows.

Photo of the Mark VIII tank model by R.S. Douglas
Buxton Museum and Art Gallery

The place looked as if it had not been disturbed for the last three hundred years.

He carried in his bag and box, being careful not to bang the walls, though these walls would take a lot of knocks, they looked about two foot thick. Lots of other climbers and cavers had stayed at the old house and he could see why.

Inside there were no cramped, unlighted passages, dangerous winding staircases or dark rooms as he expected. The place was wonderfully light and airy.

As he went back to the bus for his remaining bag, he noticed outside the gateway an iron ring let into a solid block of stone. Curious, he asked their hosts, Mr and Mrs Montney, about it, to be told it was one of the old time bull rings used in this country centuries ago for bull baiting. To this ring was fastened the unfortunate bull, then to be tormented. It was hard to imagine such a cruel event in such a peaceful spot.

Early the next day they set out for Jug Hole, quite a formidable cavern with an outer grating or grille to keep the casual explorer out. But Randolph's group were no amateurs, and were in possession of the key, so they hopped inside. As his eyes adjusted to the dimmer light, Randolph followed the others. First was a lot of crawling. Then the fun began. A vertical shaft 18 or so feet deep led down. Another of the group went first, using back and foot work. Then it was Randolph's turn. he was annoyed to find his right leg wasn't working well, so he hopped up again and let Jim have a go. As he stood there he could feel his hammer toe throbbing like a 'steam hammer'

At the second attempt he managed to do the trick and landed softly at the bottom. They went on and on, coming across some fine formations. A grand days collecting.

Late on saturday, after supper, Randolph and Jim retraced their steps, reaching the top about 12.30. then winding down the rugged slope into Snitterton again. Everyone else was in bed, so the two of them set into a good supper of sandwiches and a large jug of milk, had a chat and a smoke and then turned in to bed at 2 o'clock.

The day after they slept in until eleven. Randolph was still having a lot of trouble with his toe and chafing boots, so to rest it they got a loan of a 'dog cart' and had a drive to the nearby mining village of Winster for a look around.

Back at Snitterton, Randolph decided to go for an after-dinner walk alone. He was getting fed up with the pain on his toe and went in search of corn plasters No such luck. Resting his feet before the return walk, he called in for a pint of Bass at a public house and realised how much he missed his pal Hetty. If only she was with him now to see what a fine sight the river was tonight. just one mass of red from the blazing sun reflected in the water. Quite a lot of mill girls were bathing to try and keep themselves cool. He must remember to tease her about watching them, when he wrote to her later.

At 1.30am he stayed up and did just that, quietly writing and painting the cottage on an envelope, as Jim Puttrell snored loudly and contentedly in the background.

There were many more outings and adventures with Jim for Randolph and Hetty. Their collection of specimens grew along with their friendship.

But Randolph was still honing his modelmaking and craftsman's skills in between all the exploring. When they were busy exploring Snitterton and elsewhere, he made his friend Jim a vase, using the case of an old shell from the war.

He carefully crafted on one side the date, 1921. On the other he worked Jim's initials, JWP, wound about with rope. He carefully cut out a pick they used for getting specimens, and a few stalactites too. To finish it off he added spheres of semi-

Above and left, the shell case made into a vase and given to Jim Puttrell in 1921 *Private Collection*

precious stones. Something meant to harm was turned into a thing of beauty. A small wonder created from the ordinary, by the man who loved wonders.

The other things that Randolph was making were pretty wonderful too, and other people agreed. In January 1922 he was awarded a Diploma of Merit for a model he had entered in the Model Engineer Exhibition in London, where his work was highly commended. The award was for a model cottage of cardboard, given for neat work and realism.

But it wasn't all work and explore - there was time for a little indulgence now and then too. One such occasion was when Randolph joined Jim Puttrell and others at the Derbyshire Pennine Club's Annual Dinner, at the Barley Mow pub in Kirk Ireton.

The dinners were well known as a sumptuous feast and Randolph tucked into the various delights put before him, including celery soup, leg of mutton, roast duck, trifle and apple tart.

After dinner there was a bit of banter and a few performances. Randolph sat back and enjoyed the entertainment. There were recitations and songs. Someone had written a long poem called The Spasm, about the DPC members, set to the tune of 'John Peel.'

In Derbyshire we have a club,
The fellows in it like good grub,
And they eat it when they've paid their sub,
At the Annual Dinner at the Barley Mow.
Randolph joined in the chorus with the others:
Chorus: The Barley Mow, the Barley Mow;
At the Annual Dinner at the Barley Mow.

Our visitors, you'll all agree,
Are welcomed here right heartilee,
We'll try to fill their hearts with glee,
Also their tummies at the Barley Mow.
Chorus:
One verse in particular amused Randolph, as it was about Jim:
Jimmie Puttrell is a man with a 'past';
He's a stiff-built bloke, and he won't climb 'last';
And I don't think you can set him fast,
Even at the Dinner at the Barley Mow.

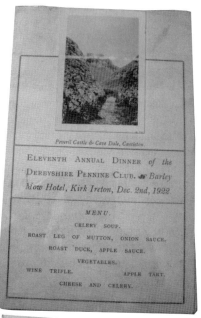

Randolph took a pencil from his pocket, opened his invitation card and signed his name. After signing he passed it around and got everyone else to sign it too. It would be a good night to remember and add to his pile of mementoes, a night with friends who all shared his love of exploring the treasures underground.

Another kind of treasure was found underground in December 1922, when Howard Carter broke into the tomb of the boy king Tutankhamen. It must have been an exciting time, reading of the growing hoard of things that were discovered.

Barley Mow menu *Buxton Museum & Art Gallery*

A Diploma of Merit, awarded to Randolph for a model cottage, on January 14th, 1922.
Buxton Museum and Art Gallery

Randolph had a thing about Egypt. The painting of a mummy was still there at the top of the attic stairs, and mummies had featured in many of his ideas for stage illusions and escapes. The Egyptians had a fascination with the afterlife too, as he did himself.

It was probably one of the things he and Houdini had found to talk about. And now his friend had touched upon it in his latest film, The Man From Beyond, which explored the subject of reincarnation.

It was all about a man who had been frozen in ice, on an arctic shipwreck. 100 years later he is discovered and thawed out. He is Howard Hillary, (Houdini of course, indulging his habit of using his own initials again). who doesn't know a century has passed and when he sees Felice, a woman who looks just like his now long dead love, he thinks it is the same woman. When he does find out the truth, he still believes it is his old love, reborn again.

At the end of the film, the two lovers peruse a copy of an Arthur Conan Doyle book about spiritualism. Houdini had become friends with Doyle and had also attended a seance with Doyle's wife, a medium, in June. She had scribbled words supposably channelled from Houdini's mother, but Houdini was not convinced, leading to his friendship with Doyle becoming strained.

Randolph more than likely saw the film when it played Sheffield. No doubt reincarnation was another subject mulled around in his curious mind. He had collected many magazines and articles about this subject and that of spiritualism.

He knew that life was precious and often short, like that of his poor mother, and the war had taken so many lives. It was painful to think that there was nothing beyond death. Life had to be lived to the full, with adventures taken and love treasured. There were so many fascinating things to see and do, or learn about in the world. He and Houdini never stood still, they both embraced life and constantly searched for new ideas, new experiences, whether it be spirits or stalactites, movies or miniatures.

In 1923, Randolph put the finishing touches to one of these miniatures. It was a model of Speedwell Cavern in Castleton and it was a gift for his friend Jim Puttrell. The cavern was one of their favourite places to explore, so it was a perfect subject. He had used a postcard to get the background and some of the details of the entrance. He had taken great care to paint the colourful flowers around the front door and along the wall. Randolph looked it over as he sealed the glass around it. It was a nice little piece. Maybe he would make more, to sell or give to other friends. But this one was for Jim. He carefully signed it on the back: *R.O.D to J.W.P. 19/8/23. Then with an eye to any future sales, added; RO Douglas, Sheffield. Copyright.*

The postcard Randolph used as reference
Buxton Museum and Art Gallery

The model given to Jim Puttrell, with (above) Randolph's inscription on the back *Private collection*

Two envelopes sent to Hetty, one from London and one from Sheffield *Private collection*

Model of a watermill, with
overshot water wheel, by Randolph
Buxton Museum and Art Gallery

26
Maker of better models

Just after making Jim's cottage, Randolph was off to London. He now went most years to see the model making exhibitions, or engineering shows, entering his own models which seemed to do well. As usual when he was away from his dear Hetty, he missed her, and sent one of his illustrated envelopes with a letter. On August 12, the subject winging its way to Walkley from the capital was of a rather grumpy pierrot, gazing at the stamp. Randolph wrote, wishing Hetty was with him as *"all the glamour and excitement is quite alright in a way but you want the right pal to share it with."*

It had been a busy year for trips. In February he was up in Scotland. From there he sent Hetty a letter, in an envelope painted with tartan, a thistle and a drawing of the Forth Bridge. Jokily he signed it 'Rob Roy'. He had seen some footage of Scotland in Houdini's film Haldane of the Secret Service, with a scene shot in Glasgow.

The last film by Houdini, Terror Island, had not gone down too well. It had some exciting scenes, with underwater exploits, a submarine and Houdini as hero rescuing the heroine from 'savages' but Randolph had heard of cinema audiences sniggering at some of the far fetched plot devices. And Haldane didn't get very good reviews either. Variety Magazine said of Houdini *"The only asset he has in the acting line is his ability to look alert."*

The plot was centred on a 'Chinese' gang of counterfeiters hiding in a monastery near Paris, but there was only one Houdini escape - from a waterwheel.

Houdini's film career wasn't going too well at all, thought Randolph, though he carefully cut out all the related news stories and publicity material his friend had sent him all the same. And maybe he was inspired, or even helping with ideas for, the Haldane film, when he had sketched out *'Stunts to overcome B.4. prisoner can possibly escape from the Chinese Gang.'*

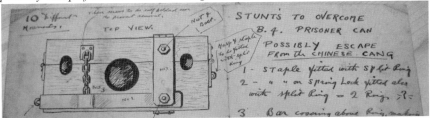

A drawing of 'stunts to overcome....'   *Buxton Museum and Art Gallery*

149

RANDOLPH · O · DOUGLAS
MODEL MAKER

SPECIALIST IN SCALE MODELS
OF FACTORIES, CITIES,
ARCHITECTURAL, CIVIL AND
MECHANICAL ENGINEERING,
REPRODUCED IN MINIATURE FOR
EDUCATIONAL, EXHIBITION
AND PUBLICITY PURPOSES.

40 Carrington Road, Endcliffe,

Sheffield,

Randolph's letterhead *Private collection*

Randolph meanwhile was not tied to a waterwheel, but he had made a lovely model of one. He was making a big effort to get his model making skills more widely known. By December 1923 he had got a letterhead and was busy taking some examples of his models around firms, canvassing for work. The firms were favourably impressed, though he wondered why the people he talked to all seemed to work in dark holes...it was hard to show all the details he put into his models to the best advantage. Maybe he would make a few with lights in...

The models he was making were exquisite, with unbelievably small details, tiny treasures of workmanship, and all done with the naked eye.

All this work was good for his employment prospects as a modelmaker, but it meant he had less time free to see Hetty. And he liked to see her as much as possible. They were still very much devoted to each other and over the next couple of years it became even more clear that they were meant to spend their lives together.

Randolph made his sweetheart special gifts. In 1925 he crafted a beautiful jewellery box, perhaps similar to the one he had crafted for the woman in Houdini's life, Bess, back in 1914. It was decorated with a turquoise coloured heart, bearing the date and had a tiny lock, which he carefully personalised with the words 'Randin Fecit' (Randin made this).

The box made by
Randolph, for Hetty, in
1925, and close up of
the lock *Private collection*

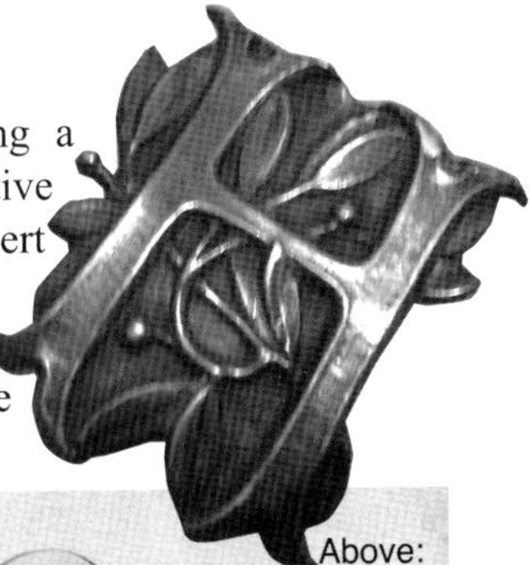

Randolph also made Hetty some jewellery, including a brooch of her initial. He was such a multi-talented, creative man, but with a talented and creative father like Robert Strachan it was not surprising.

Robert was doing lots of wonderful work himself, including trophies and cups for Cooper Brothers and he had also made a lovely plaque for the Artscrafts Guild.

Above: Randolph's brooch for Hetty *Private collection*

1925 was an especially good year for him. He was proud to have been elected Master of the Guild and sat for a photograph, wearing his regalia. He signed it and gave it to Randolph, knowing his artistic son would be proud too. But as well as that, he had produced a piece of work for royalty which had gained him a most cherished letter.

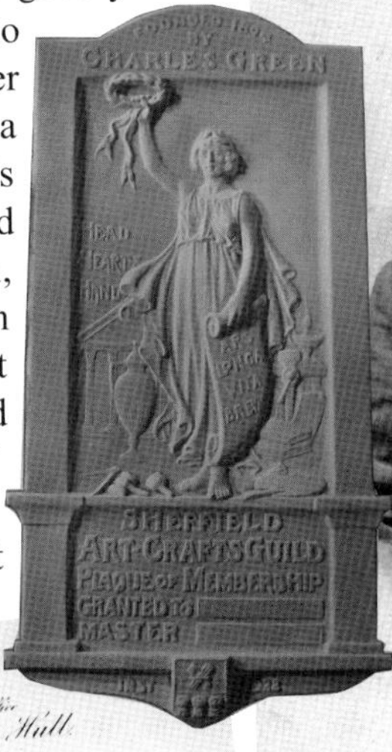

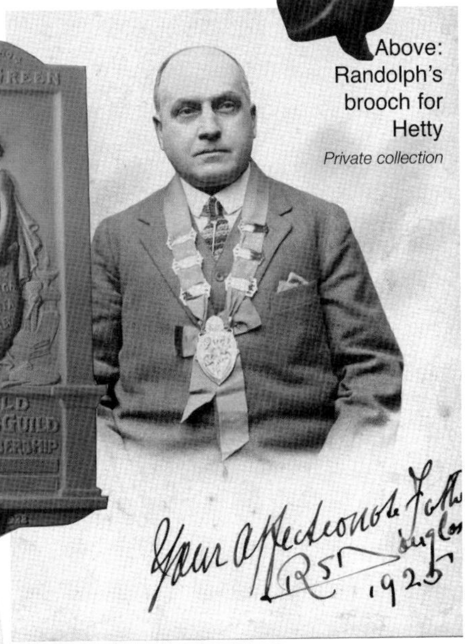

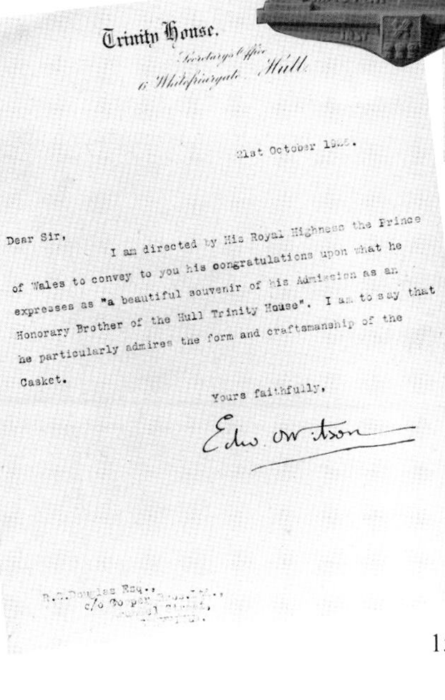

Trinity House.
Secretary's Office
6 Whitefriargate, Hull.

21st October 1925.

Dear Sir,

I am directed by His Royal Highness the Prince of Wales to convey to you his congratulations upon what he expresses as "a beautiful souvenir of his Admission as an Honorary Brother of the Hull Trinity House". I am to say that he particularly admires the form and craftsmanship of the Casket.

Yours faithfully,

R.S. Douglas Esq.,
c/o Cooper Bros.

The Prince of Wales had been presented with a splendid casket and had directed the letter from Trinity House to Robert, to congratulate him on a *'beautiful souvenir of his admission as an Honorary Brother of Trinity House'* and that he *'particularly admires the form and craftsmanship.'*

High praise, but well earned.

Above: The Artsguild plaque made by R.S. Douglas *Goldsmiths Journal January 1927,*
The regalia photo, *private collection*
Left: Letter from Trinity House *private collection*

The casket by R.S. Douglas, which was presented to the Prince of Wales   *Private collection*

Examples of work by R.S. Douglas *Private collection*

As the year drew to a close, Randolph could bear it no longer having to be apart from his sweetheart.

In July, when she had been away in Epworth visiting relatives, it had been unbearable, even though his usual letters with their beautifully painted envelopes had winged their way there and he had received loving words in return. So that decided it - they would get married.

As they seemed to be made for each other it was probably not that big a surprise really for Robert and Kitty. So their son was to wed - but first they needed a place to live.

For a while Randolph had been listing all the keys, locks, minerals and assorted wonders he had collected over the years.

What he needed was a place to show them all off, like a cabinet of curiosities.
And he had seen just the place.

In November 1925, there was plenty to celebrate on the 27th.

For one thing, it was Peggy's birthday; maybe she came home to visit - she was married now, but they were often meeting

A tiny cottage, made by Randolph
Private collection

up. Also, the Artcrafts Guild were holding one of their general meetings, this time being entertained at Carrington Road by Robert, as Master. So there were plenty of refreshments and some happy chatter that night at the Douglas household.

As well as this, they were all greeted by a delighted Randolph. He had just that day completed his purchase on the cottage he had seen. Hetty had liked it too.

It was big enough to make them a home and also to give a place for his eclectic collection. There were congratulations all round as he described the new home to be. It was in Castleton, just down a little street in the lee of the ancient Peveril Castle, at Stones Bottom. It was near the famous Peak Cavern, and of course not far from the Speedwell Cavern, which he, Hetty and Jim often explored.

It would be perfect.

A real cottage, purchased by Randolph in November 1925   *Author photo, with kind permission*

It was March 31st, 1926, Randolph's 30th birthday. And a special day in another way too - it was his wedding day. Beside him was his new bride, Harriet (Hetty), Bown no more, but Douglas. They had chosen the Register Office at 31 Union Road to be married, the same place as Robert and Kitty made their vows. They must have been re-living their own day a little as Randolph and Hetty walked up to the Registrar to make the same promises.

Proudly Randolph had signed the register, stating his trade as 'model maker.' Robert signed, as 'modeller and designer.' Like father like son.

Hetty had of course had signed her name too, adding her profession 'silver warehouse woman.' Her father signed himself 'Henry Bown, Horse Keeper.'

Henry worked for the well-known Sheffield firm of Tomlinsons. It was his job to look after the horses and also drive the carriages. Maybe the firm provided a horse and carriage for the happy couple.

Randolph's sister Peggy and her husband were there and his brother Ambrose. Hetty's family were over from Walkley, including her sisters Doris and Clarabell and her brother Harry. And friends, too, joined the celebrations. Jim Puttrell would more than likely be a guest, and so would other of their exploring friends.

Tomlinsons, ready to drive the Prince of Wales in 1909. Hetty's father is driving the first carriage and his hat is just jutting into the 's' of dragonettes. *Private collection*

Robert Strachan and Jim had already met, and they had been together not long before, in February, when Jim gave a lecture to the Artcrafts Guild. He had talked about his collection of semi-precious stones and minerals, some obtained 'at considerable risk.' No doubt Randolph and Hetty had been there with him on some occasions, adding to the collection and taking a few risks at the same time too. But now they were all together to witness an adventure of a different kind. Randini was tying another knot - *the* knot in fact. Another role, this time of husband, was in store.

Perhaps Randolph had invited Houdini to his special day. But his old time role model and friend was back home in America, and still busy with his latest passion, exposing fraudulent mediums.

Houdini was having a particularly public duel with a woman named Margery, whom Arthur Conan Doyle and many others believed in. There seemed to be veiled threats going on, with Margery's 'dead brother' sending messages to Houdini that his time was almost up. But this didn't stop Houdini, and he was touring with a show about how mediums could dupe people, complete with lantern slides and demonstrating how so-called 'spirit hands' and ectoplasm could be produced.

He had also issued a challenge to mediums to produce something he could not produce himself by less unworldly means.

It was all a culmination of his times of disguising himself, attending seances and then, as he spotted any phoney methods, ripping his disguise off and shouting. *"I am Houdini, and you are a fraud!"* Not the best way to win over the spiritualists. But he was determined to stop the frauds from exploiting others. He knew only too well how desperate people were to keep some contact with those who had gone. And he also knew, from his early days as a mediumship act with Bess, how easy it was to fool willing people.

Randolph would probably know all about Houdini's campaign and the spiritualists warnings. He was always getting the newspapers delivered from America and kept in touch with all the news stories concerning him.

It was a worrying time as his headstrong and tireless friend, no longer so young and invincible, pitted himself against many people who wished him harm. Randolph hoped he knew what he was doing - Houdini always seemed so relentless to be right. All the touring and campaigning was a lot to deal with physically, and probably emotionally too, and would be a heavy toll on a body that had already been pushed to so many limits

But on his wedding day, the world seemed a happy and harmless place to Randolph, as he and his new bride went off to their new home, and new life, at Stones Bottom in Castleton.

An old postcard of The Douglas Museum, The Stones, Castleton *Private collection*

27
The House of Wonders

R andolph and Hetty, Mr and Mrs Douglas, opened the door to their
new home. The Pharaoh style door knocker he had fitted rattled as
they closed it behind them. Randolph still had a fascination with
Egypt. So had Houdini - he had lately been working on a buried alive
escape called 'The Mystery of the Sphinx,' and would no doubt have
approved of the appropriate knocker for the one-time Randini.

And he would probably have liked the cottage too. Randolph and
Hetty did. They gazed around the room. Most of their belongings were
sorted out and Randolph had made a good job of getting it cosy,
but there were still a few things to unpack.

There was a pile of books and Hetty's knitting bag, stuffed with
wool and patterns, on the big wooden settle under the window.
And the large wooden table was stacked with boxes.

It was a little cold so they set to making a fire in the huge range. Hetty
placed a kettle on the swinging trivet and as it
heated they unwrapped a few more things. Toby
jugs were carefully placed on the shelf above
the deep set window, and Randolph crammed a
few more of his locks into the chest he had placed in the
kitchen, next to the door to the outside toilet. More books from
the boxes were pushed into the large bookcase next to the fireplace.

The door
knocker from
the cottage
Private Collection

The kettle whistled and called them to a teabreak. They
sipped drinks as they stood looking through the French-style
doors into the garden, with its apple tree. It would be a longer
task getting things just right, but they had made a good start.

It had been a lengthy task too, getting all Randolph's
treasures from the attic at Carrington Road, but now they
were all piled and waiting in the part of the cottage which
was to be his very own cabinet of curiosities - a House of
Wonders, The Douglas Museum.

He had planned it all for ages, listing locks and exhibits, and
things he could perhaps sell to all the visitors he expected.

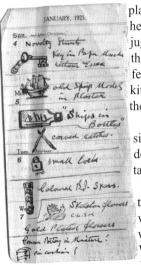

List of ideas for items
to sell *Private Collection*

157

And now it was all a reality. A new challenge. Randolph and Hetty worked hard getting the museum ready. There were to be two floors, but no shortage of things to display - all the keys and locks in Randolph's impressive collection, mineral specimens, cave formations and semi-precious stones, as well as all the odds and sods that had appealed to Randolph for one reason or another. He was interested in everything and he wanted to share his enthusiasm for life's infinite variety with all.

They had got all the glass cabinets sorted out and the museum began to take shape. The entrance would be the cottage main door, but they built a little hatch, with a curtain, to sit by and take the money from any visitors.

In the entrance hall it was a bit tricky pinning up a hide shield and swordfish swords, but they managed, and added next a few photos of themselves exploring in Speedwell Cavern- they would be a good talking point.

The ground floor had a few glazed cases. Randolph carefully filled the largest, taking up the objects one by one; an old brass pocket sundial, a swiss cow bell, a saxon spear head found at Matlock, a tinder striker and a 17th-century snuff box. Next he lifted one of his favourites - the six-inch-high Iron Maiden tooth pick holder, sent specially for him from Nuremberg by Houdini. Carefully he labelled it 'Presented by Mr Harry Houdini,' remembering the thrill he had got unwrapping it all those years ago, a young teenager with a headful of dreams. He had not made those dreams a reality, but life was still pretty good. His health, the stealer of his escapology hopes, was holding up, he was in his own home with the thrill of a new museum to run and best of all, he was married to his dear 'little pal' Hetty.

Coming back from his daydreams, Randolph carried on with the case filling, unpacking and mounting an amazing array of objects. He placed in the cases onyx, agate, quartz, clay pipes, a sea horse, a watertight matchbox used by Derbyshire miners, a South African comb, sand from the Isle of Wight, and stalacites. On the wall he hung a map of Derbyshire from 1610 and his Diploma of Merit from the Model Engineer Exhibition in 1922. The diplomas would remind people nicely about the standard of his modelmaking talents, though the models themselves spoke volumes. For they were all there in the House of Wonders too, and wonders they most certainly were. Randolph had worked hard on his tiny creations. He wanted people to be amazed by his own work as well as that of nature and others, and he had produced some of his best work to date to fill the cases and draw in the crowds. They were mentioned on a flyer that he had got printed, with the header. 'This museum will interest you!' as bold a statement as any Houdini bill.

The tiny motor
made by Randolph
*Buxton Museum
& Art Gallery*

158

There was a working motor he had crafted, so small it would fit under a thimble, tongs carved from just one match, a perfectly scaled - down saw, only 5 inches long and a safe the size of a stamp. Another lovely miniature Randolph had made was a greenhouse, so small it would fit on your thumbnail. Inside it there were forty two tiny plant pots in rows, complete with plants.

One morning he had sat in his workroom, at the left hand side of the cottage over the kitchen, and written out the Lord's Prayer on a slip of paper so small that it would pass through the eye of a needle. This too was now an exhibit, waiting to draw gasps of awe.

The greenhouse, with the roof off, and, below, on the author's thumb nail *Buxton Museum and Art Gallery*

A 5" long saw made by Randolph and a handbill for the museum *Private collection*

HIS MUSEUM WILL INTEREST YOU !

THE

DOUGLAS MUSEUM

A HOUSE OF

WONDERS

CASTLETON,   DERBYSHIRE.

This house is situated at the foot of Peveril Castle, on the way to th.. Peak Cavern. Here the visitor can see a unique collection from all parts of the world.

CAVERN   FORMATIONS.

The Finest Collection in the District.

is to be seen here, consisting of Stalactites, Stalagmites, Curtains, Cave Nests, Pool Formations, etc.   RARE MINERAL and GEOLOGICAL SPECIMENS.

LOCKS 4,000 YEARS AGO.

A fine collection of LOCKS and KEYS showing the progress of the locksmith's art, 4,000 YEARS AGO to the present day.

A CURIOUS TREASURE CHEST.

An Iron Bound Chest over 300 years old.   An interesting point about this exhibit is that the keys which unlock the chest are HIDDEN in the CHEST itself and the hiding place must be found before the Keys can be extracted.   The Keys operate SIX LOCKS, two of which are MUSICAL CHIMING.

Some Wonders of the World.

THE SMALLEST ELECTRIC MOTOR IN THE WORLD.

Perfect in every detail the whole of which will stand under a SMALL THIMBLE.

THE SMALLEST SAFE.

The door of which a penny postage stamp will easily cover.

A GREENHOUSE ON YOUR THUMB NAIL.

A TINY GREENHOUSE, complete with its plant-pots and flowers in full bloom.

HOW SMALL CAN YOU WRITE?

Handwriting that will pass through the eye of a small needle.

A TINY HOUSE.

Standing in its own grounds and fitted with Electric Light.   A beautiful example of miniature architecture.

ANN HATHAWAY'S COTTAGE.

STRATFORD-ON-AVON, with its OLD WORLD GARDENS. A model remarkable for its minuteness of detail.

A WONDER IN CARVING.

A PAIR of TONGS carved from an ORDINARY MATCH, which when closed will fit inside another hollowed out to receive it.   The chief point of interest in the TONGS is that they have been carved from ONE SOLID MATCH and not made in TWO PIECES.   These along with many CURIOUS objects of general and LOCAL INTEREST will occasion wonder in the most disinterested person.

NO VISITOR SHOULD MISS THIS HOUSE OF WONDERS.

OPEN DAILY - Including Sunday.   Proprietor :—R. O. DOUGLAS

VISITORS ARE PERSONALLY CONDUCTED ROUND AND OBJECTS OF INTEREST EXPLAINED

TAYLORS, Printers, Wombwell, Yorks

159

Model of Ann Hathaway's cottage *Photo, private collection, actual model on show at Castleton Information Centre*

He had made some more Speedwell Cavern models, like the one he had given Jim, and models of the Douglas Museum itself. But one of the more impressive ones was a model of Anne Hathaway's cottage at Stratford-on-Avon. At just six-and-a-half inches long it was exquisite, with a glorious garden. A little piece of 'Olde England.' Very little, in fact.

Specimen cabinets and glass cases, downstairs in the Douglas Museum   *Private collection*

160

Randolph O. Douglas
MAKER OF BETTER MODELS

OUR REF.   YOUR REF.

THE MUSEUM,
CASTLETON,
VIA SHEFFIELD.

A photograph of the upper floor in the Douglas Museum and Randolph's re-done letterhead for his new address   *Private collection*

The upstairs of the cottage museum was crammed too, with a bizarre range of items Randolph had collected and hoarded over the years. These included his grandfather clock, an elephant's skull, Buddhist prayer wheels, spears, a musket, a spinning wheel and some colourful collections of butterflies and beetles. One glass container he had acquired was labelled 'Radio Hypnotic Crystals'. He wasn't quite sure what they were, or what they did, but it sounded interesting.

Miniature models of the museum, in plaster, cardboard and brass
Private collections

161

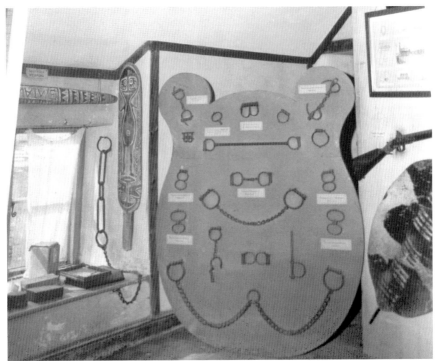

Handcuffs on the padlock-shaped display board, upstairs in the museum   *Private collection*

It was also upstairs that Randolph made a display of his lock and key collection, including the one he had made in 1916 from shell cartridges, an ancient wooden one from Egypt and the keys to Sheffield Manor, Debtor's Gaol and Tickhill Castle. He and Hetty had cut out a big padlock-shaped board to hang his handcuff collection on. At least if he wasn't using them, draped in iron as the Great Liberator Randini, he could use his expertise to tell people about them. He had a better idea than most of how effective they were.

But it was on the stairs between the two floors that Randolph put some of his most important items. Bridging the gap between the Randini locks and shackles on one level and the models and specimens of his new life as a cave explorer on the other, were news cuttings and photos of Houdini, one of his life's constants.

Randolph had proudly framed all the newspaper cuttings he had collected about Houdini, either sent by the man himself, or taken from the American newspapers that were sent over for him on order. Lots of his money went on magazines and papers, catalogues and leaflets of one kind or another.

And now the cuttings were all on show, next to a peacock's tail, a beaded grass skirt, a 'slave whip' and 'slave leg irons.'

But in pride of place was the photograph taken of Randolph and Houdini, standing shoulder to shoulder, outside the Empire in 1920. That was the last time they had been together, though letters and Christmas cards had been exchanged regularly since then. It seemed a long time ago, thought Randolph as he straightened the picture on its hanger, stroking the glass with his hand to wipe off a little of the packaging dust.

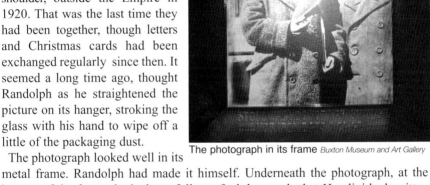

The photograph in its frame *Buxton Museum and Art Gallery*

The photograph looked well in its metal frame. Randolph had made it himself. Underneath the photograph, at the bottom of the frame, he had carefully crafted the words that Houdini had written that March day in his autograph book:

'Stone walls do not a prison make, nor iron bars a cage.'

Randolph and Hetty stood outside their own stone walls, looking up at the wooden signs now in place - signs on the front and gable end of the cottage and proclaiming the delights to be found within 'The Douglas Museum. The House of Wonders.' Everything was ready - and they opened their eclectic little treasure house at Eastertide, 1926.

Hetty sat by the door, and collected the small fee for entrance. Once inside, Randolph showed people around personally. He enjoyed explaining the objects and showing off his workmanship, seeing the amazement on people's faces as they saw the detail in his tiny models. And there was often a murmur of appreciation as he switched lights on in some of the little factories and buildings he had created.

Sign from the museum *Buxton Museum and Art Gallery*

To show other models off to best advantage he used a hand-held flashlight. pointing the light at various objects to pick out details.

163

A CASTLETON MUSEUM.

INTERESTING EXHIBITS. .

The Douglas Museum at Castleton, which has been opened to the public this Eastertide, should appeal to all classes of sightseers, for the exhibits consist of geological specimens of interest to the scientist, historical relics and curiosities which occasion wonder in the most disinterested person. The geological exhibits contain specimens from the Derbyshire caves, stalactites and stalagmites, which look like beehives, and stalagmite straws, rods 18 inches long. The cave nests also are of interest; they are cuplike holes in the limestone formed by dripping, and containing little egg-shaped stones, which have evaded dissolution. From southern rock formations cases of agates and fossil sponges of beautiful colours and unusual shapes, are found. An unusual collection which is seen here is the lock and key collection, which traces the lockmakers' art from 2,000 B.C. to the present day. The model lock of 4,000 years ago is similar to the Yale lock of to-day, but was on a much larger scale and made of wood, but the principle is just the same in this Egyptian pin-lock as in the elaborate present-day specimen. Tracing the variation through the centuries, the heavy Elizabethan locks, hand-made, forged and welded by hammer, appear clumsy yet intricate in their design. Other locks are Secret Escutcheon German XVI Century; prison padlock, German XV. Century; and the Old English Para-toptic lock, which has two keys which open or shut the lock independently. The more modern locks contain Chubb padlocks and door locks of a century ago, and hundreds of keys of all ages, shapes and sizes are seen in other cases.

The curiosities include a smuggler's book, a Dutch dictionary, which has its middle pages stuck and a secret cavity made in them to contain contraband, a model motor, the outer casing of the dynamo of which is only ¼in. in diameter and is driven by a 4-volt. battery, the whole of which would go under a small thimble. A tiny nickel safe, perfect in every detail, has a lock which is eleven-sixteenths of an inch long, three-eighths broad and three-thirty seconds thick, the rest being in proportion. Another interesting exhibit is a thread six inches long, and which is in a small needle, and a magnifying glass shows clearly the "Lord's Prayer" written along the thread. .

The most skillful models made by Mr. Randolph Douglas are perhaps the architectural models which are extremely minute, and include a model of Anne Hathaway's Cottage, the garden and flowers being included oin detail: a Swiss cottage, and a greenhouse about 1in. high, inside of which can be seen through a magnifying glass, plant pots containing flowers. There is also a pair of tongs, carved perfect in detail, from one match-stem, a Swiss cow-bell, pocket animal, Saxon spearhead (found at Matlock), cedar cones from Mount Lebanon, cases of beetles, moths butterflies and weapons, a treasure chest from Spain (16th century), which when pressed in two places reveals a key which opens a secret escutcheon, revealing a further keyhole and which causes warning chimes, six keyholes are found thus before the chest is opened. All these are included in a large and varied collection

Newspaper cuttings collected by
Jim Puttrell *Sheffield Local Studies Library*

The Lord's Prayer on the tiny strip of paper, going through the eye of a needle, was a favourite.

A reporter from the 'Derbyshire Times' came to look over the interesting new Castleton museum and its exhibits, and wrote quite a long review. Now Randolph had another item to add to his cuttings collection.

His friend Jim Puttrell added it to his collection too. Jim also had scrapbooks of cuttings about Derbyshire, caving and such. Into one of these he pasted the article about the opening of his friend Randolph's home and haven for the weird and wonderful. No doubt some of the specimens and cave formations on show he had helped get, or donated.

Just a month after the glowing review, the newspapers were full of more downbeat stories - of a General Strike to be called by the Trade Union Congress in support of the miners, who were already on strike. Mine owners wanted longer working hours and lower wages. All industries were being urged by the TUC to join in to try and paralyse the country in protest.

On Monday May 3rd, the local press carried a national appeal for volunteers to help during the strike with maintenance and food supplies to go to the Town Hall and a 'national emergency sermon' was given at St Paul's church. But after attempts to avert it, the strike went ahead. Pits and factories were idle, buses and trams stopped.

Perhaps the impact was felt less out in Castleton, but everyone would know about it. Getting there from Sheffield without public transport would be hard, so maybe there were less visitors to the museum to show around. On the other hand some may have taken the strike as an opportunity for a walk out into the countryside whilst away from their jobs.

Strikers in Fitzalan Square, Sheffield   *Sheffield Newspapers*

The strike carried on until the 12th. There were some skirmishes as strikers tried to stop volunteers from driving buses or loading food, but overall it did not get as nasty as it could have been. Perhaps people were still hoping for a calmer and more harmonious world after the horrors of the war. On Thursday May 13, The Guardian newspaper said, *"There was with most of them a sort of understanding that never existed before and they had a common trench language they never had before. How long this thread between them would have lasted in the sharper conflict of another week one cannot surmise, but happily the real test never came."*

At the House of Wonders, life there, whether affected by the strike or not, was working out pretty well. Visitors were enjoying the new attraction and Randolph and Hetty were enjoying their new roles as museum owners, the carers and sharers of a world of exhibits . The year passed by and the summer was beginning to turn to Autumn. The castle ruins were not so busy and the nights were getting shorter. In the cottage the black range was getting more use as the chill crept into the air a little earlier each evening and Randolph and Hetty relaxed by the fire after another day. 1926 had been pretty good, they reflected; getting married, moving into a new home and running the museum. But before the year was out, it had sad news in store.

165

YORKSHIRE TELEGRAPH AND STAR,
MONDAY EVENING, NOVEMBER 1, 1926.

HOUDINI.

DEATH OF FAMOUS
"HAND-CUFF KING."

STOMACH BLOWS?

Harry Houdini, illusionist and "handcuff king," died yesterday at Detroit after two operations (says Reuter).

An Exchange message from Detroit quotes the "New York Sun" as saying that Houdini's manager, Mr. Stuckel, has issued a statement attributing the magician's fatal illness to blows upon the stomach inflicted ten days ago by a student at McGill University, Toronto. While lecturing Houdini invited the students to come to his dressing - room for further information.

Gaol-Breaker.

He repeated the trick in a village hall, where his success was witnessed by a New York manager, who engaged him for six months. The manager had Houdini handcuffed and put in gaol, to demonstrate his powers of escaping. There followed tours of Europe, where Houdini escaped with ease from many gaols, including those at Leeds, Liverpool, Sheffield, and Huddersfield.

A few months ago Houdini allowed himself to be confined in a coffin equipped with a telephone instrument, and submerged in a swimming pool for an hour and a half. Rahman Bey, the Egyptian mystic, who had previously stayed under water for an hour, declared that the feat was only possible while he was in an hypnotic trance. Houdini, who was assisted out of the coffin in a state of exhaustion, afterwards explained that it was only necessary for the person thus imprisoned to take short, even breaths to conserve the oxygen in the limited air supply.

Escape from Sheffield Police Cells.

Houdini frequently appeared in Sheffield, where he delighted large audiences with his escapes from ropes and handcuffs fastened upon him by members of the audience. On one occasion, it will be recalled that the famous "Handcuff King" permitted himself to be handcuffed and put in a double-padlocked cell at the Water Lane Police Station. The officers in charge of

SHEFFIELD MAIL, MONDAY, 1 NOVEMBER, 1926.

"HANDCUFF KING'S"
DEATH MYSTERY.

BELIEF THAT HOUDINI
WAS HURT BY BLOWS.

FROM OUR OWN CORRESPONDENT.
DETROIT, Monday.

Startling allegations have been made by the physician who attended Mr. Harry Houdini, the world-famous illusionist, who died here, yesterday.

The doctor attributes the "Handcuff King's" death to blows on the stomach, dealt by a student at the McGill University.

The student, says the doctor, called on Mr. Houdini in his dressing room some time ago and, commenting on the magician's strength, said: "You would hardly feel a blow on the stomach, would you?"

"HANDCUFF KING" DEAD.
Houdini's Great Strength and Remarkable Escapes.

NEW YORK, Sunday.
A Detroit message states that Houdini, the "Handcuff King," has died after a few weeks' illness.—Ex. Tel. Co.

Houdini's many remarkable escapes from chains and sealed compartments have been performed in all parts of the world.

One of his extraordinary acts was to escape from the so-called "Chinese water torture cell."

Houdini was lowered head first into a tank filled with water, his feet being fastened in stocks brass bound.

When he was submerged a cover was padlocked on the tank, which was enclosed in a curtained cabinet. By his unaided effort he escaped within two minutes.

His success, it is stated, was partly

Cuttings about Houdini's death, from Randolph's scrapbook   *Buxton Museum and Art Gallery*

166

28
The last escape

Randolph looked at the headline in disbelief. There it was in black and white. *"Death of famous hand-cuff king."* It was hard to take in, that the man known by name to thousands, and whom he had known as a personal friend, was gone. Could it really be that one blow to the stomach had killed the man who had withstood so many physical extremes and pitted himself against so many challenges?

It seemed that the unexpected blow was delivered to Houdini's stomach by a student visiting him in his dressing room. Randolph knew that Houdini would have needed time to prepare himself mentally and physically before any test of strength. Not having the time to do that would have left him vulnerable.

Since this event, Houdini had been in pain, but battled on until the end of a show in Detroit on October 24. After the show, he had collapsed with a fever and had been rushed into hospital. Two operations later, a ruptured appendix and peritonitis were deemed to be Houdini's final challenge against death. This time he lost.

He died in hospital, with no triumphant return, no applause; just a final exit from a man tired of fighting. Houdini had made his last escape. It was October 31st, the suitably mysterious Hallowe'en, when the veil between life and death is said to be thinnest. He always did have a great sense of timing.

Randolph sat by the window in his workroom on November 7th, gazing up the sloping path towards the castle. He didn't know what to write. How could words help when Bess had lost such a special and unique man? But he had to say something, let her know he was thinking of her. He expressed his sympathy simply and told her that he had *'been anticipating a Christmas card which has been his custom for some years and which I have very highly prized."* He was tentatively trying to imagine a future without the man who had been his inspiration since childhood. No letters or cards, no sharing of ideas and information. It would be an emptier world without the larger than life Hand-cuff King, his friend, Mr Harry Houdini.

The funeral had been held on November 4th and thousands of mourners had attended. Even in death Houdini was putting on a crowd-pulling show. And, as fitting for a master mystifier, he had left people talking and even puzzling about his death. There were some rumours that the spiritualists would have been keen to get rid of Houdini and his embarrassing public attacks, and that maybe they could

NOVEMBER 14, 1926

CROWD PAYS TRIBUTE TO HOUDINI AT FUNERAL

The body of Houdini, the world-famous Illusionist and handcuff king, being borne from the Elks Club, New York, to the waiting motor-hearse. The funeral took place at Cypress Hills. Rabbis Drachman and Tintner officiating.

Cutting from Randolph's scrapbook *Buxton Museum & Art Gallery*

even have poisoned him. No one could prove it of course - a final potential mystery.

Such devious means may have seemed more believable in some ways than the fact that a ruptured appendix had finished off a legend. A sensational showbusiness icon suited a more sensational end.

It was with a heavy heart that Randolph pasted in the cuttings. Reports of his friend's death and funeral from various newspapers were the last things he put into his special Houdini scrapbook. Next to them was an earlier article he had stuck down, before his friends death. It was Houdini talking about his own end, entitled 'Breaking life's fetters.' Randolph read it again with a new perspective:

"If I were to die to-morrow I could not complain. I would pass out content with the fullness of life and with the knowledge of experiences such as few men have had..... Men like myself, who are continually risking their lives, are inclined to brood upon the Great Beyond." He talked of his brush with death in the Grim Game plane crash, and how his time was *"not yet ripe to pass into the existence to come. When it does I hope I shall meet it fearlessly."* Maybe this made Randolph feel a little better.

Houdini probably knew all about Randolph's museum; but now he would never see it. He would never see on the top floor the display of locks given to Randolph from his own collection, some of the more interesting ones he had found when he was in Nuremberg. There were German wrought iron padlocks and keys from the 15th and 16th centuries. He had known his friend Randolph would be the one to appreciate them. And now they were in a glass case, in pride of place in a Derbyshire village, a tribute to a special friendship.

Everyday, people looked at them and saw the cuttings and photograph of Randolph and Houdini on the stairs, heard of their friendship as Randolph walked around the museum talking about his collection.

But did they also hear how Randolph had given Houdini one of his most iconic escape ideas? Perhaps not.

It must have been strange for him, showing people around after that sad Hallowe'en, talking of Houdini, now dead. It may have seemed another line drawn under his own shelved dreams of Randini. And one of the articles about Houdini and his exploits he had pasted in his book perhaps filled him with a sad irony. It was from the Vancouver Sun of March 1, 1923:

"So when you see Houdini wriggling out of a strait jacket in front of this office today, hanging by the ankles thirty or more feet from the pavement and admire him, remember that you yourself could have done such a feat with ease if you had only had energy and ambition enough to put your capabilities to fullest use."

Randolph <u>had</u> done it with ease - and before Houdini did it too. He had indeed had the energy and ambition. He had even had the idea. But what the reporter didn't mention you needed was health. That was the difference. If he had been as fit as Houdini and carried on, performing the stunt himself, maybe people would have been writing about him doing the feat and he would be the one admired for it. As it was, he was an almost forgotten part in the story of Houdini.

But Randolph was now hoping to be written about for other amazing feats. His models and museum were the main focus of his work now, and he was getting publicity from various articles in the press. He was also getting some well known visitors. On 17th July 1927, he welcomed another famous magician to The Douglas Museum, Murray, an Australian escapologist, who had played Sheffield Hippodrome the week before with his 'packing case escape,' probably watched by Randolph. He signed the museum visitor's book:

YOUNG SHEFFIELDER OUTRIVALS LILLIPUT
MINIATURE MARVELS. FLOWERS IN A TOM THUMB GREENHOUSE

...A young Sheffielder, now living at Castleton, has taken up modelmaking for business firms, wealthy Americans and others. He is Mr. R.O.Douglas and he can make a model of anything from a battleship to a sewing machine.

He showed the writer a greenhouse so small that it will stand comfortably on one's thumb, yet it is complete down to the tiniest flowerpot. Looking through the glass of the house the rows of flower pots and blooms can be plainly seen.

Fascination of Detail

Then there is a model of Ann Hathaway's cottage at Stratford on Avon, drawn exactly to scale - 1 inch to 16 feet - which means that the building is reduced nearly 200 times. Yet not a detail is missing, every flower is there in the garden, and even the separate bushes which comprise the hedge can be distinguished.

Ever since he was a lad Mr. Douglas has been fascinated by the making of tiny models. "The detail work appeals to me," he said, "I am never satisfied unless I have included everything"

Sheffield Daily Independent Wednesday 29th June 1927

Murray's name in he book *Buxton Museum and Art Gallery*

Murray had not long after Houdini's death, done his own version of the trick invented by Randolph too. As early as November 1926, just a few weeks after Houdini's death, there was a photograph of him doing the escape hanging 200ft in the air above Piccadilly Circus in London. They must have had quite a bit to talk about as Randolph showed him around the museum. Maybe Murray had made a special effort to get to see the home of the man who had invented the escape for Houdini. They must also have talked about other illusions too, as Randolph sent him a letter just a couple of days after his visit. On July 26th a letter came back:

Dear Mr Douglas,

Many thanks for your letter of the 19th which I have not had an opportunity of answering before. The design is very useful and it will be very good for distribution on return visits. Thanks for the idea. Despite the weather being too good for show business we are keeping our end up and cannot complain. Thanks for the good wishes from Mrs D and Self which are heartily reciprocated. Wishing you both all the best for the present and future.

Yours Sincerely, Murray."

Murray had also told Will Goldston, one of the foremost magic dealers, about the 'design,' a version of the milk can escape done by Houdini. Maybe it was an idea that Randolph had worked on with him, or designed for him and had decided to sell on. Or maybe it was a new twist on it, and Randolph was determined to keep involved in illusion design, even if Houdini was not there to share it.

The same day as Murray's letter was sent. Goldston sent one too, expressing interest in buying the illusion and, finding it a fair price, asked Randolph to send it:

"In reply to your letter of the 7th, we understand that your can is fitted with an inside lining which pushes up with the collar and lid, allowing the performer to escape. Should this be the case, please forward to the above address, covered and securely packed. Kindly advise that this has been done. Send your bill per letter post.'

Murray was playing at the Hippodrome, Preston, in March 1929, and Randolph was there. He looked down at his programme. It was odd to see the photograph on the back, an escapologist hanging upside down in the escape he had initiated, and know it was not Houdini. Others had always copied, but now it was different - now there was no original.

Programme for Murray in 1929 *Buxton Museum and Art Gallery*

170

It was still unbelievable, that Houdini had gone forever. Poor Bess was finding it hard too. The newspapers had been saying that Houdini had spoken to her through a medium, relaying a code they had decided on before his death; then were saying it had all been a fake. It was sad. Bess was drinking heavily which didn't help. She didn't really make much contact any more. Even the Christmas cards had stopped. Houdini's secretary didn't like her keeping in touch. Maybe he was a bit jealous. And that was that.

No doubt Randolph enjoyed Murray's show and perhaps he went to chat back stage afterwards, the way he had with Houdini. He was at home in the company of magicians and illusionists and they perhaps knew of his reputation as a good ideas man.

He was having plenty of ideas for the Douglas Museum too, ideas for things to sell, for publicity posters and gadgets.

And back in Sheffield his father Robert was still being creative at Cooper Brothers. On July 17th, he and the staff posed for a photograph, examples of the fine

July 17, 1929, Cooper Bros. *Private collection*

work they did hung about them on the walls. At home in Carrington Road he still tapped and burnished in his little studio, whilst out in Castleton his son was tapping and modelling works of his own. The two men were creating intricate wonders, one using precious silver, and one pieces of cardboard, but both were using admirable skills.

Posters by Randolph *Buxton Museum and Art Gallery*

171

Photographs of some of Randolph's modelling work. Top: shredded wheat factory. middle: village, and bottom, the cement factory model in Castleton Village Hall *Private collection*

29
A model career

R andolph worked hard at his amazing models. And people began to take notice. During the 1930's he was written about in many newspaper articles and got lots of commissions from firms and individuals. Some models were shown at a modelmaking exhibition in Wembley and at the British Industries Fair in Birmingham, where the Prince of Wales warmly eulogised his work. Models he made ranged from the very tiny, to huge, but all with just as much detail painstakingly added. One model, a cement factory, was so large that Randolph had to hire out a cafe in Castleton to work on it.

He made a great range of wonderful things, a tiny set of dental surgery equipment, including a tiny chair, and a picturesque little village, which was sent abroad as an example of a typical English scene. He had to be conversant with many trades to turn out models correctly, when he made part of a locomotive model, for example, for a firm; it had to stand the inspection of railway experts as well as the general public.

Reporters were always dropping in to look around the cabinet of curiosities he and Hetty called home. One sunny afternoon another called. Randolph made him welcome and showed him around. The tour ended with the man looking through a magnifying glass at the Lord's Prayer on a tiny strip of paper, threaded through a needle.

Randolph writing the Lord's prayer an a tiny strip of paper
Private Collection

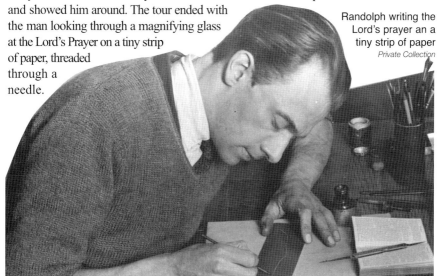

173

A postcard from Randolph to
his father *Private collection*

Randolph never used any magnifying lenses to work.
He could do it all with the naked eye.
The man was duly impressed with the
marvellous works and the time it must
take to produce them and wondered
what the maker did to relax after
such effort and dedication. He asked
Randolph, "Well, what's your recreation?",
as he picked up his stick and pack.
"Crosswords," said Randolph. "They're
restful, but sometimes my patience runs out."

AUGUST 19, 1931.

Model-making Hobby.

I believe that the most patient man in the north of England must be Mr. C. Douglas, who spends his life making models in his little stone cottage nestling in the shadow of Peveril Castle, in the heart of the Peak District.

Day after day he toils in his workshop, carving and moulding scale-size models of houses and country cottages, complete even with tiny working locks, which are no bigger than a finger nail.

Mr. Douglas showed me during the week-end his latest model. It is a miniature Lancashire cotton mill, and it contained actually 200 glass windows, scale furniture, looms, boilers, and even a "clocker-in." The model lay in the palm of Mr. Douglas' hand.

"Model-making is a good profession, but apprentices are scarce," Mr. Douglas told me. "The work needs tremendous patience."

His hobby is collecting locks, and he ... in the ...

EVENING CHRONICLE, TUESDAY, NOVEMBER 20, 1934

This Man Makes the Little Things That Count

From Our Own Correspondent

Buxton, Tuesday,

MODELS of the Statue of Liberty, the Manchester gas-

Cathedral in Match Box

MODELS of the Statue of Liberty, the Manchester gasometers and St. Paul's Cathedral that fit into three match boxes have been made by Mr. Randolph O. Douglas, who lives in a cottage at the foot of the Peveril Castle, Castleton, not far from Buxton.

He has made, too, a greenhouse which stands on his thumb nail and contains 42 plant pots and flowers in bloom, and a working electric motor which is so small that it can be covered by a thimble.

holders, and St. Paul's Cathedral that fit into three match-boxes, have been made by Mr. Randolph O. Douglas, who lives in a cottage at the foot of Peveril Castle, Castleton, near Buxton.

He has made, too, a Lilliputian greenhouse. It stands on his thumbnail, and contains 42 plant-pots and flowers in bloom; also a working electric motor which is so small that it can be covered by a thimble, a safe with eight moving bolts, and to operate them a key measuring 1¼ by 5 milli metres.

Mr. Douglas has written the Lord's Prayer on a strip of paper threaded through a cotton needle, and he has carved a pair of tongs from an ordinary match.

He has a collection of locks that are 4,000 years old. At one time he made locks for Houdini, the famous escapologist.

All these Lilliputian models are made ...

The man looked at him in disbelief. He couldn't image anyone producing the tiny works he had seen would ever run out of that.

Other people around the time were making tiny models too. And a few were in Sheffield. Randolph kept cuttings about them all along with cuttings about his own work. Indeed miniature model making and writing had been a favourite occupation of those with enough patience for many centuries. Randolph was following on after along line of people, including as far back as Cicero, who recorded that a copy of Homer's Iliad had been written on a piece of parchment small enough to be enclosed in a nutshell.

Randolph always liked looking at other people's work, He made a habit of going to London to the modelmaking exhibitions there. In February 1931 he was at a fair, staying at The Bedford Hotel again. It was a 'wonderful show' and no doubt provided some inspiration.

News cuttings about Randolph from his collection Buxton *Museum & Art Gallery*

The countryside around his home also provided some inspiration, as well as recreation, for Randolph.

He was still exploring with Hetty

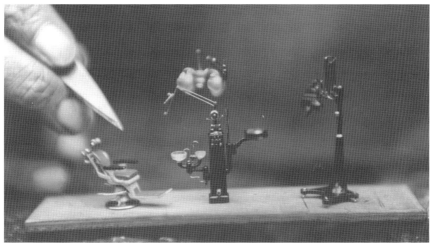

Dental equipment by Randolph. The hand and scalpel blade add scale   *Private collection*

and Jim and in the 1930s was no doubt excited by a new discovery. The Derbyshire Pennine Club had found a place called Nettle Pot, above Winnats Pass in Castleton. Randolph did some drawings of the system and would probably have been shown around it by Jim.

He also drew out a plan of Perryfoot Cave, also near Winnats Pass. One of the tight squeezes in this cave is called 'The Iron Maiden.' Maybe Randolph had a hand in naming that one if had been on the early explorations!

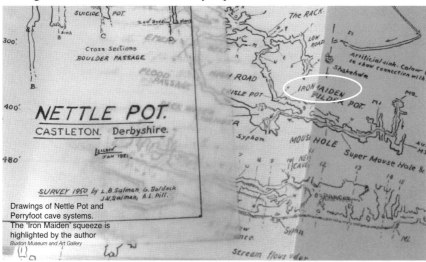

Drawings of Nettle Pot and Perryfoot cave systems.
The 'Iron Maiden' squeeze is highlighted by the author
Buxton Museum and Art Gallery

Randolph working
on a model
Private collection

In May 1932 Randolph was alone at the cottage as Hetty had gone off to Blackpool with her friend Ruth, He had their two cats Swiggles and Tiger for company though and they rubbed around his legs as he took the chance to catch up on some model making. He had an exhibition to get ready for July, to show at the centenary of the Royal Hospital on West Street, Sheffield.

He also painted Hetty an envelope and sent a letter off to her and Ruth of course. He smiled as he sketched the two girls, leaning on a big stick of Blackpool rock, and wearing their best hats and coats.

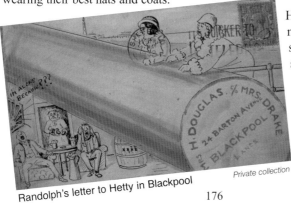

He drew himself and another, man, probably Jim, drinking strong beer to drown their sorrows and singing along to a melancholy song.

The lady coming in the door is carrying in two big dummies to use to shut them up. Hetty would find that funny, he thought, as he dropped it in the post.

Randolph's letter to Hetty in Blackpool

Private collection

Randolph put the finishing touches to one of his bigger commissions, three models of the Robinson factory sites around Chesterfield. Robinson was an old established firm, making packaging and boxes. They were expanding the sites and wanted a record. He had worked hard as usual, including every little detail and he surveyed his work as he carefully placed the last few plants and shrubs in the garden of the Portland site model.

There were tiny trains too and an art deco style tower with '1930' on it and a tiny shed. At the end of the garden path were tiny gates.

It was done. He screwed on the name plate last, the final flourish. The new little brass nameplates were a nice touch, he thought, as he gave it a wipe to remove the wood shavings from the base board

Randolph's Portland site model and details. A £1 coin is added to give scale
Chesterfield Borough Council Museum Service

Robinson's Wheatbridge site, wih detail of the tiny van and man on a buggy ferrying cardboard *Chesterfield Borough Council Museum Service*

He put the finished model alongside the other two, of Robinson's Wheatbridge and Walton Dam sites. The Wheatbridge one had lots of windows, all perfectly made and even. Along the road tootled a characterful little van, painted with the words, 'Robinson & Sons Ltd, Chesterfield. Manufacturers of cardboard boxes.' Following on the road opposite was an even tinier little vehicle, with a man ferrying piles of cardboard. The chimney bore the date of its construction, 1895 - the same year Randolph was born. The world had changed a lot since then. But Randolph was making his own little versions of the world, frozen forever under glass domes, and in glass cases, that would be the same forever, or at least until the cardboard and paint wore away.

Randolph working on a factory model. One of the newspaper cuttings from his collection
Buxton Museum and Art Gallery

178

The Robinson sports facilities, at Walton Dam, with detail of
the diving board and one of the huts. A 50p piece adds scale
Chesterfield Borough Council Museum Service

More newspaper articles were written as people discovered the little house of
wonders and the man who was always creating a few more. More people were
finding their way to the countryside on Sundays as a means of recreation and
rambling was becoming more popular as rail transport improved. People from the
industrial cities of Sheffield and Manchester took the train out into the Peak
District to roam the hills and enjoy the fresh air. There was a lot of unemployment
in the 1930s and rambling was a free pleasure that could be enjoyed by all.

As the number of people walking increased, they wanted to be able to get around
more easily, and to get more access over the countryside. The unrest over this came
to a head with a mass trespass, on April 24th, 1932. Walkers on Kinder Scout, a
mountain at Edale, close to Castleton, deliberately trespassed on private land.
It was an orchestrated protest to highlight
the right to roam, but also became a kind of
class struggle between Socialists and land
owners. Some of the trespassers were jailed,
but many people thought the sentences
harsh. There was a rally at Winnats Pass,
Castleton, a few weeks later, with thousands
gathered. Randolph couldn't fail to have
noticed that, even if he hadn't seen the publicity
the trespass had gained in the press. Maybe
it even got him a few extra customers.

ON KINDER.—The struggle between combined Sheffield and Manchester ramblers and gamekeepers yesterday, in which one keeper (seen on right) was injured.

Sheffield Daily Telegraph, Monday
April 25th, 1932 *Sheffield Newspapers*

179

Randolph's father Robert often brought friends or fellow craftspeople to his son's quirky little museum. The Sheffield Artcrafts Guild had another outing there in May 1933, a welcome break as Robert and other members were busy working on an exquisite book, to hold a record of the Guild and its members. It was leather bound, embellished with gold, ivory, silver and jade.

The leader of the day out to Castleton and Hope was J. B. Himsworth, another great Sheffield craftsman. His daughter Joyce was also a member of the guild, and was a well known silversmith and enameller producing exquisite work. No doubt all these talented people could appreciate Randolph's talents too.

Randolph was reminded of his friend Houdini every time he walked around the museum and showed off the photographs and all the locks. He was always proud to acknowledge his connection with the famous man. In May, one of the newspapers that Randolph collected, The World's Fair, had an article that acknowledged it too.

The writer was a man who Houdini personally and had probably met Randolph too, as he seemed to know a lot about him. Randolph sat down in his study, by the window, and read the article:

"Houdini was a very reserved man and never mixed with many people, and he had no time to talk to the average person unless he was interested in magic.

He used to visit a friend who had the same ideas as himself, Randolf Douglas, who has one of the finest collections of locks in the country, some of which Houdini sent him from various parts of the world...Houdini by the aid of a certain manipulation could open all the locks in the country. Mr Douglas can do the same. He can open any lock you bring before him".

Shame they had spelled his name wrong, but it was good to have such publicity and to be spoken of as being as proficient as Houdini at opening locks and to remember their special friendship.

Randolph read on, as the piece mentioned Houdini's jail escape in Sheffield. It seemed like yesterday he had been excited to hear all about the amazing Houdini and his escape from Charlie Peace's cell. Maybe he didn't know about all of it until now, or maybe Houdini had told him about his spot of vandalism...

"Now after Houdini had gone away it was brought to the notice of the Sheffield Watch Committee that he had broken the locks and that there was a sum of over two pounds to pay for new ones...I talked it over with him some time after, and he told me that the locks were old fashioned and out of date, and gave him a bit of trouble and that was why he smashed them. It is not what you do but how you do it that counts."

The article brought back vivid memories of all the shows he had seen Houdini perform, and the early days at the Empire, when his younger eyes had devoured all the Handcuff King's feats. It had been a time full of hope for his own act. *'Mr Douglas can do the same...'* At least there were still some escapology links he was carrying on with, and being likened to Houdini for. Randini was still around in part at least, in the Douglas Museum at Castleton.

Randolph still made frequent trips over to Sheffield and to the music halls. In December, the Empire made the paper when a tiger ran amok. It had even been reported in 'The Times.'

The keeper was cleaning out the cage of Bengal tiger Rajah's cage, when the animal lunged and attacked him, hurting his shoulder, Rajah was beaten off with shovels and dashed into the theatre's cellar where meat for the performing animals was kept. The screams of terror stricken cleaners mixed with the tiger's roars as for three hours Rajah managed to dodge firemen, police and trainers. Eventually he was forced out with a high powered hose, trapped in the music room where he smashed a few instruments, then lured back into a cage.

The poor tiger still had to go on for the evening show after his bid for freedom. The poor keeper went to hospital.

The press were still often writing about Randolph and the museum too.

In October, there was another article about a talented Douglas, but this time Robert Strachan, not Randolph.

The Artcrafts Guild had put on a big exhibition, opened by the Lord Mayor. A Daily Independent reporter visited Robert in his studio at Carrington Road.

Kaiser Bill, Robert confided to the visitor, had won one of the cups he had made at one of the pre-war Cowes regattas.

Robert in his studio at Carrington Road *Private collection*

Derbyshire.

COTTAGE WITH MANY TREASURES.

A Museum in Miniature.

CASTLETON CRAFTSMAN'S REMARKABLE SKILL.

Derbyshire villages hold many surprises. They remind one of those lucky packets for kiddies—you buy one wondering what is inside.

They all seem alike—just a cluster of cottages with a public-house or two and a main street, and that is all. Turn down a little lane and the surprise awaits you.

So it was at Castleton yesterday. Wandering down a side track, right under ancient Peveril Castle (writes a "Sheffield Telegraph" reporter) I came upon a quaint old cottage which contained many treasures. Actually this little building housed a museum, the tiny rooms being tastefully arranged and staged. But although this discovery came in the nature of a shock, an even greater surprise awaited me when I had a chat with the proprietor, Mr. Randolph O. Douglas.

Through Magnifying Glass.

Mr. Douglas has an artistic and mechanical turn of mind, and this has found expression in designing and making a number of wonderful models so small that a magnifying glass has to be used to bring all their marvellous points to the naked eye. Here are a few of the things he showed me.

Sheffield Telegraph, August 2nd, 1935 *Sheffield Newspapers*

Randolph, far right and Hetty, fourth from right, welcome a party of visitors   *Private collection*

It was Randolph's turn again, however, in May 1938, when a reporter from 'The World's Fair' newspaper came over to talk to him. Kitty was there too that day and joined them for the interview.

Randolph, even though he was once hoping to be out on stage performing, was quite shy and quietly reserved. He thought carefully before he spoke. But once the reporter had got him talking about Houdini, he found he was quite a genius who but for untimely ill-health might have blazed a name equal, or even transcending, that of his famous prototype.

Randolph showed his visitor the prized, framed photograph of himself and Houdini outside the Empire, still hanging at the top of the staircase. He also showed his Houdini letters and the scrapbook, crammed with photographs and press cuttings taken from papers from all over the world. He explained that he had sometimes bought a year's bound volumes of magazines just to go through them and pick out anything relating to Houdini.

It was good talking so much about his old friend again. Randolph, sat back in his chair as the reporter scribbled, and told the tale of how they met:

"Ever since I was thirteen years of age I have been fascinated by the mechanism of locks and other things, and every lock I could get hold of I used to dissect it and assemble it again. Hundreds have passed through my hands, and from that stage I turned to handcuffs and so on".

Randolph's model motor in a 'Can You Beat it?, in the Daily Express   *Buxton Museum and Art Gallery*

"When I first met Houdini - I was living in Sheffield at the time - he soon realised that I was not the usual type of 'fan' or autograph hunter and I think I impressed him with my knowledge of locks and the art of escapology. He did one thing which he told me he never made a practice of, except with intimate friends; he visited my home personally and often had meals with us."

Kitty joined in then, telling of how Randolph had drawn the Torture Cell and how he thought it worked, which Houdini had said was correct, and taken the drawing as a memento. She was proud of his contributions to Houdini's career and went on to tell the reporter about the one that had become one of the most famous:

"On another occasion my son demonstrated a strait-jacket effect while hanging upside down. I remember it vividly because it took place in the attic, and I had to help my son to get suspended from the ceiling!"

Randolph caught her gaze, and they both smiled, remembering that far ago day when they had impressed the great escapologist.

When the newspaper was published, they sent Randolph a copy. He took it over to join Hetty, who was sitting knitting on the settle in the lounge, as she listened to the 'Light Programme' on the radio.

Randolph flicked through to find the page. There it was, with a heading that made clear his part in the world of escapology. He tilted it so Hetty could read it too. Her Randolph's story was there, under a title that he had earned, one he should be remembered for. She read it out proudly... *'Man Who Helped Houdini.'*

Two match holder
cottages made
by Randolph
Private Collection

30
War work

1938 held rumours of another war. But by September, after the Munich treaty, when Chamberlain made his 'peace in our time' declaration, and waved his piece of paper signed by Hitler, it all seemed a narrowly escaped threat. So it was perhaps with a little more sense of relief from encroaching danger that Randolph went off to see the Australian escapologist Murray, back in the area at the The Attercliffe Palace that October.

Maybe the two of them met backstage and chatted over old times, swopped tales of Houdini and shared a few ideas.

Out front, as the New Palace Orchestra played 'The Liberty Belle,' Randolph looked forward to another night getting lost in the world of magic and illusion, as he glanced through the programme. People needed a little magic and laughter after coming so close to another terrible battle. So it was an ideal first half, with the Lennox Sisters rocking in rhythm, the talents of Hal Julian, a comic, and the Messengers of Mirth from BBC Radio, Rusty and Shine, to entertain and get people in good spirits.

After the intermission and a few more orchestra tunes, Zoma the Unusual Zylophonist and Aerial Gymnast Les Storks were amongst the delights on offer; then it was Murray's turn: 'Presenting an array of Mysteries that even Sherlock Holmes could not solve.'

Did the mention of Conan Doyle's famous creation remind Randolph of the feud between Doyle and Houdini and sadden his spirits? Maybe, but if not, surely Murray presenting 'The Water Torture Cage, the Greatest Escape of the Age' reminded him of his lost friend and their times and talks together.

After Murray and his act, declared on the programme to be filled with 'Thrills! Mystery! Sensation! Laughs!, the national anthem was played and then a final 'Cheerio From Attercliffe' rounded things up, with singing drummer Fred Archer leading the theatre's signature tune...

"We wish you adieu, until the next time....May the sky ever be blue..."
went some of the words.

But those blue skies would soon be full of the hum of war planes and seared by searchlights.

Time at the Castleton cottage was often pleasantly spent with Randolph's sister Peggy and her children- his little nieces. They loved coming to see Uncle Randolph and Aunty Hetty. It was such a a fascinating old house they lived in, with so much to see and explore... and such a pretty little garden too. Outside, there was the fine apple tree they could see through the window and inside there were so many treasures to look at. Not all grown ups were as ready to wonder and keep their curiosity burning as their slightly eccentric and always interesting uncle was.

And Uncle Randolph sometimes gave them wonderful little gifts he had made too. One of these gifts was a little cottage each, which held a box of matches. They would treasure these for a lifetime.

Cottage made for his niece
Private collection

But there were the less happy times too, for Randolph.

1939 was a sad year, as his dear friend Jim Puttrell died.

It was a sad year for the whole country too, as war once again snarled at the heels of life and liberty. On September 1, Hitler invaded Poland.

On 3rd September, the morning was bright and sunny and, as usual, the radio on the sideboard was playing in Douglas Cottage. At 10.00 the BBC told listeners to standby for an announcement of national importance. Every fifteen minutes listeners were told that the Prime Minister would make announcement at 11.15. So when the time came, Hetty and Randolph were probably expecting something ominous. As some people feared, the ultimatum to withdraw from Poland had been ignored. They listened on as the Prime Minister gave out the news.."*consequently this country is at war with Germany. Now may God bless you all.*"

Another war, after the one that was supposed to end them all. It all seemed so unreal on that fine Autumn day in the little village of Castleton.

But things soon changed to make it real. Winnats Pass was resurfaced for an alternative route through Castleton, and rationing began early in the new year. On the edges of Sheffield, Burbage Rocks and the moors were used for target and troop practice.

Cinemas and theatres in Sheffield closed on September 5, after a ban on large gatherings. Luckily for fans such as Randolph the ban only lasted about ten days.

By May, 1940, Churchill was in charge of the country and the year saw the Dunkirk evacuation and the Battle of Britain More personally for Randolph, his father and Kitty had moved to Christchurch, near Bournemouth, to join his brother Ambrose who had re-located to a job there, so he did not see them all as often.

186

A lot of Randolph's time was taken up with work over in Sheffield. The city was even busier with steel production than usual, for the war effort, and Randolph did his bit to keep the vital steel works running. Many Sheffield men were at home fighting the war this way, in protected occupations in the steel industry.

Randolph was working mainly at Hadfields, one of the big works in the Tinsley area of the city.

Each morning he bid goodbye to his little pal and wife Hetty and left to get the 8.04 am train from Hope, the nearest station to Castleton. He carried his case of tools with him.

Randolph's employment was making, repairing and maintaining equipment of various sorts. His deft touch and mechanical creativity made him good at the job,

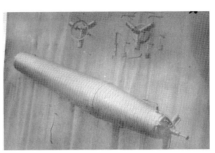

Top: Photo of a rather strange looking piece of equipment from Randolph's files and probably made by him. It is hard to tell the scale but it could be a gas sampling device. Also shown are two diagrams for things he was making, perhaps a damper arrangement.
Buxton Museum & Art Gallery

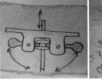

sometimes working on delicate instruments. He listed all the jobs and the hours taken. Work included mending 'stone breakers', making a wire cutting jig, recorder clock repairs, making a klaxon horn piece, repairing a flow meter at the Alsing Road site, mending an underload testing furnace and doing x-ray hangar repairs.

He could turn his hand to them all - it was maybe easier for him than escaping a heavy burden of chains and padlocks.

Randolph's list of jobs undertaken *Private collection*

Date	Nature of work	Time Spent	Dept	Order Changeable
July 1941	X Ray Film develop hanger repair	3 0	X Ray	3498/177
" "	Grinding Drill	1 30	" "	" "
" "	X Ray centering device repair	3 0	" "	" "
" "	Test	31 0	Test	/227
" "	Stone Break	103 70	Power Dept	T.224
August	Repairing Recorder clock	4 0	O.H	3394/080
" "	X Ray clips	30	X Ray	3498/177
" "	Repairing Drayton AM Regulator	7 0	Gas Producer	3394/080
" "	Test	22 30	Test	/227

187

During the war, a man called Clayton Hutton visited the biggest steelworks in Sheffield to buy steel strip, to magnetise for miniature compasses. The same day a lorry left, carrying the steel strips to London, as Hutton was working there for M19, designing and masterminding production of escape aids for prisoners of war. The tiny compasses could be hidden in buttons and such as a vital help for escapees..

Other things they were making were mini chess sets with aids hidden inside, and games with maps hidden within the playing board. All these secretive devices needed fine and intricate craftsmanship to make things small enough to be hidden. At the War Office one day, a man came in and told Hutton he could draw on a very small scale. He brought a grain of rice with the Lord's prayer written on it, which he done with the naked eye. Also he had adapted a single match. A wedge shaped piece was cut from the middle third of the match, so that it could slide freely in and out; and underneath this a secret message was written.

At Hutton's request the man drew a detailed, tiny map two inches square. Miniature skills indeed. But it was not Randolph.

Whoever this man was, he was younger and he died just after meeting Hutton. But Randolph was surely capable of these things, though if he ever did help with these tiny, hidden escape aids, his part in it is still hidden too.

Randolph could easily have met Clayton Hutton. Hutton had met Houdini - at the Birmingham Empire in April 1913 - when he and others, on behalf of his father's saw mills, issued Houdini one of his famous challenges. The challenge was done on May 2nd 1913. Hutton and others constructed a packing box on stage and challenged Houdini to escape from it. Of course he did.

What Hutton didn't know then was that after going to see the saw mills, arriving in a hansom cab, and wearing a fur lined coat and gaudy carpet slippers, Houdini had persuaded the carpenter to adapt the box a little to his own specifications for escape, and not say anything. This of course was a known pattern of the Houdini challenges - getting a local firm to issue one, but setting it up himself really.

Randolph may have been there at The Empire in Birmingham to watch Houdini take up his packing box challenge. He often followed Houdini's show to other cities. Maybe he met Hutton then as he helped set up the challenge at the theatre.

But whether Hutton remembered the young pal of Houdini's and decided to utilise the young mans skills years later, in wartime, well who knows? Hutton did contact scientific instrument makers to assist him in his tasks, and Randolph was working on delicate instruments, gauges etc during the war. But back in 1913 when the challenge to Houdini was taken up, Randolph was not making models or instruments, he was still Randini the fledgling escapologist.

Maybe Hutton and Randolph met, but if they didn't, he may have crossed paths with others who worked for Military Intelligence.

The government's 'secret service' were around in Derbyshire, and had requisitioned Smedley's Hydropathy Centre at the spa town of Matlock, not far from Castleton. The hydro was used as a training centre for various intelligence activities. One person who attended there was the writer Evelyn Waugh, who studied photographic interpretation.

Being in Sheffield so much for work, Randolph saw first hand the terrible devastation the Luftwaffe inflicted on the steel-producing city, one of their prize targets.

The worst damage was in December 1940. At seven in the evening on the night of Thursday, 12th, the air raid sirens screamed as the 'blitz' came to Sheffield. It was a clear night, with a full moon brightening the blackout of the city. Ideal for bombers; and the city was hit badly. It was hellish, with buildings ablaze and collapsing, homes flattened on top of families, and people huddled in shelters as planes droned overhead for eight long hours.

The Sheffield Empire, scene of many nights of wonder and magic for Randolph and the place where he had first met Houdini all those years ago, was amongst the places hit. Henry Hall and his orchestra were top of the bill that night. As they played, a huge blast rocked the theatre. But they kept playing. The audience was cleared for safety, but some went down to the boiler room to shelter and were entertained there by the orchestra as bombs were falling. The theatre suffered serious damage to the frontage, and to the right dome, which was never replaced.

Maybe Randolph and Hetty were there that evening, or maybe they were safely home in Castleton, looking out at the eerie red glow in the sky over Sheffield.

The Sheffield Blitz. A gutted tram is silhouetted by blazing buildings   *Sheffield Newspapers*

The damaged Empire, after the bombing on Thursday 12th December, 1940 *Sheffield Newspapers*

The morning after was chaos. Transport was non-existent and streets were blocked with rubble, still burning. Many people had to walk to work. Randolph could have been one of them, warily walking up through the damage from Sheffield rail station,.

He would have passed the Marples pub, standing in Fitzalan Square, the same square people had crowded to see a new-fangled tank during the first war. The pub had taken a direct hit, leaving many sheltering there dead. And perhaps he walked through the Wicker Arches on his way out to Hadfield's steel works at Tinsley, where a tram car lay ripped in half. Terrible scenes. But the steel works had escaped.

Another dose of skyborne terror came on December 15th. This time the steelworks were not so lucky and some suffered hits, including Hadfields. But there was no major damage. Luckily the 15 ton drop hammer at Vickers was not hit. This was turning out crankshafts for the vital Spitfire and Hurricane planes. Perhaps the decoy city out on the moor towards Derbyshire, had worked. Troughs, lights and flames were laid out there to imitate the burning city and attract the German planes away from the real one. But in just two nights, the lives of over 660 civilians and 25 servicemen were lost. Many thousands more injured and homeless. Randolph's old home areas of Greenhill and Endcliffe didn't escape. Lots of businesses too, were wrecked and disrupted. Perhaps Randolph was called in to open the odd safe whose combination was lost, or locks that had lost keys amongst the rubble.

In 1941 Pearl Harbour was attacked and America joined in the war. But this time there was no Houdini around doing his bit to help troops learn to escape.

And on February 11th, 1943 Bess Houdini followed her husband to wherever he had gone. Randolph was saddened. He had not been in contact with Bess for years, but her death was another part of his old life gone, another tie with his friend Houdini unknotted forever.

Thoughout the war, people were determined to make time for an uplifting show or two. Cinemas, dance halls and theatres were still busy and the stars of stage and screen were a welcome distraction from the conflict and cares.

Randolph was one of the people who kept to his theatre trips, stepping over the rubble still lining the streets of Sheffield as he made his way to the Empire. On November 8th, 1943, he was watching a magical show again- this time it was The Great Lyle, with his 'Cavalcade of Mystery.' The Empire had only just re-opened, in September 1943, after being closed since August 3rd . On that day a bad fire had gutted the stage. Special permission had been given to repair it at a time when building was restricted. An indication of how valued the theatre and its morale boosting shows were.

The war seemed endless. More bombings, more deaths. It was going on even longer than the one before. Broken buildings, sirens, blackout and rationing were all people were beginning to remember.

In May 1943 there had been a morale boost with raids on German dams, by Lancaster bombers with 'bouncing bombs.' These 'Dambusters' practiced at stretches of water on British soil first. One of these was the Derwent Reservoir, not far from Castleton. Perhaps the throb of a Lancaster's engine overhead, as it made its way to the reservoir, brought Randolph or Hetty out of the cottage to take a look.

At last the war ended, at midnight on May 8th, 1945, when the village of Castleton was one of hundreds of places celebrating VE Day. But the emotional effects of war didn't end then of course; and the practical effects were still biting. Rationing was still in force, and Randolph and Hetty queued with their Ration books at the Castleton shops.

Randolph and Hetty;s ration books Buxton Museum & Art Gallery

The austere and worrying time of war perhaps made everyone even more determined to make the most of their time now it was over with. Randolph, after working at Hadfields on all the various jobs, may have felt it was time to do the things he was happier with to earn a living; to leave more time for his modelmaking. So it was just a year after the war, in July 1946, that he sat down and wrote a letter to Hadfields, telling them that he was now self employed.

His income came a little from the small charges of visitors to the Douglas Museum, but mainly from the models he was producing for various firms throughout the country. He was probably happier, working in his cottage studio, overlooking the Stones, and showing people around his collection of wonders.

191

Sketches, by Randolph, perhaps ideas for things to sell in the museum *Buxton Museum & Art Gallery*

31
Endings

It was a severe winter in 1947. And there was another cold blow, just two years after peace had finally come. Randolph's father, Robert Strachan, died. Randolph looked sadly at the article in the Sheffield Telegraph of February 1st. He was glad his father's skill was recognised. He had gone from them all, and they would miss him badly, but at least would leave behind him in the world many beautiful works of art to be remembered by.

Randolph had inherited all his father's tools; chasing hammers, riffles and swiss files. kept in a copper box.

He could see his father now, in his mind's eye, as he carefully picked up one of the hammers, turning it in his hand. He contemplated the wonderful things it had made in the employ of the man who had owned it. He could visualise him, tapping designs into a bowl, absorbed in creativity at the studio in Carrington Road; and he remembered back to the days in Greenhill, when he first saw magical things conjured forth from pieces of metal by his father's talented hands.

And now Randolph, Robert's talented son, was living out his days in his own house of creativity, conjuring forth magical things and bringing wonder into the lives of others. People came to see the things he had collected about him and to hear tales about the far off objects picked out by his torchlight in the dim light of the cottage; to be told of the dark enchantment to be found in sun starved, glistening caves full of quartz and Blue John.

They came to marvel at the tiny greenhouse, unbelievably small writing passing through the eye of a needle, and a motor that could fit under a thimble. It was a place to escape from the ordinary, to dream a little, as Randolph did, and revel in the unusual.

Made Casket For Prince

ARTCRAFTS GUILD FOUNDER DIES

FOR many years one of the leading designers and art-craftsmen in Sheffield, Mr Robert Stachan Douglas, has died at Christchurch, near Bournemouth.

He was a founder of Sheffield Artcrafts Guild and master for a number of years. He was also president of the Silver Trades Technical Society.

Mr. Douglas was a regular contributor to local artcraft exhibitions and specimens of his work were purchased by the city for the Weston Park Museum and Art Gallery. Probably his most ambitious and beautiful piece of work was the enamelled casket presented to the Duke of Windsor when, as Prince of Wales, he was made a member of the Trinity House Brethren at Hull. The Prince sent his personal congratulations to Mr. Douglas.

Mr. Douglas designed and made models and cups for many European royalties.

Until his retirement in 1940 he lived at 40, Carrington Road, Sheffield.

Mr. DOUGLAS

Did he really once have the skeletons of two lovers murdered in Winnats Pass hidden under his bed? One friend of his told people it was so.

And there was always a sense of the unexpected with Randolph.

People may not suspect at first that the quiet and unassuming man leading the tour around the little Castleton museum was once the young showman who spent his youth wrapped in a mesh of locked metal, the Great Randolph, Randini The Self Liberator. But they saw his photographs and cuttings and listened to his tales of Houdini as they peered at the incredible collection of locks and cuffs, said by some to be one of the best in the world. Then they would see him in a different light. His dream had not worked out the way he had hoped, but at least he had had one.

And now he was preserving that dream, along with his glass trapped miniatures, along with the ancient fossils and the stalactites. He had created his own world full of the important things in his life, of things that needed to be wondered at and cherished. And he invited people in to share it.

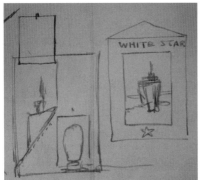

Sketches for a display featuring a liner
Private Collection

So years of passing wonderers came and went; and Randolph worked hard at his many models. In the 1950s one thing he was working on was a 4ft model of the 'Windsor Castle' cruise ship for Union Castle. He did many other displays for companies too.

But amid all the work, he and Hetty enjoyed having guests. People of the village often dropped by the cottage in the evening, and listened to Randolph tell stories as he idly whittled a piece of wood into a toothpick.

And family too, often called over to Castleton. Doreen, daughter of Hetty's sister Doris, along with her husband Harry, was a regular weekend visitor. Their little boy, Christopher, loved the visits and pattered down the lane to his Uncle Randolph waiting at the cottage door, who greeted him by his nickname, Christopher Robin. He enjoyed the inevitable tea and biscuits too.

And Randolph's sister Peggy, her husband and their daughters, still came over regularly, or the couple visited them in Sheffield. Everyone enjoyed their company.

Hetty baked excellent cakes, and knitted and crocheted dresses and jumpers for her friends and family, when she was not at her post collecting money by the museum door. She wore knitted jumpers herself too, self confident and totally unselfconscious about comments that maybe they were a little too revealing. *'Randolph likes me free'* she said proudly. Very appropriate for an escapologist.

And appropriate for this popular and devoted couple, unbound by the convention of the nine to five, unfettered by the ordinary.

Randolph also spent his time making little models and trinkets to sell at the Douglas Museum. Pictures made from foil were one of his specialities.

He enjoyed saving colourful sweetie wrappers to use for these, and creating local scenes by expertly placing pieces of the paper behind an ink outline he had drawn. Carefully he put his 'Douglas' signature on the latest one he had created, another picture of Peveril Castle, He pressed it into its small frame and stood it next to others already on the table, putting the left-over pieces back in his tool box.

Foil pictures by Randolph, and the tool box he used *Private Collection*

Then he wandered out to sit on the bench in front of the cottage, alongside Hetty, as the warm evening drew to a close. It was a favourite spot of theirs, watching the world go by, and chatting with passing neighbours.

Randolph's health, always a problem, was slowly getting worse, and he was often tired. It was a frustration as his head and heart were full of ideas and enthusiasm. He still got out a lot though, with friends and family taking him trips in their cars. They sometimes went up 'on the tops,' over hills he and Hetty had explored the hearts of, in those younger days, along with Jim. It was hard to believe now that he had scrambled down potholes and squeezed through tiny gaps as they explored the hollows beneath. It was even harder to believe that he had once squashed in a tiny box for over three hours, with his knees up to his chin. But then he had been Randini and the future was his for the taking, so he thought. Now he was Randolph, and happy in the present, in his little country cottage with Hetty. But Randini was still alive there too, in the exhibition of locks, in his memories, in his stories.

The Peak District was a National Park now, since 1951. More and more people were discovering the joys of the places there that Randolph loved. And many of them were delighted to discover his special little museum, tucked away on a back lane in Castleton. The visitors book was full of names from all over the world.

He smiled, knowing that his home would be long remembered by those that passed through it. They would have a favourite exhibit to tell their friends about and maybe they would talk about the man who was friends with the famous Houdini. He would like that. And so would Houdini- he had wanted to be immortalised and he certainly was. His name was now a by-world for amazement A fitting place for him to be remembered then, in a House of Wonders.

The front of the Cottage, where Randolph and Hetty used to sit out on their bench

It was 1956. It could always be a little chilly in the cottage, even in summer, and by December the range needed plenty of wood on it to keep out the winter cold.

But this year brought in a cold that could not be helped by heat.

Randolph was dying.

Hetty was by his side, but the illness he had fought for so long was finally winning. He could escape it no more and he was tired of fighting. There was so much he did not want to leave behind; his long cherished treasures, his much loved places, his darling wife Hetty. But still, he slipped away.

It was December 5th, and he was surrounded by all that was dear to him, at his home, in the Douglas Museum. His House of Wonders was the place where his life was reflected, lived and ended, as his eyes, always so eager and curious, closed for the last time.

And then the little cottage held one wonder less.

Randolph
Robert Osborne
Douglas in his
later years
Private Collection

The Castleton churchyard that is Randolph and Hetty's final resting place

After

Randolph was buried in St Edmund's Church, Castleton. The active mind and hands of this amazing. multi-talented man were stilled forever, as apoplexy and emphysema claimed him.

He was laid to rest in the tranquil graveyard, just a stone's throw from Stones Bottom, The Douglas Museum and Hetty.

He was just 61, but it was longer than Houdini had lived. Like Houdini, Randolph lived his life with a mind and heart ready for new experiences and challenges, putting his full concentration and dedication into all he did. But unlike Houdini, he was almost forgotten.

After Randolph's death, Hetty took over the tours of the Douglas Museum, showing guests round with a well-rehearsed script, proudly showing off her husband's collection and modelwork. She told them too, of his famous friend Houdini, whom Randolph had met when he was 'quite a boy,' and whom he had helped.

Hetty used the same torch Randolph had always used, to light each item as she went around the rooms. The chrome was worn through to the brass, with years of her husbands grip as he pointed it at his works and treasures.

When Randolph had gone, up until her death, on April 21st, 1978, just days after her 80th birthday, Hetty ran the Douglas Museum. For twenty-two years, she remained custodian of the treasures her husband had spent a lifetime collecting.

When she died, Hetty was buried with Randolph, and they were re-united at last. Their cottage was sold, and the little museum that had been open for over fifty years was closed. Wonders were packed away in boxes, cabinets emptied, and cases unscrewed from the old stone walls. The families of Randolph and Hetty took away some mementos, and the Douglas Museum existed no more.

Three cardboard boxes, according to Randolph's instructions, were sent to the Magic Circle in London and the contents are now in their archives. These consisted of magic books, letters and photographs from Houdini, and Randolph's autograph book, with the sketches and signatures of the many famous magicians he had met.

Some of Randolph's work. including the model of Anne Hathaways cottage, and miniature lead mining tools, can be seen in the Castleton Information Centre.

The bulk of Randolph's Collection, however, is now in the Buxton Museum and Art Gallery and is occasionally out on display. If not on display, it can usually be seen on request.

The cottage that was home to Randolph, Hetty and the Douglas Museum, House of Wonders, still stands at Stones Bottom, in Castleton. It is now a private residence, called Douglas House.

And Randolph and Hetty lie in the quiet church-yard nearby, he and his little pal still together.

Mention the name Houdini, and most people in the world will have heard of the famous escapologist, Handcuff King and bane of the Spiritualists. His name is still used almost every day to describe a miraculous escape, or a clever illusion. His is the name people will still probably mention, if asked for the name of a master escapologist, not that any of more recent people doing similar stunts today. What he worked so hard to achieve, and put down on film to immortalise, has worked. Houdini has become a legend - and legends live much longer than men.

Mention Randolph Douglas and most people will never have heard of him.

But as you walk past his old haunts in Castleton, or read about the Handcuff King, remember Randolph. For now you know.

As well as being a talented silversmith, caver, artist, engineer, model maker, wonder collector and museum keeper, he was the man who helped Houdini.

A list of the contents of the House of Wonders

The items which were displayed in the Douglas Museum in Castleton
Compiled by Harry Emmerson in 1978

A wooden clockwork sign that Randolph made to advertise the Douglas Museum House of Wonders *Buxton Museum and Art Gallery*

ENTRANCE PASSAGEWAY
Hide shield
Carved wood head
Swordfish Sword 44" long
Swordfish Sword 28" long

1 glazed frame 32^1/2" x 23" containing 8 prints of Peak Cavern & Peveril Castle

2 Framed photographs 8^1/2 x 6^1/2 of Mr & Mrs Douglas in Speedwell Cavern

GROUND FLOOR MUSEUM
Glazed case 50" x 14"
(wall mounted) containing:

Model Iron Maiden
(Presented by H.Houdini) 6" tall

17th Cent. brass snuff box with combination lock

Brass pocket sun dial 1^3/4" diameter
Brass sovereign scale
Swiss cow bell from Arrolla
2 Cedar apples from Mt Lebanon

Saxon spear head found near Matlock
2 Chinese card markers 3^1/2 x 2"
Lacquered wood and inlaid ivory
2 Chinese razors
3 Chinese opium pipes (water pipes)
Tinder striker

Glazed case 25" x 23"
(wall mounted) containing:

60 various agate specimens (chalcedony) - carnelian - onyx - black ribbon agate - chrisophase - fortification agate - brecciated quartz - moss agate - landscape agate

Glazed case 26" x 16"
(wall mounted) containing:

Miniature Spear & Jackson saw 5" long
Model Milners safe 1^1/4" x 1"
Miniature electric motor 12 high
Lord's prayer written on strip of paper passing through the eye of a needle
Match within a match carving

Glazed case 39" x 18"
(wall mounted) containing:
67 agate specimens

Glazed case 42" x 15"
(wall mounted) containing: *(Pictured below)*

Hollowed out smugglers boot
Seed pod 'lingua de vaca'
Carved ball within a ball
Match tongs
4 Cromwellian clay pipes (Derbyshire)
Sea horse
Pipe fish
Tinder striker
Japanese dwarf tree
Brass watertight match box used by Derbyshire lead miners

Iron extending candle holder found near Rivelin Sheffield

Bottle coloured sand. Isle of Wight
Wooden native comb. (S.Africa)
Convicts tinder box Central Prison Preteria S.A
Carved boxwood marking board with carved ivory inserts. Pekin China 1898
Kaffir stone drinking vessel. S.Africa

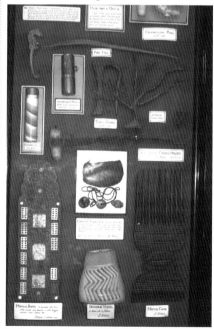

Wall mounted case from Douglas Museum
Buxton Museum and Art Gallery

Contents of The House of Wonders

Ivory sedan chair 3" tall

Glazed case 80" x 26" x 13" (free standing) containing:

40 approx specimens of stalactites - stalagmites - stalactitie curtain - cave floor formations - rock pool formations - stalactite shelf - cave floor. Castleton, Matlock

Model leadminers tools (pick shovel hammer etc)
Model lead miners stoves (Weasley 1930)
Model factory. Cardboard on base 10" x 25"
Model Ann Hathaways Cottage in glass case $6^1/2$ x $3^1/2$ x 3

Model cottage in domed glass 4" dia 5" high
2 Model Speedwell Cavern in glass cases $4^1/4$" x 4" x 3"

Model plough silver on wooden plinth 4" x 2"
Model of *(illegible)* on wood base $3^1/4$" x $2^1/4$"
Model of falling valve and boiler sight glass in glass topped bot 2"

Model cottage in cardboard 1' x $1^1/2$"
Model Greenhouse with plants $7^1/8$" x $3^1/8$"

Plaster model Brighton parish church
Perspective model shredded wheat factory

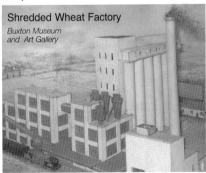

Shredded Wheat Factory
Buxton Museum and Art Gallery

Welwyn Garden City in case 14" x 14" x 6" (illuminated)

Map of Derbyshire 1610 in frame 19" x 17"

Diploma of merit from Model Engineer Exhibition to R.O.Douglas 1922

Glazed case 25 x 13 (wall mounted) containing:
2 carved coconuts
Carved figure wood $2^1/2$"

Carved ivory card case 4" x $2^1/2$" x $^1/2$"
Carved wood card case 4" x $2^1/2$" x $^1/2$"
Wood and ivory inlaid card case 4" x 3" x $^1/2$"
Carved ivory carriage and oxen on base 4" x 2"
Carved ivory scent case $3^1/2$"

Carved ivory ball within a ball $1^1/2$" dia

Bracelet with head in relief

Mother of pearl plaque carved with Bethlehem scene 8" dia

Mother of pearl game counter carved with chinese scene $2^1/4$ x $1^1/4$

Display box, glazed, in three sections ?? over fireplace 51" x 25" containing:

10 Rock specimens of rock crystals +
Brazillian pebbles from S. America
+ water crystals from Mexico

6 Rock specimens of Serpentine (Lizard) Mesolite (Giants Causeway) Serpentine (Shetlands) Quartz Crystal in USA

9 Rock specimens of pudding stone - flint Conglomerate - jasper conglomerate - fissile sandstone - Marble

2 Petrified birds nests (Matlock)

4 Specimens including Sardony (Sidmouth), insect in amber

5 specimens including slickensides (Castleton) quartz geode (Clifton) quartz crystal (Cumberland) stalacmites in sardonyx

6 specimens including asbestos (Cornwall) steatite and serpentine (Lizard)

2 specimens stalagmitic barytes (Middleton Derbys)

13 specimens including native copper (Cornwall) copper pyrites (Cornwall) azurite - yellow copper - peacock copper - chalcopyrite - fibrous malachite - compact malachite

11 specimens including amethyst in agate amethyst chalcedony - amethyst 'button diamonds' opal - avanturine - rose quartz - crocidolite - bloodstone - ambolon stone

1 Board 6 x $2^1/2$" with 2 specimens labrodorite (labrador)

1 Board 5" x 4" wih 13 opal specimens (Queensland)

1 tube 3" long opal chippings (Brazil)

1 imitation opal made by R.O.Douglas

1 imitation adventurine made by R.O.Douglas

Board 8 x5" with13 specimens of precious stones from Pedras Do estado mines Brazil

1 pedestal dish 5" dia x 3" high

Ashford marble slab inlaid with 'star' pattern $5^3/4$" x $3^3/4$" x $1^7/8$"

Ashford marble slab inlaid with flowers $6^1/4$ x 6 x $^1/2$"

Ashford marble slab inlaid with flowers $5^1/4$ x $3^1/2$" x 1"

Ashford marble miniature lamp $3^1/2$" dia

Ashford marble tablet inlaid with flowers $2^1/4$" x $1^1/2$" x $3^1/8$"

62 rock samples (polished) including jasper - agates - stiphonia petrified wood (Sidmouth) - wood agate - chalcedony

1 large piece coral

Glazed case containing
4 coral specimens16" x 14"

Glazed case 12" x 12"
containing fossilised shells 40

Beehive stalagmite (Castleton)

Piece of rock on which Royal Charter was struck at Moel Fro Oct 26th 1852 $4^1/2$" x $4^1/2$" x 4"

Water colour, Bingham Park Sheffield 1914

Framed print $19^1/2$" x 12" N W view of Castle in Castleton 1727

Frame $31^1/2$" x 22"containing 11 old prints

Framed print of Peak Cavern Castleton 11" x 13"

Model of 3 masted barque in glazed display case 40" x 29" x 14"

Glazed display case 8" x 15" containing 11 rock specimens - chormite

Glazed display case 12" x 12" containing 11 rock specimens - agates

Model TAS manual incomplete

Old lead miners boot from Hazard Mine Castleton

Lead miners blasting straw case

Coraline formation from cave pool Matlock in domed glass case 6" dia 12" high

Domed case 15" high containing 19 stuffed tropical birds

Model by R.O.Douglas - Dam + water wheel in glass case 11" x 7" x 5"

Model beam engine in domed glass case 15" high

Glazed display case 6" x 31" x 17" containing:
59 specimens flour spar crystals + blue john
3 Polish spar eggs
Dish on pedestal blue john $6^1/2$" dia $7^1/2$" high
30 specimens dog tooth crystals (Derbyshire)
16 specimen calamites - fossils in tin bath

Various specimen calamites - small fossils in box 36" x 6" x 6"

22 shells in cardboard carton 12" x 7" x 7"

Cave moss and cave pearls in cardboard box 7 x 4 x $2^1/2$"

36 various fossil shells in wooden cigar box 8 x 6 x 2

Cardboard box containing pitchalo? and thorite 5 x 2 x 1

Cardboard box containing various fossil shells 16 x 10 x 5

Clockwork museum 'House of Wonders' sign 17 x 18 x 4

STAIRCASE BETWEEN BOTTOM & TOP MUSEUM
Framed sign 36" x 26"
Framed sign 26" x 13"
Framed sign 32" x 22"
Set slave irons from Gold Coast W.Africa
Peacocks tail from India
Beaded 'grass skirt'

Slave whip made from tree branch Jamaica

Framed picture Houdini 20" x 18" showing various news clippings of Houdini (17)

Framed picture as above

Copper framed picture 16" x 18" showing Houdini and Mr Douglas

TOP MUSEUM
Carved wood native weapon (African) 48" x 8"

Glazed diplay case 36" x 26" containing:
Ancient Egyptian lock & key (wood)
Chinese padlock key (Pekin) Decorated base
2 Brass animal shaped padlocks & keys (Chinese)
2 Padlocks & keys (Nuremberg 17th cent)
Reproduction wooden Egyptian pin lock
Padlock & key made from cartridges badges etc made by Mr. Douglas 1917

Padlock & key made from cartridges + pull through 1916

Padlock & key with spiral spring action (India)
7 other various padlocks & keys

Glazed diplay case 42" x 34" containing:
Wrought iron padlock & key with secret escutcheon from Harry Houdini collection German 16th cent

Elizabethan door lock steel engraved lock plate from Kent 15th cent

Prison padlocks. Wrought iron. From Nrmberg. From H. Houdini collection. German 15th cent

Padlock & key. Wrought iron barrel shaped with screw action. German 15th cent. From H.Houdini collection

Padlock & key. Wrought iron . German 17th cent

Padlock & key. Wrought iron . English 17th cent

Chest lock & key. Wrought iron. Spanish 17th cent

Lock & key. Sheffield Manor House

Padlock from Nuremberg. German 16th cent

Door bolt from Debtors Gaol Sheffield 18th cent

Door lock from Debtors Gaol Sheffield

Leg irons & key from Debtors Gaol Sheffield

Glazed case 43" x 16" containing:
26 specimens of tumbler locks keys etc from 17th cent to 19th cent

Glazed case 33" x 17" containing:
18 specimens of locks & keys etc 19th cent
Iron door lock & key15" x 12"

Glazed case 25" x 31" containing:
40 keys. Roman to 16th cent. Including Tickhill Castle Key

Glazed case 25" x 31" containing:
28 keys. from16th to18th cent.

Glazed case 25" x 31" containing:
30 keys. from18th to19th cent

Glazed case 25" x 31" containing:
100 approx keys curious for their shape

Glazed case 50" x 36" containing:
54 various locks mostly 19th cent

Armadillo basket

Glazed case 17" x 15" containing:
200 approx various beetles

Glazed case 36 x 33 containing:

112 moths butterflies dragon flies etc

Elephants skull

Large carved wooden ladle 26" long

Sword fish sword 26" long

2 Carved wooden S Sea native weapons 46" x 6" & 45" x 8"

Set leg irons from old Newgate Prison London

Padlock shaped board 61" x 47" containing 18 various handcuffs

Grandfather clock 75" high. Brass face.

Set convict irons from Siberia

Painted gourd

Framed print $13^1/2$" x $11^1/2$" of Newcomen steam engine 1778

2 Buddhist prayer wheels

wood cut block for printing prayers (Tibet)

Zulu war rattle

Carved native canoe paddle 41" long

2 Carved wooden native ladies head rests

Ornamental steel dagger 20" long

2 Native spears

Native sword in leather scabbard

3 Hide shields

3 Arrows feathered metal tipped

Tower musket English 1690 - 1820

Spinning wheel

Broken ship chronometer (German) 7" dia

3 small boxes containing 1 butterfly 2 beetles

Small stone lamp $2^1/4$" dia

Flint axe head

Crystal formation 3" dia approx

'Scrimshaw' tooth of sperm whale

Sulphur specimen from Sodom & Gomorra

Clay pipe & accompanying letter. Found in London whilst making underground railway

Tobacco tin containing 9 flints for flintlock guns

Model case 11/2" x $1^1/2$" containing model stalactities & stalagmites etc

Plaster model of Peak Cavern entrance $4^1/2$" x 3"

Silk screen picture of Japanese lady 30" x 16"

Chain mail hat

Roll of various Derbyshire prints

Wooden Chinese puzzle pagoda 12" x 9" 9"

Large seed pod 12" x 4"

ROD model of Rogers Tomb Christchurch $4^1/2$ x $2^1/2$ x 2"

Card 9 x $6^1/2$ containing various model artifacts by Mr Douglas

2 framed photos Mr & Mrs Douglas in caves $8^1/2$ x $6^1/2$

3 Small cardboard models of farm buildings

Toy tightrope walker

Beaded horn

Seed pod 4" dia & 6" long

Tea infuser spoon Castleton

Carved wooden fan

Ebony necklace & bracelet

Empty Mills bomb (hand grenade)

2 wooden quivers of 'poisoned' darts

Oriental hand weigh scale in wooden 'violin shape' case

2 embroidered Oriental pictures 20" x 17"

Beaded S Sea Island skirt

2 wooden Burmese combs

2 wooden Solomon Island combs

Pair chopsticks wrapped in Chinese newspaper

Old stone mould? 1" x 6" x $5/8$"

Cardboard box containing 5 old Vestas

Large egg 5" long x 3" dia (Emu)?

Pair embroidered ladies shoes Oriental $5^1/2$" long

206

Stone slab $5^{1}/4$ x $3^{1}/2$ x $3/4$ with engraved statue of Achilles to commemorate one of Wellington's victories (printing block?)

Velvet covered board 10" x 5" with models of world's largest diamonds 16

Box 4" x $2^{1}/4$" x $3^{1}/2$ x $2^{1}/4$" containing Tibetan Sandscript prayers from mill in museum

Wooden puzzle ball 3" dia from ???

Embroidered sampler

Leather purse containing 3 native bracelets

Cup & saucer (white)

Cowbell 4" high

2 window brackets from Haddon Hall

Piece landmine fabric. Southampton 1941

Small statuette 4" long $2^{1}/2$" high. Wolk feeding Romulus & Remus

Seed pod 7" long x 3"

2 Japanese discs

Globe glass 2" dia containing 'Radio Hypnotic Crystals'

Tin box 17" x $8^{1}/2$" x 4" containing variety of padlocks & keys

Tin box $7^{1}/2$ x 4 x $3^{1}/2$ containing variety of keys

2 'Ostermiilk' tins containing various padlocks & keys

Hide chest 24" x 15" x 15" containing large variety of handcuffs locks & keys

Cardboard box 11" x 4" x 4" containing various keys

Cigar box 9 x 5 x $2^{1}/2$ containing various padlocks & keys

Cardboard folders containing catalogues & cuttings of locks etc

Various folders catalogues cuttings magazines prints etc

Carved spoon & chain from Tasmanian Prisoners

2 Photo albums of postcards

11 Postcards, loose

23 albums cigarette cards

Dublin exhibition catalogue 1853

2 vols Cassells Household guide

Clock & watchmaking Reid

Guides to Ruskin Museum

Illustrated Guide to Church Congress Exhibition 1922

Clocks Watches & Bells Beckett

Collection of Medal Models . Consisiting of 9 moulds 5 castings

34 local theatre posters etc

Book dated 1769

Table knife inscribed 'Florence Nightingale'

34 Prints of local scenes

Printed sheet of info relating to AR & Diaboli

Painted church scene

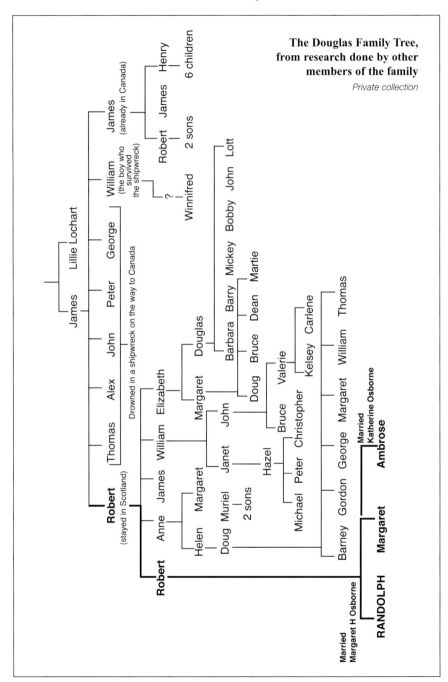

**The Douglas Family Tree,
from research done by other
members of the family**
Private collection

Notes to chapters

1: The Boy in the Box

steel lined trunk...
In the photograph Randolph is reminiscent of a magician called Herbert Brooks who used to cram himself in a tiny trunk for an escape illusion. He was said to have replicated the trick done by another magician named Maskelyne. Maskelyne offered a reward of £500 for anyone who could replicate his trick.
   Another person who managed to replicate a box escape similar to Maskelyne's was Dr. J W Lynn. In the photograph, his assistant, The Great Carlton, is inside the box in a very similar position to Randolph. It is from an article in The Strand magazine, which gave details of how to build the box,
   Randolph drew diagrams of 'The Great Box Trick' dated February 21st 1911. The little sketch of a person crouched in the box is from those. Whether he copied the box diagrams or worked it all out for himself I am not sure. Maybe he was inspired to his 'seige' by these people, as well as Houdini.

a German high-wire act... In 'The Secret Life of Houdini' by William Kalush and Larry Sloman, there is a description of this. When Ehrich (Houdini) was almost seven he saw a travelling circus in his childhood home of

Dr Lynn and his assistant The Great Carlton, from an article in The Strand Magazine in Randolph's scrapbook *Buxton Museum and Art Gallery*

Appleton, Wisconsin, USA. A wire walker called Weitzman enthralled him and he went home and tried walking on a rope himself until he perfected it. The man risking his life and exciting the crowd made a big impression on him.

2: The Bonds of Love

brought him to Sheffield...
It may be that Robert came to Sheffield, with its fine silversmithing reputation, to find work after his training, and met Margaret then. The family story though is that they met at art college in Edinburgh, Margaret was a painter and at the time she would have been at college, she is not shown on the census of her parent's home at Woodside, Chesterfield Road, Sheffield. It was unusual for a woman then to go off to college, but the Trustees Academy, (also known later as Edinburgh School of Design), in Edinburgh, did admit women.
A quote from the Book of Old Edinburgh Club vol 27, 1949, about the School of Design by John Mason, says:
"On 13th December 1797 the Trustees Society proposed that females should be

Herbert Brooks *From an article in the Magic Circle Archive*

209

admitted to the Academy on two evenings in the week.....who approved of the daughters of tradesmen and manufacturers being afforded opportunity of acquiring a knowledge of drawing...." The daughter of one of the well known Osborne file manufacturers would certainly fit the requirement.

meeting at Shrewsbury Road...
The details of meetings and events, outings etc concerning The City of Sheffield ArtCrafts Guild are taken from the guild's minutes and notebooks, held at Sheffield Archives.

Houdini married his beloved Bess...
There is some debate amongst Houdini scholars about the date of the wedding, or if they were actually officially married at all.

his bride...
The date of July 19th 1894 is from the marriage records, Norton Parish Church, entry 158. On this Robert is listed as a chaser, living at Havelock Street, Sheffield. His father Robert is listed as wine merchant and Margaret's father, Henry George Osborne, is listed as a file manufacturer.

salamander..

The font at Norton, which dates from 1220, has a sala-mander carved on it (pictured). A salamander is seen in mythology as a creature that can withstand or live in fire and so may be used on fonts to represent purification. St James is a lovely old church. The ivy is now cleared from the arch.
  The 'needle' monument to Chantrey still stands and his grave, surrounded by railings, is to the left of the main door of the church.

a fine village...
Greenhill was a small village in Derbyshire when Robert and Margaret moved to Yew House. Now it is a suburb of Sheffield, but the road and house have changed very little. Greenhill Hall is long demolished, but the water pump is still there. The forge is still there too, now a private residence.
  The house that was the Douglas family home still looks much the same, covered in ivy, and the windows are the same as the ones in the photograph of the family taking tea in the back garden.

visit Margaret's parents...
Margaret was from Greenhill, in the parish of Norton, then in Derbyshire, now part of Sheffield. Her family home was there, probably near Yew House.
  In the Sheffield Kelly's street and trade directory for 1893, there is a Frank Osborne

Sheffield Local Studies Library

Author

Greenhill Main Road, around 1910 (top), and in 2009. The ivy covered house at the end of the terrace on the left was Randolph's childhood home

listed at Woodside, a hamlet not far from Greenhill, and a Henry Osborne, Margaret's father, listed at Greenhill.
  In the Kelly's Directory for 1895, the year Randolph was born, Henry George Osbornes address is given as Greenhill and his trade as Steel file saw and machine knife manufac-turer. In the 1898 Kelly's directory, he is listed, at Greenhill, as a file manufacturer.
  In the 1881 Census, page 8 entry 40, at Woodside Hamlet, Norton Civil Parish. parish of St Paul's (Norton Lees) Margaret's family are listed:
Henry George Osborne, Head, 34.
File maker (forger) Born Dore
Jane Osborne, Wife, 34, Born Norton
Arthur William, Son, 10 Born Norton
Margaret Helen, daughter, 8 Born Norton
Jennie, daughter, 5 Born Norton
George Henry, son, 2 Born Norton
Katherine, daughter, 9mths Born Norton
Jane Needham, servant, 28 Born Norton
William Greaves, apprentice, 15 Born Sheffield.
  In Greenhill, in 1898, the family lived next to the Rev Vaniah Odom, curate of Norton Church, who resided at 'Rock House.' Incidentally Rev Odom's name came up on the Blackpool parish church register, as he married there in July 1885, to one Mary Ann Harrison.
  Living at 'The Hall' at Greenhill in 1898 was Charles William Cowlishaw, farmer. Robert Strachan Douglas is listed on deeds for Yew House as 'farm manager'
  There seems to have been quite a few with the name Osborne living around the area of Norton and Woodside, on the Chesterfield

Road. Other Osborne's lived at Norton Woodside, perhaps relatives of the family.
   In 1895 J William Osborne is listed in the Kelly's Directory at 53 Woodbank Close. Charles Frank Osborne and Thomas Osborne, file manufacturer and general merchant, are listed at Norton Woodside, at number 175 Chesterfield Road. Next listing to them, at number 261 Chesterfield Road, Woodside, is the Woodside Brick Co.
Later, the houses were later re-numbered, and more were built.
   In 1902 Thomas and Frank Osborne, file manufacturers, are listed at number 285 Chesterfield Road.
   In 1902 Frank Osborne, who lived next door to Margaret Helen Osborne's family according to the 1881 census listing, is listed at number 285 Chesterfield Road.
   This ties in with the area still known as Woodside. It is just before Woodseats, and is now a retail park, built on the site of the old brick works, with the quarry still showing behind the shops.
   So I am not sure if Margaret's family lived in the Woodside area,which was grouped with Greenhill then, or actually in the heart of Greenhill village. I have assumed the village, as in 1893 the two places were listed separately

3: A little Douglas

William Hutton and Sons...
The firm was a well known Sheffield business, making fine tableware.Buildings which formed the frontage of the firm still stand on West Street, Sheffield. The makers mark for the firm is a crowned H in an oval, This is stamped on Randolph's spoon, identifying it as from Hutton & Sons

Sheffield Empire was booming...
Details of the acts and descriptions of the Empire are taken from a notebook listing all the acts which is held in Sheffield Local Studies Library. The book 'Sheffield's Lost Theatres' by Bryen Hillerby tells more.

Part of Hutton's still stands, on West Street Sheffield

the Douglas crest...
Information from various websites and heraldry books about the name Douglas. The name Douglas seems to be mainly listed as coming from the Gaelic 'dubh glais' which means 'dark water'.
   One of the first of the Douglas family mentioned is Sir William, who fought and died for William Wallace. His son, Sir James, was the one who was a friend of Robert the Bruce and is said to have taken Bruce's heart to the Holy Land. Because of this a heart was used in the family emblem. The Douglas motto is 'Jamais arriere' which means 'never behind'. The North American version of the Douglas clan badge has a winged heart and the motto 'Forward' so it seems it is this version which Robert chose to use for Margaret's brooch.

stayed in Edinburgh to look after his wine selling business...
In the Post Office Directory for Edinburgh around this time there is only one wine merchant by the name of Douglas, at an establishment called Douglas and Mason. This was at 96 George Street, Edinburgh.

shipwreck...
The story of relative's drowning in a shipwreck is a long held story in Randolph's family and was told to me by his remaining relatives.
   Details of the steamer Montreal and the people drowned are from accounts in the 'New York Times' on August 1, 3 and 5, 1857. The St Lawrence river was notorious and many ships were lost there,
   The Douglas family were in the passenger list for the John McKenzie, from where many people boarded the Steamer Montreal.
   The list was in the 'Montreal Gazette' of 1857. This clarified which shipwreck they had died in.
   An article of August 1, 1857, in the New York Times, also listed the family. It was entitled *"Burning of the steamer Montreal. Corrected list of the Persons Supposed to be Lost'.*
and in the list are found
"Mr Douglas, father of William, who is saved; Mrs Douglas and a sister of either Mr or Mrs Douglas, together with six children.'

4: A curious eye

Art Nouveau style clips...
W. Hutton and Sons were famous for this type of fine silverwork, including clips that look like the ones Margaret wears. If Robert was working there he could well have designed and made them himself.

studio...
The photographer's studio address is on the photograph. The descriptions of the street and church are based on old photos in Sheffield Local Studies Library.

Vulcan...
A metalworking god of the Greeks and Romans. Very appropriate as the symbol of Sheffield and part of the city's coat of arms.

frieze...
The fine stone frieze shows the various Sheffield industries. On the right hand side is a woman carrying a horn of plenty, the fruits of labour, next are those labours, smiths, grinders, smelters and miners.

On the left is a woman carrying a blazing torch, representing the light of knowledge. Next to her are sculptors, painters, metalworkers, buffers and finishers.

Empire Theatre..
The Empire Theatre Palace of Varieties stood on Charles Street and Pinstone Street, in the centre of Sheffield. It survived the Blitz and still entertained the crowds until April 1959. In July 1960 it was demolished to make way for a row of shops.

Sheffield Empire *Sheffield Newspaper Archives*

The site of the Empire, in 2008 *Author*

Hodgson...
The man who caused Houdini such distress- William Hope Hodgson (1877-1918) was every bit as driven as the master escapologist himself. A small, delicate child, he had run away to sea at the age of thirteen, only to be returned until he began a formal apprenticeship some years later. His dream quickly became a nightmare, however; his almost pretty looks made him a natural target for bullies. He responded by studying boxing, body building and the martial arts; *'The primary motivation of his body development was not health, but self-defence. His relatively short height and sensitive, almost beautiful face made him an irresistible target for bullying seamen. When they moved in to pulverise him, they would learn too late that they had come to grips with easily one of the most powerful men, pound for pound, in all England."*
Sam Moskowitz "Out Of The Storm"
Hodgson set up a physical training school in Blackburn which, sadly, was a failure. Among his customers were members of the Blackburn police force. His behaviour towards Houdini generated controversy; the escape artist had some difficulty removing his restraints, complaining that Hodgson had deliberately injured him and jammed the locks of his handcuffs. His "duel" with Houdini has to be seen in the light of him fighting for his own financial survival. He lost on both counts and, in attempt to make money, started to write fiction. His monstrous science fiction work "The Night Land" is regarded as a cult classic, along with "The House On The Borderland" and his occult series "Carnacki The Ghost Finder". He was killed in Ypres, April 1918 by an exploding artillery shell.

Siberian Transport cell...
An account of this escape is told in 'The Secret Life of Houdini' by William Kalush and Larry Sloman.

5: On stage with Dink

Herbert's Dogs...
The reviewer from the 'Sheffield Daily Independen't who was at the show was very impressed with the 'great Houdini' saying *'one of the best programmes that Sheffield people have been privileged to witness.'* He was impressed by 'Metamorphosis,' where Houdini and Bess change places whilst put in a sack and locked in a trunk. But he seems to have liked the dogs almost as much, which may not have done much for Houdini's ego!:

'*Clever as Houdini is, his is not the only smart turn on the evenings entertainment. There is a wonderful collection of performing dogs...these are marvellously trained to all sorts of jumping, leaping and somersaulting and a French poodle amongst their number displays amazing intelligence indulging in antics which send the house into roars of laughter and concluding with a unique performance of high diving.*'

other members of the Douglas family followed Robert's example...

Randolph, his sister Peggy and Peggy's children took up the idea of mirror writing and used it often, said Randolph's niece, when I spoke with her on one of the numerous occasions she kindly took time to do so.

he pushed up his elbows...

The description of how Houdini gets out of a strait jacket is based on the description in his own book 'Handcuff Secrets.'

Mirror cuffs...

Descriptions in 'The Life and Many Deaths of Harry Houdini' (Ruth Brandon) and The Secret Life of Houdini tell of the Mirror challenge. In the latter, Kalush and Sloman tell of how it seems to have been an elaborately pre-planned stunt, as the silver presentation cuffs appear to have been made before the date of the challenge.

he would have seen Houdini challenged...

The episode is described in the Sheffield Daily Independent of Monday, May 3, 1904:
HOUDINI HARASSED
At one time it looked as though the visit of Harry Houdini, the Handcuff King, to the Empire Theatre, at Sheffield, would pass off very tamely indeed and it was not until the performance at the second house on Friday night that anything out of the
ordinary took place. Then...Houdini was challenged by a local 'handcuff king' named Tom Sharp, to release himself from an extraordinary sort of handcuffs, which
certainly did not look like regulation manacles. It took Houdini an hour to extricate himself, and after he had accomplished the feat Houdini extracted a promise from Sharpe that the latter would present himself at the Empire on Saturday night and allow Houdini to fasten a pair of handcuffs on him (Sharpe). Naturally there was a full house at each performance on Saturday night in the hope of seeing something new, and people had to be turned away. There was a great scene on Friday night when Houdini accomplished what many thought would be an impossibility, but this was nothing compared to what happened at

the first performance on Saturday evening.
After introducing his business in the usual manner, Houdini asked three times if Mr Sharpe was present and wished to fulfil his promise. On asking the third time a young man came on the stage and stated that he had been sent by Mr Sharpe to say that Mr Sharpe would not accept Houdini's challenge in the manner the latter wished, and that it was unfair, because Houdini would not let Sharpe see the manacles before they were put on. This Houdini denied, and said he had given Sharpe the choice of three pairs of handcuffs. The incident terminated and Houdini then asked in the usual manner for handcuffs to be fastened on him. The young man who had represented himself as being sent by Sharpe, remained upon the stage, and immediately produced an assortment of handcuffs, and challenged Houdini to release himself from them, offering to forfeit £1 to a local charity if Houdini succeeded.
And then followed a most remarkable scene. Houdini took up a pair of handcuffs, examined them critically, then threw them on the stage, and shouted, 'Yes I will.' He then took up another pair , and after looking closely at them he rushed to the front of the stage, and in a most dramatic style declared that the manacles had been tampered with in the same way as those brought the previous evening by Sharpe. Houdini declared that the collar had been 'sweated' and the key hole made smaller. He than asked if there was a mechanic or a locksmith present, and a gentleman in the stalls answering in the affirmative the manacles were handed to him, and he was asked to compare them with a pair of handcuffs borrowed from a policeman, as both pairs were supposed to be English.
After a slight delay, Houdini said 'Don't hesitate for a moment; speak your mind; don't bother about me.' but the gentleman said he was unable to give a decision on the point.
At this moment a message was sent to Houdini to the effect that the youth who had issued the challenge was Inspector Brookes' son. This the youth denied, there upon Houdini asked what was his name. After great pressure, but very reluctantly, the young man declared his name was Brown.
Houdini stared back, and in a dramatic style, said, 'Yes I know you now! You are Brown, of Matlock. It was you who wrote to me for information.' This Brown denied. Houdini then declared to the audience that he had had several letters from Brown, of

Matlock, who stated that his parents were well off, and he was collecting handcuffs and information respecting the business of people styling themselves as 'handcuff kings' with a view of confronting and exposing them, but that if he (Houdini) would help him he would not interfere with him. 'I wrote and told him,' (continued Houdini) 'that I would have nothing to do with a man who tried to take away the bread and butter from another man, I have letters at home from this man which I will fetch and read at the second house.'

After a pause of a second or two, Houdini shouted excitedly, 'No, I shall fetch them now and you shall see.'

With this Houdini rushed off the stage and out into the street, hatless, just as he had appeared on the stage. During the time he was away there was an excited buzz of conversation all around the house and the orchestra began to play, when Brown stepped to the front and made a statement which was not properly heard.

Then Houdini marched on the stage with a large pile of letters in a correspondence rack, and he and his wife and assistant began to look for the letters. They appeared unable to find the right letter for a time, but at length Houdini jumped up with Brown's epistle in his possession. This he read to the audience, proving he had been in correspondence with a man at Matlock

Turning to Brown Houdini said. 'Did you write these letters or did you not. If not, I'm a liar. If you did you're a ---' (but Houdini did not finish this part of the sentence).

'I did not.' replied Brown.

'Then write now and let the audience compare the handwriting.' said Houdini.

Pen and ink were brought and Houdini asked him to write: 'I hereby state that you have falsely stated.' but this Brown would not write. Houdini then told him to write what he liked and sign it Will Brown (the name of the writer of the letter). This he did, but on picking up the paper Houdini seemed nonplussed, and handed the two lots of writing to the spectators in the stalls. There was little or no similarity but it was the general impression that Brown had disguised his writing.

After a brief pause, Brown then said: 'For the last time I challenge you to escape from the manacles after I have fastened them on in the way I wish.'

'No.' said Houdini, 'You can fasten my hands behind, but you must not double me up.'....The handcuff king retired into his tent

and in a short time he emerged triumphant with the handcuffs undone. There was a most dramatic finish, and the audience nearly went wild with delight, cheering Houdini and hooting Brown.

At the second house there was not even standing room and excitement ran high as Houdini's turn approached. Some eight men walked on the stage, but the first pair of handcuffs that Houdini selected he looked at very carefully. He than turned to the audience and said he had been expecting this for some time.

'These are Inspector Brooke's handcuffs. I have had them described to me and could tell them in a minute.' ...

The young man who had brought them on stage was Brooke's' son. Houdini still took the challenge and opened the cuffs in about three minutes and he came out free. Just how much of these provocations were initiated by Houdini for better publicity it is hard to know.

Houdini tells of the Sheffield Empire event and quotes some of the above article in his book 'Handcuff Secrets.'

A newsaper cutting about Inspector Brooke's death is in Randolph's scrapbook at Buxton Museum. The cutting mentions the Houdini incident, but says Houdini declined to take up the challenge of Brooke's cuffs. The funeral was held at Norton, at the church where Robert and Margaret Douglas were married.

Whether Randolph was at these shows is hard to know, but there is an intruiging envelope drawn by him in the Magic Circle Archive.

It shows a man running with a briefcase. He is running past buildings including the Angel Hotel and Skidmore Pork Butchers. These places, (though it was the Angel Inn) were on Button Lane, which was just opposite the Empire Theatre.

It is tempting to think that this is a sketch showing Houdini running back to the Empire armed with his letters from Sharpe, to show to the audience. The building on the right, named 'Binns' cloth shop, is not on a map of around 1904, when the event occurred. By then it seems to have become a tram terminus shelter. In Sheffield local Studies Library there is a very early drawing (1890) of Button Lane, that does have a similar building. Maybe Randolph saw this drawing and used it as a reference to try and draw the area around as it was years before.

In Randolph's drawing there is a cameraman too, so perhaps it is done to be like a scene from the Houdini's Serial, which concerns suitcases getting mixed up and the odd chase.

The envelope Randolph sent to Houdini, showing a man running near Button Lane towards The Empire Theatre *Magic Circle Archives*

The 1890 drawing. The buildings match those in Randolph's sketch *Sheffield Local Studies Library*

A later photo of Button Lane. Skidmore Pork Butchers is there, but the little hut once on the left is not on the maps *Sheffield Local Studies Library*

little Margaret was ill...
Family anecdotes tell of this illness at age 4 and her having a governess. Maybe home schooling was just for a while until she recovered, as in the 1911 census, Margaret is listed as at school.

sharing the family home...
Katherine is listed there in the 1901 census

Greenhill School...
Illness record, temperature, lessons etc at the school are from the headmaster's journal at the Sheffield Archives

7: A fondness for locks

badge..
The Artcrafts Guild badge pictured, made by Robert S Douglas, was owned by guild member and Master George Beeston Himsworth, a designer silversmith and writer, whose name is inscribed on the back.
His daughter Joyce Himsworth was also a talented silversmith and enameller. Examples of their work can be seen in the Metalwork room of the Millennium Gallery, Sheffield, in the same case as the badge.
  Details of Roberts pressure of work, the Artcrafts Guild meetings, lectures, excursions etc are from records at Sheffield Archives.

tender letters back home...
The fact that Robert wrote letters everyday is anecdotal from family members. The quote about *'shopping for our darlings'* is taken from a transcript of an interview with Randolphs sister Margaret on May 19th,1987, held at Buxton Museum and Art Gallery.

Birchinlee..
Details of the Artcrafts Guild excursion are from the records at Sheffield Archives.

every lock that came into his hands..
Randolph says this of himself in an interview in the Worlds Fair on May 28th 1938

long suffering sibling...
Anecdotal from Peggy's daughter, who was told about her mummy being tied up by 'Uncle Randolph.'

8: Unfinished portrait
hard winter...
The weather descriptions and illness records are from the journal of the headmaster of Greenhill School, which is now in the Sheffield Archives

pneumonia was diagnosed...

The details of Margaret's illness,symptoms and operation are from relatives and also from her medical notes. She seems to have become ill after the operation for empyema.

painting..

The painting now hangs in the home of Margaret's niece, who told me the story of the painting and how Margaret had died on her daughter Peggy's birthday. Margaret's death certificate confirms this.

Mickleover..

The institution later became known as Pastures Hospital and is now flats. It opened in 1851 and had patients coming from all over Derbyshire to be treated

'day by day and grain by grain'..

This quote is from Nicholas Nickleby by Charles Dickens.

a romantic affliction..

The sad ebbing of life from the awful disease, TB or consumption, was often used as a romantically skewed plotline, for example in La Traviata, and La Boheme. TB is now known to be caused by a bacillus. It knew no boundaries, it was a terror without class distinction. A good percentage of the population at the time probably were infected with TB, but the disease did not always develop.

Many famous artists, writers and poets succumbed to it, including Keats, the Bronte sisters, Chekhov, Chopin, Ruskin, and Orwell. The disease is now treatable with drugs, though drug-resisitant strains are emerging.

the cemetery..

The description of the chapel of rest, spire etc at the Derbyshire Lane cemetery are from a photograph of the entrance at the time in Sheffield Local Studies Library.
The cemetery and buildings are still there, but the spire is now gone.
The date of the funeral was found on burial records from Norton Church.
The weather on the day is taken from the bulletin in the Sheffield Daily Independent of December 1st 1910.

9: Escaping the past

Carrington Road...

The street index directory for 1910/11 at Sheffield Local Studies Library lists a Mr Tom Percival, Clerk at the house the Douglas family lived in on Carrington Road. In the 1911/12 one it doesn't seem to be listed, perhaps due

to the house being empty at the time of the survey, or no one being in.
The family were definitely living there by September 30th, 1911 as the marriage certificate of Robert and Katherine gives the family as living at that address. After that the street indexes give Robert Douglas, Designer, as head of household.

The attic is up 3 flights of bannistered stairs, with a door at the bottom of final flight.The ceiling is no longer a high A frame as it is lowered with boarding. No trace of a big beam or anything is left visible.

Entering the front door, to left is bay window room which was used as study and sitting room, on the right is what was a lounge and where a study/studio for RDs dad was, there is now a kitchen.

A flight of stairs leads down from that level into the old kitchen on the right side and on the left another room- perhaps used for a servant. They did have a maid; Randolph in letters refers to her as having tidied up and then leaving. So if there was a maid's room, she didn't seem to live there later.

help with the housekeeping...

In the 1911 census, Katherine Osborne is listed as housekeeper at Carrington Road.

new domain...

The road, houses and shops are described from the photograph of Carrington Road in 1910 and also from visiting the house, by kind permission of the owner.
The decoration and content of Randolph's attic room is described from studying the photographs shown in the chapter.

Carrington Road 2009 *Author*

...and in 1910 *Sheffield Local Studies Library*

216

Notes

10: Magical Inspirations

box trick...
The number 33 indicates the drawing may
have been from a series of tricks and may be
an explanation copied from a magazine by
Randolph, showing details of Maskelyne's
illusion, or that of one of his imitators.

four shillings and sixpence...
This would be about 22.5p in the decimal
currency today. It was a large amount to be able to
spend at the time. Houdini never had much to spend
on equipment in his early years.

gaudily magnificent...
The description of the theatre is based on
information in 'The Lost Theatres of
Sheffield,' by Brian Hillerby.

steel blue eyes...
Houdini's appearance is summarised in the
book 'Houdini!!!' by Kenneth Silverman.

characteristically startling...
these words are from a review in the
Sheffield Daily Independent, March 8, 1911

placed in a sack-like arrangement ...
descriptions of the evening are from Sheffield
Daily Independent, March 11, 1911

illusion after illusion ...
The acts Chung Ling Soo did are taken from
those listed in the programme for that night.
Descriptions of the acts are from the book
'The Glorious Deception' by Jim Steinmeyer.

11: Randin's first show

Tuesday September 26th, 1911 ...
Randin's first show is known as he wrote
those words on the back of the ticket pictured
in the chapter for the concert at St Vincent's
CYMS that night. The ticket is now in the
Douglas Collection, Buxton Museum & Art Gallery.

sea monster ...
The challenge that Houdini took up on the
same day as Randolph's first show is
described in 'The Secret Life of Houdini'
(from a cutting from Boston Herald.
September 27th, 1911, in the Robinson
Locke Scrapbook 247 in the collection of the
New York Public Library).
The escape was set at Keith's Theatre.
From descriptions in the newspaper and a
cutting with a photo on, the 'monster' could
have been a very large turtle. The creature
was turned on its back on the stage. The
abdomen had been sliced open, rimmed with

metal eyelets and
laced with steel
chains which were
fastened with locks.
The chains were
slackened to allow
Houdini to climb in,
wearing handcuffs
and leg irons.
He sprinkled
perfume where his
head would be. The
chains were tight-
ened and padlocked
and a screen placed
around the scene.
Fifteen minutes later, Houdini, pale and
grease covered, was free, standing in front of
the creature holding his shed handcuffs and
leg irons.. The 'monster' still had padlocked
chains around it.

Scott had challenged Randin ...
In the transcript of the interview with Robert
and Margaret's daughter Margaret (Peggy), in
May 1987, Margaret says that Randolph was
challenged by Commander Scott, the Chief of
Police, that he could not escape if shackled by
Scott, and that he escaped in a minute and a half.

a wedding ...
The date is from the wedding certificate. It
lists the venue as 'The District Register Office
in the District of Ecclesall Bierlow'.
Looking in the Kelly's Directory for that year
shows this register office, which covered the
area of Carrington Road, to be at union Road
in Sheffield. The registrar listed at that
address is Joseph A Beard, who has signed
the certificate.
By the time of the wedding Robert's father
had died. Katherine's father is still alive and
listed as File Manufacturer.

bad winter ...
Weather records taken from the Greenhill
School records in Sheffield Archives

Randolph spent more money on chains ...
From his notebooks listing what he bought
and in which year, held in a private collection.
Though he is dreaming of being an escapologist
he is listed in the 1911 census as an
'apprentice designer and modeller.'

sensation ...
The quote is from a letter Houdini sent out to
theatre manager Howard Watson, on Buckingham
Street London, when he was in Hull on Feb 1st
1913. From the American Memory Collection.

HOUDINI ESCAPES FROM MONSTER

Gets Out of Sea Freak in 15 Minutes and Receives an Ovation at Keith's.

Harry Houdini went Jonah one or two better at Keith's Theatre yesterday afternoon when he not only escaped from the in'ards of the "What-is-it?" sea monster, but incidentally removed a pair of handcuffs and a pair of leg-irons en route. It took him exactly 15 minutes to do the trick amid the cheers of an immense audience greeted him when he stood, grease-covered, palid and perspiring beside the turtle-like monster which he had been chained. Lieut.-Gov. Frothingham, seeking to forget the anxieties of the campaign, stood in the wings of the stage and witnessed the exploit. He invited Houdini and the latter's tiny wife to visit him at the State House.

217

12: Face to face

needle mystery...
This is described in the book 'Hiding The Elephant', by Jim Steinmeyer.

water torture cell...
The description of the stage and the act is based on description in various Houdini books, including 'Hiding The Elephant', by Jim Steinmeyer and also on the Sheffield Daily Independent review of April 22, 1913

declamatory voice...
Houdini's voice was recorded doing this introduction in 1914. It can be heard on the DVD box set 'Houdini the Movie Star' by Kino.

challenge, Sales & Teather...
Details of the Sheffield Empire box escape are from a newspaper article. entitled 'Houdini Wins' in Randolph's scrapbook at Buxton Museum & Art Gallery.

piercing eyes...
Randolph's description is from details on his army papers. A friend of Randolph's, G W Marshall. in an interview transcript of 21st August 1987, (now in Buxton Museum and Art Gallery) says Houdini had very piercing eyes.

box endurance test photo...
Randolph showing this is just a suggestion. He may have done the box test after seeing Houdini in 1913, as he signs it 'Randini' This tribute to Houdini may have been suggested by Houdini himself after they had met in 1913.

cakes..
In the transcript of the interview with Peggy, in May 1987, she says she used to prepare the tea. for their famous visitors. It was the first of many visits. A Worlds Fair article of 28th May, 1938, Randolph says *'he (Houdini) visited my house personally and often had meals with us.'*

mummy...
A man called G W Marshall, a close friend of Randolph's, was interviewed by the Museums Service on 21st August 1987, at John Turner House. He says Randolph painted a mummy at the top of the stairs. Mr Marshall 'met Houdini on many occasions at the Douglas' home.' He says Randolph did invent tricks for Houdini. Mr Marshall took a photo of Randolph in the attic room, with cases of butterflies etc. The description of Randolph's room is based on this and other photos of the room, perhaps taken by Randolph himself, which relatives have. Mr. Marshall also says Randolph was a

member of The Magic Circle, but there is no record of this. A transcript of the interview is in the Douglas Collection at Buxton Museum and Art Gallery

Water torture drawing...
Thanks to William Kalush for his help with this sketch. He informed me that the drawing Randolph did, shown in the photo, has 'May 2nd' written in the corner, but not the year.
A possibility is that Randolph drew the Water Torture Cell in April in Sheffield after seeing it at the Empire, as I have suggested, but posted it on to Houdini in Birmingham on May 2nd.
I have written of Houdini being shown the drawing at Carrington Road and not at a theatre or Birmingham, because of a quote in the Worlds Fair article of 28th May, 1938, which suggests this. In this article Randolph's (step) mother Kitty says:
"Houdini came to our house one day and Randolph had done a drawing of Houdini's torture chamber and method of working, based on what he had seen at the Empire the previous night when sitting among the audience. Houdini was astounded, and admitted that my son had correctly interpreted the secret of the trick, and he was so interested that he begged the drawing for a memento.'
The fact that Houdini went to the Douglas home the day after Randolph had done the sketch among the audience 'the previous night' suggests that it was the Sheffield Empire run that the exchange occurred. Birmingham is quite a way from Sheffield (61 miles/91.15km). If Houdini was already playing there it seems unlikely that he, or a visiting Randolph, would have travelled back to Carrington Road the next day and then back to Birmingham again, in the middle of a run. It is possible though; the distance from Sheffield to Birmingham maybe wouldn't seem that much to an American, or a well travelled showman.

lion's den..
The story about the Suffragette, a Mrs Lloyd, is taken from an article in the New York Times of February 24th 1913

13: Perfecting a craft

Boston key
An article in the Sheffield Daily Telegraph of Saturday, July 19th 1913 tells of the new Town Bridge opening and the ceremony.
There is also another article in the Douglas Collection, recorded by well respected and thorough author and researcher Professor E Dawes. This also tells of the event, and how Douglas made a key.

14: A most terrible thing

iron maiden
The device that inspired Houdini to send such an excited postcard to his friend Randolph was a man-sized, man-shaped container that looked rather like a mummy case with a hinged door or doors.

The inner side of the doors were covered with spikes meant to pierce the body of the unfortunate victim and inflict a lingering death; a face plate could be opened and closed for a final interrogation.

This Medieval Murder Machine was presented as the last word in torture and impressed not only Houdini but many other terrified tourists, most notably Bram Stoker, the author of 'Dracula.'

A research trip to Nuremberg with the actor Sir Henry Irving, for a production of 'Faust,' led to Stoker writing 'The Squaw' published 1892, in which a loud-mouthed tourist is killed in the Maiden by a vengeful black cat He describes the Maiden:

"There were several long spikes, square and massive, broad at the base and sharp at the points, placed in such a position that when the door should close, the upper ones would pierce the eyes of the victim and the lower his heart and vitals."

Unfortunately, both the Master Mystifier and the Vampire King were had - the Iron Maiden was a fake based on a literary joke. Though it purported to date from 1515 it was probably made around 1892 based on a colportage - a sort of sensationalist tract rather than a natty song by an American composer- by one Johan Phillip Siebkenees.

He, in turn, may or may not have been inspired by St Augustine who, in his City Of God, writes of Marcus Attillius regulus, who was "packed into a tight wooden box, spiked with sharp nails on all sides, so that he could not lean in any direction without being pierced."

Whatever, the irony remains of the great Houdini falling for the illusion hook, line and sinker.

Some details above are taken from Wikipedia. The scene of Houdini in the Nuremberg torture room with the iron maiden and the fact that he sent a model of it to Randolph are based on a letter from Houdini, dated Stuttgart, Germany, Oct 12th 1913. It is now in The Magic Circle Archives.

The Iron maiden model was later displayed in The House of Wonders and is now in the Douglas Collection at Buxton Museum and Art Gallery.

Some of the Nuremberg locks, labelled as from the Harry Houdini collection, were also later displayed at the The Douglas Museum House of Wonders. Randolph could have been sent them by Houdini at a later date, or perhaps he was even sent them by Hardeen or someone after Houdini's death in 1926, the same year that The Douglas Museum opened..

A 'Spanish Maiden escape' was an idea by Houdini but not performed. His notes about it are in a book called Houdini's Escapes compiled by Walter Gibson, originally published in 1930.

This idea was more than likely inspired by the iron maiden. Torture implements seemed to fascinate Houdini. He also did notes for a rack, a torture gallery style scene and he owned an electric chair. He and Randolph also correspond later about a page on 'Mongolian tortures' (in a letter of March 25th 1914, now at The Magic Circle archive).

note to his friend...
The Iron Maiden postcard to Randolph form Houdini is in the Douglas Collection at Buxton Museum and Art Gallery.

15: The self liberator

Greenhill Council School...
Details of Randini's appearance, and the different acts in the Grand Concert, are from a poster advertising the event in Randolph's collection at Buxton Museum and Art Gallery.

play the Empire..
In the transcript of the interview with Peggy, in May 1987, she says Randolph played the Sheffield Empire when he was about 20 (1895 + 20 = 1915). I could not find any records about this performance around that year. Perhaps Randolph appeared in an act with another name.

Looking through the Empire acts around then, there is tantalisingly an 'R H Douglass, Monologue Artiste', there on January 2 1915, (also there on Aug 24, 1908), but this is somebody else as he toured the country and was also older than Randolph I think.

water torture cell sketches.
It is tempting to think of Randolph sketching down these ideas for alterations/changes to Houdini's Water Torture Cell as the two of them chatted together, or perhaps as Randolph watched the illusion on stage and tried to add his own ideas to it. In a correspondence with magical illusion designer and author of 'Hiding The Elephant' Jim Steinmeyer, he commented that one of the drawings shows the Water Torture Cell raised in the air, which would help dispel the idea some people had of there being a trap door underneath the tank for Houdini to escape from. This seems a bit unfeasible though as, being full of water, and a man, it would be extremely heavy.

16: Faithfully yours

Human shaped case...
Perhaps Randolph was the one who gave Houdini the idea for the Spanish Maiden escape he described in his notes and not the visit to the Iron Maiden?

January 1914...
This month also had an event that Randolph may have gone to see, as the Sheffield Daily Independent advertised on January 1st that 'The Kinetophone is here' Edison's Most Marvellous Talking Pictures' at the Cinema House in Fargate, in the city centre from Monday next.'

proposed by some...
The book 'The Secret Life of Houdini' by William Kalush and Larry Sloman, puts a meticulously researched and convincing argument for this forward,

go backstage...
In the transcript of the interview with Peggy, in May 1987, she says Randolph at HH's insistence, used to go backstage with him, after he had finished his challenge on a Friday night, in case anyone 'did a dirty' and he was trapped.

eight foot plank...
In the book Houdini's Escapes, compiled by Walter Gibson, Houdini describes the plank escape, and how he got out of it:
"I am lashed to an eight foot plank, with broomstick behind my knees and hands secured at each side. Long soft cord or rope is used for fastening the stick to my knees. I get into a sitting position, the stick is placed behind my knees. The rope is in the center of the stick and is fastened to the knees; then both my hands are placed under the stick and tied firmly to it.
"I am now laid on the plank,...I am lashed to the plank with heavy rope starting under my arms, crossing over my body and back to my neck; the neck is fastened with the same rope, tying it off at the end of the board. My feet are now tied together with heavy rope...
"There are two methods of release. One is to be able to pull the feet out. This can be done with a great deal of effort...when my feet are loose I can get my mouth to the rope that holds my hands and untie it with my teeth.
"Second method; After working awhile I can push the stick out from my hands, this will make me virtually loose."

a quick sketch...
In the drawing we can see the ropes as

described above. There seems to be a dog-like squiggle on the right of the sketch, just coming onto stage or peering from the wings. Perhaps it was one of the performing dogs often at the Empire, overcome by curiosity at all the wriggling!

china doll...
In the transcript of the interview with Peggy, in May 1987, it says 'Mrs Houdini was a dainty lady, and she once brought their mother a lovely china doll'. The doll passed down to Peggy's daughter, who described it to me.

Jewel box
The letter written by Beatrice Houdini to Randolph on February 19th, 1914 is where the words come from. This letter is now in The Magic Circle archive.

avid collector of magazines...
There are dozens of magazines and newspapers Randolph accumulated in the Douglas collection, magic, model making, films, Houdini ephemera in newspapers etc. In the World's Fair article of May 28th 1938 the interviewer of Randolph at The House of Wonders says *'The owner thought nothing of buying a whole year's bound volumes of pictures and magazine periodicals just to go through them and pick out anything relating to Houdini."*

brief paragraph...
The words are from a review of the Empire acts in Sheffield Daily Independent, February 2nd, 1914

17: Suspended

bordering on the supernatural...
positively the last appearance in England.
These words are used in the newspaper ad for the Nottingham run on Monday June 8th 1914.

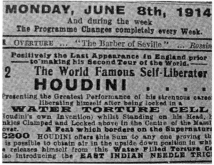

Ad for the Nottingham show   *Private collection*

220

Notes

He opened with the Crystal Casket...
The list of illusions that night is on the Revue poster. Descriptions of the Magical Revue illusions, including De Kolta's Expanding Die, are found in Jim Steinmeyer's 'Hiding The Elephant.'

take it all in his stride....
World's Fair article of May 28th 1938:
'So intimate were they in discussing escapology and demonstrating tricks that devoid of any natural hero worship...'

up the small staircase....
I can describe the stairs etc. as I was kindly allowed to visit the attic by the present owner of the house.

all in one straitjacket.....
In the transcript of the interview with Peggy, in May 1987, she says Randolph always used an 'all in one straitjacket, sleeves stitched together.'
She also says Randolph 'certainly did pass on illusions to Harry Houdini - but would never take any money for them.'

noticed the rope.....
The beam and high gable ceiling of the attic are now covered by a lower panelled ceiling. In the photograph of Randolph's room, there seems to be some kind of winch or pulley and rope next to his bed head. Could this have been the rope he used when giving Houdini his iconic new straitjacket escape demonstration? It does seem a bit too thin to haul up a person, but Randolph was only a slight nineteen year old at the time. It doesn't seem to go up to a roof beam though, judging by the angle of the rope. Maybe it was for another of Randolph's ideas.

What (Randolph) Douglas did next would change the course of magic's history...
These words are used about the incident by William Kalush and Larry Sloman in 'The Secret Life of Houdini' (page 303)

nodding to Kitty.....
The episode with Randolph, Houdini and Kitty in the attic is based on the interview in World's Fair article of May 28th 1938:
" My son demonstrated a straight-jacket effect while hanging upside down.
I remember it vividly because it took place in the attic and I had to help my son to get suspended from the ceiling; Houdini was again impressed and it was not long after that he started with the trick in America."
It must have been a great thrill for Randolph to be able to contribute to Houdini one of his

What looks like a pulley, handle and rope above the bed head in Randolph's room
Private collection

most iconic escape tricks. It is a little like, for example, a David Bowie fan today giving the star a song, and him performing it at a concert where it becomes an instant hit.

He had come up with a winner.....
In a correspondence with 'The Secret Life of Houdini' author William Kalush about why the upside-down straitjacket escape was so important he says that Houdini, with this stunt, was the first magician to bridge the gap between the outdoor spectacle that circus would often use and magic. It also gave more time for dramatic build up than other stunts Houdini did, and people could see him better and for longer as he performed. It could be done in most weather in a flexible location, usually a newspaper building so the press were always on hand. The places chosen were places where there was more space for a big crowd to gather.
  The suspended straitjacket played an important part in the indelible image Houdini created; it became an iconic image in cultural history and magic.

221

18: War and wonders

Bramall Lane....
The troops had to move elsewhere to practice as the club were complaining over the loss of grass. Details of the Battalion and its moves are from the book 'Sheffield City Battalion' by Ralph Gibson and Paul Oldfield.

Herbert Brooks
The description of Herbert Brooks and his tiny trunk escape come from an article entitled 'What Others are Doing' and an article from the British Magical Society, current programme, both in The Magic Circle archive. The trunk escape and card tricks formed his act.

David Devant.....
The description of the illusions in Devant's show come from the Hippodrome programme for October 24th, 1914, and an article called 'My Illusions' in The Strand magazine written by Devant and kept at the Magic Circle archive.
  The description of the 'Biff' motorcycle trick is from the book 'Hiding The Elephant by Jim Steinmeyer, p229.

***a young
soldier.....***
This is the photo of the young soldier with his pipe and tobacco, in the Sheffield Daily Independent of Wednesday 4th November 1914.

a performance of Oriental splendour.....
The words are from an ad in the Sheffield Daily Independent of Monday December 28th, 1914.
  A review of the day after says:
'the packed audiences which crowded the Empire Palace last night watched with breathless interest the many wonderful and clever illusions. ...many startling illusions which are new to the city.'
  As well as Soo they all saw Hugh J Emmett a ventriloquist, Tom E Hughes a 'rag bag of vanity' broken down swell, Frank and Vesta 'some remarkably clever dancing' John and Lilian Grand, responsible for a playlet entitled 'At Home and Abroad'
  The reviewer also says. *"Griffen and Ardell are a couple of eccentrics who make the most of their acrobatic business; Fred Weldon 'plays an instrument which he names the phonofid-dledeoddity, is able to combine the ludicrous with the sublime.'*
  Marjorie Dawson was in a crinoline 'singing songs of the period when it was worn'. This

all followed a rave week of 'Princess Caprice and 'Velanche's Dogs 'who provide an exciting episode in their footballing competition.'

Soo had revamped his act.....
Descriptions of the Soo's illusions can be found in the book 'The Glorious Deception' by Jim Steinmeyer

19: Houdini hung

Pages from Randolph's autograph book....
Van Berne (later using Bern) also gave Randolph a signed photograph. The drawing of Van Bern in the book shows a glass jug. This is from his wine and water trick. The jug was shown filled with water, then poured into a wine glass where it turned into red wine. When tipped back in the jug it changed back into water.

Photo of Van Bern signed to Randolph

Clempert.....
The details about Clempert's life and acts are form an article in the Magic Circular,
  'A Rich Cabinet of Magical Curiosities' by Edwin A Dawes MIMC. Below is part of the programme for the show

> 7. (Russian).
>   Starring Engagement of the Daring Russian Bombardier, Our Loyal British Ally—**JOHN CLEMPERT, The Napoleon of Mystery,** in His Latest Invention—" The Siberian Water Torture Prison."

in the interests of public health.....
The words are from the ad for the Karenzo act in a newspaper from Randolph's collection.

the Leons.....
Description of the act is from information sent to me by the Magic Circle, including from the book 'The Great Leon' by Mike Carcney.

Houdini was busy.....
Drawn form various Houdini books and articles including 'The Secret Life of Houdini.

Edith Cavell.....
The death of Edith Cavell was reported in the Sheffield Daily Independent on October 16th, 1915, under the headline ' A Lady Murdered. Illustration of Tuetonic Justice (?) in Belgium.'

Willard.....
Words from an newscutting in the Douglas Collection at Buxton Museum and Art Gallery.

writhing about on the rope.....
Described from the footage of Houdini's upside-down straitjacket escapes on the DVD box set of Houdini The Movie Star by Kino. Also, Houdini wrote how he manipulated his way out of a strait-jacket in his 1910 book 'Handcuff Escapes.'

Hetty Bown.....
Descriptions of Hetty and where they met are taken from family reminiscence, Randolph's private letters, kindly made available by his relatives, and photographs.

Randolph's fond nickname for Hetty in his letters is 'my little pal.'In the interview with Randolph's friend Mr Marshall, he states that Randolph 'worked at Cooper Brothers, (Arundel Street) and Hetty was in charge of the girls in the warehouse - this is how they met'.

Arundel Street was an amazing mixture of artistc and industrial skills. Here is a sample from 1913: 55-69 Sheffield School of Art, 31 Silversmiths and casket maker, 83 Ecclesiastical art worker, 85 stained glass maker, 89 cutlery and scissor makers, and an ebony teapot handle maker, 44 Cooper Brothers, 72 Butcher Works, 152 George Osborne fried fish dealer (any relation I wonder!).

In 2009, once again Arundel street is flourishing, with a new school of art moving back there and the old Butcher Works opened as workshops for Sheffield craftspeople. Full circle and Cooper Buildings have stood through it all.

Cooper Brothers in the 1950s *Sheffield Newspapers*

Cooper Brothers was partly demolished (above) and the remaining part of the site, now called Cooper Buildings, is a Science Park.
Sheffield Newspapers Archives

Troops on Surrey Street, at the side of the Town Hall, in Sheffield during World War 1
Sheffield Newspapers Archives

20: 'Am now a soldier'...

great rush of recruits....
Descriptions of the rush to join up in December 1915 are from an article headed 'Mighty Rush To Win With Voluntaryism' and 'Well Done Sheffield' in the Sheffield Daily Independent of Saturday, December 11th 1915 and an article entitled 'Brave, Sheffield' in the Sheffield Daily Independent of Monday, December 13th 1915 in Sheffield Local Studies Library.

The dates of Randolph's attestation, mobilisation date, number etc are taken from his army papers.

The place Randolph was sent to at Cocken Hall and the hut number etc is known from the address he gives on his letters sent home.

He seems to have been enlisted in January at Pontefract, where there was an army depot. He could have done some basic training there for a while before being sent up to join the troops at Cocken Hall.

The 3rd Battalion of the York and Lancaster Regiment's role in WW1 was that of training /reserve Battalion. Their wartime station was Sunderland and their main task was to train recruits to serve with the Battalions overseas. Private Douglas could have ended up serving overseas with virtually any regiment.

signal box....
The photograph shows the signal box at Fence Houses station in 1990. It was opened in 1914. The sidings were associated with a nearby coking plant. The level crossing was automated on 18th May 1991, and the box demolished. Information and photo kindly supplied by John Hinson.

Fencehouses is a small village in County Durham. Cocken Hall is a 17th century mansion once used by nuns. In July 1914 it had been empty for eight years, but was owned by the Earl of Durham.

attacked by militant suffragettes....

On July 14th 1914, the caretaker of Cocken Hall found graffiti declaring 'Votes for Women' and leaflets strewn around the grounds, Inside there had been an attempt to set the house on fire. The staircase was smouldering. The incident was reported in the Northern Echo and even in the New York Times of July 15th, 1914.

Later in 1914 the hall became home to the Durham Light infantry, who used it as a army training centre.

Some time after the war the hall was flattened.

envelope sent to Hetty...

Hetty lived on Western Street in Walkley. The area is now totally rebuilt and lies in the shadow of tall flats and close by the rumble of the tracks of trams the second time around, Sheffield Supertram.

a brother...

The date of birth for Ambrose is known from relatives and also from his birth certificate.

The Scottish Rifles..

The dates of Randolph's transfer, his new regiment and number are taken from his army papers. Details of the regiment are taken from the website for the Cameronian Museum in Hamilton. The staff of the museum also helped with details about the uniforms in the photograph.

rheumatic endocarditis..

Details about this illness are taken from the NHS Direct Health Encyclopaedia.

paragraph 392 XVI KR..

The KR stands for King's Regulation.

I found a medal index card in The National Archives for a Randolph Douglas, in the 1st Reserve battalion of the Royal Engineers, number 231123, the rank of 'sapper' also discharged physically unfit for further duty.

It could be our Randolph, but I have not managed to solve it, as the dates don't fit-Enlistment 26-1-17, discharge 27-12-19. Randolph does not have these later dates on his service records as far as I can tell. Perhaps it is a coincidence, or a mistake?.

If he did sign up again later I have not found any indication of it in letters etc.

21: A new direction

met often...

The meeting place and comments about the early mornings, Simple X, brass dust, uncle staying etc are all taken from Randolph's letters to Hetty.

Simplex

The information about which firms were making parts for the Simplex car came from Kelham Island Museum, Sheffield. William Brothers, at Green Lane, Sheffield, did brass brushing, brass and alloy castings. This could be where the brass dust came from.

toothache...

Randolph tells Hetty about this in his letters.

Zeppelin raid

A monument plaque to this air raid is on a wall at Effingham Road, Sheffield. It says: 'On this site on 26th September 1916, nine men, ten women and ten children died.'

22: Sticking it

adopted birthday

Houdini was born on March 24th, in Budapest, but he later told people April 6th was his birthday and Appleton, Wisconsin USA was his birthplace. One explanation for the April 6th date is that it is the day his mother always wrote to him.

vanishing elephant...

The illusion is described in 'Hiding The Elephant' by Jim Steinmeyer.

Vanishing elephant as much chance....

From an article entitled 'The Story of Harry Houdini' in The New York Times of January 13th 1918

latest purchases...

Randolph listed all his purchase, costs and when bought in a notebook I was kindly shown by Randolph's relative.

Defying the Bullets...

Soo's act and the night of his death are described in the book 'The Glorious Deception' by Jim Steinmeyer.

hands as marked with lines as a jigsaw...

Randolph says this in a letter to Hetty. In the same letter he describes the workshop, and bemoans his unlit pipe and the elusive runabout.

fly press..

All British WWI aeroplanes, though not airships, were made of wood and all had steel components. It could be that he was producing small fixing components that joined bits of wood together, but he was certainly not producing major structural components which required holes to be cut or punched in them to reduce the weight of metal present in the 'piece'.

had to save gas..
The gas strike in Doncaster had probably created a shortage.

Phyllis Dare
Randolph says in letter in a private collection that they will see a show at the Empire on Wednesday April 17th. The act on that night was found by looking at the theatre listings in the Sheffield Daily Independent for that night at the Hippodrome. It was Phyllis Dare. Information and the Sunshine Girl lyrics were found on various websites by 'Googling' the name Phyllis Dare.

A man fly-punching in 1910. The machine Randolph used probably looked similar to this
Sheffield Local Studies Library

grandfather clock...
G W Marshall. in the interview transcript of 21st August 1987, says
'Randolph always put a priority on his collecting. Once, his father gave him £5 to buy a suit, but he bought a grandfather clock instead. He studied antique clocks.'
The date Randolph bought the lock is found from his dated list of purchases in his note-book, in a private collection.

23: Side by side

the robot....
This may be the first screen robot.

Niagara Falls...
Houdini filmed a rescue scene near the falls in his film Terror Island.

Arthur Conan Doyle...
He was famous as the author of Sherlock Holmes. His wife was a spiritualist and medium and Doyle championed the cause. He and Houdini had very public disagreements over spiritualism.

stone walls do not a prison make...
A quote from English poet and nobleman Richard Lovelace (1618-1658).
It continues 'minds innocent and quiet take that for an hermitage.'
Lovelace spent time in prison, for supporting the Royalists in the time of Oliver Cromwell.

a labour of love...
In the World's Fair article, May 28th 1938, Randolph says these words about his collection of magazines and press cuttings of Houdini and the way he kept them all and made scrapbooks.

24: New challenges

Tommy shanter
A large woolly hat with a bobble on top.

Speedwell Cavern...was a favourite
There are lots of photographs in the Derbyshire Pennine Club archives of the friends exploring this cavern and the scarily named 'bottomless pit', a subterranean lake. The cavern is one of the show caverns in Castleton, of which much is open to the public and even more to experienced cave explorers and divers.
Speedwell is set at the bottom of Winnats Pass, a spectacular route between the hills. A visitor to Speedwell goes down around 150 steps then rides on a boat on an under-ground canal, as a guide takes them through the old workings of a lead mine.

Occasional maps
Randolph did one for an article by Puttrell called 'The Bottomless Pit and Beyond.' It can be seen in Puttrell's writings in Cave and Caving, Vol 1, no.3, January 1938.

Considerable risk
G W Marshall. in the interview transcript of 21st August 1987, says that he helped get many of the geological specimens in the Douglas Collection and one particular exam-ple, from the Ecton Copper Mines nearly cost him his life, when he stepped through a cover

and nearly plunged many feet down a water-filled shaft.

Randolph probably took a few risks too, but it would more than likely have fed his sense of daring and challenge, another kind of task to vanquish, like his locks and straitjacket.

amazing his fellows...

In the same interview, Mr Marshall says that Randolph had a 'knack' of winding the rope around his arm, shaking it in a particular way, and it would come out knotted, at the distance required.

trouble from his hammer toes

Randolph refers to his sore toes and his walking boots rubbing in his letters to Hetty in a private collection.

The Beeches... Mr Brown

The details of where Randolph stayed and that a Mr Brown was there are taken from the letters mentioned above.

The Beeches, Riverside, Clapham *An old postcard of the cottages kindly sent by Ken Pearce of Clapham*

Clapham

This pretty village is an ideal place to stay to explore a popular cave, Ingleton Cave and Gaping Ghyll. Gaping Ghyll is popular as it has a spectacular fall of water about 300ft down into the cavern.

25: More adventures

he had purchased...

Lists of items in Randolph's notebooks that he purchased then.

tank...

Photos and a press cutting of the tank were shown to me by Randolph's relatives.

A researcher for the Bovington Tank Museum in Dorset, John Taylor Firth, sent me the following information about the tank:
The fact that the silver model is of a Tank Mark VIII is interesting as this tank never really was in service with the British Army.

Design work on the tank started in late 1917 as a joint British and American project and in January 1918 a treaty was signed by both governments to assemble 300 of these tanks a month from the summer of 1918 onwards at a new factory to be built in France. The tank was often referred to as the Mark VIII 'International'.

It was the culmination of tank design at that time. Its Liberty engine at 300 bhp was twice as powerful than earlier tank engines, the tank was 34 feet long and could cross 15 foot trenches and its 16 mm armour plate gave it better protection. It weighed 37 tons and its new engine gave it a maximum speed about 7 mph on roads using 4 gallons of petrol per mile.

The whole programme was frozen when the Armistice was signed in November 1918. A tank of this type can be seen at Bovington Tank Museum in Dorset.

bus arrived..

The loading of the bus etc are described in Randolph's letter to Hetty of10th July 1921, as is the cottage itself. He uses the words 'a fine little spot....hard to find these days.' Descriptions of the Jug Hole outing and the walk by the river are in the same letter

vase..

The vase was shown to me by one of Puttrell's relatives. It is not signed, but it is so much like Randolph's other work,including a jewellery box made for Hetty, with the same round precious stones for decoration, that I am almost certain Randolph made it for his close friend Jim. Randolph's relatiive agrees.

model of Speedwell Cavern..

The model is one of four known remaining Speedwell models Randolph made, two are with his relatives, one is with Puttrell's relative and one is in Castleton Information Centre. There may be more still around.

26: Maker of better models

Randolph wrote...

Randolph was staying at The Bedford Hotel, Southampton Row, when he wrote Hetty the letter, using the hotel notepaper.

dark holes...

These thoughts are based on words from one of Randolph's letters at the time.

naked eye...

Randolph did not use lenses to do his work. He also tended to work on his projects through the night so he could concentrate, say relatives and Mr Marshall in his interview.

When I asked an optician about the ability to work so small, he said that Randolph probably had good 'Vernier acuity.' This is the degree to which a pair of fine lines can be aligned to each other. and still seen to be separate. Some people can distinguish this when the lines are closer together than others. A 'Vernier Scale' is used for small measurements, a sliding secondary scale, eg on a sextant, scientific instruments and machinists' measuring tools. Randolph may have used one himself for his repair work at Hadfield's etc. The name comes from the French mathematician Pierre Vernier.

entertained at Carrington Road...
This is known because of the Artcrafts Guild records in the Sheffield Archives.

completed the purchase...
The documents held by Randolph's relatives give dates and details of the purchase.

Peveril Castle...
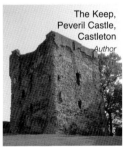
The Keep, Peveril Castle, Castleton *Author*

The original castle was built soon after the Norman Conquest by William Peverel. Most of the castle left standing today was built after the Peverel family owned it and dates from around 1176. For a short while the castle was in the hands of Simon de Montfort, until he as killed in battle and it became crown property again. The castle fell into disuse in the 15th century and became a picturesque ruin.

The keep has three floors with access at the first floor. The facing stones have fallen or been taken over the years, exposing its rubble core. The castle is now looked after by English Heritage. It is thought the spelling was changed to 'Peveril' not Peverel, when Walter Scott published his novel 'Peveril of the Peake.'

Another novelist, Houdini's friend and later antagonist, Arthur Conan Doyle, also visited Castleton and probably the castle, at one time. He worked as a doctor in Sheffield in his early career and it was probably the huge Peak Cavern, also known rather rudely as 'The Devil's Arse,' atop which the castle stands, that inspired his story 'The Beast of Blue John Gap.'

Blue John is a distinctively coloured type of Fluorite (calcium flouride) found in Castleton and Randolph had examples in his museum.

In Doyle's story, from his book Tales of Terror

and Mystery (1929) the cavern is inhabited by a wild beast that comes out at night, savaging sheep, and terrifying locals.

The Devils Arse name was given to the cavern because of rather bodily sounding noises the water makes as it swirls through the limestone cavern. 'Blue John Gap' is a much more polite name of course!

Randolph and Doyle could have met, but it is hard to know and so far I have found no reference to a meeting.

signed the register...
Details of what they had written are from the marriage certificate

lecture...
Puttrell's lecture and what it was about are written of in the Artcrafts Guild records in the Sheffield Archives.

marriage...
According to the 'Sheffield Year Book and Record' 1925, Superintendent Registrar for Ecclesall Bierlow, which is the area the marriage certificate states, was Mr Joseph A Beard, 31 Union Road, Nether Edge, Sheffield.

The side of Randolph's Speedwell Cavern model *Private collection*

The actual building, which now has a frontage added. The part of the cottage shown in the models with flowers around the door. is on the left hand side out of view. *Author*

There were for the Ecclesall Bierlow Registration District two registrar sub-districts for marriages with addresses at 102 Marshall Road, Woodseats and 9 Washington Road, Sharrow. Beard signed Randolph and Hetty's certificate and also Union Road was nearest to Carrington Road of the Ecclesall Bierlow choices.

It also seems likely that if his father and Kitty were married there it would be a place with a connection to them already.

veiled threats...
The medium Margery and the threats are described in 'The Secret Life of Houdini' by William Kalush and Larry Sloman. It is one notion, explored in the book, that spiritualists were to blame for Houdini's death.

Houdini's campaign...
Houdini did a tour with lantern slides to show how mediums could use tricks to convince people there were spirits present. The book 'Houdini Speaks Out' by Arthur Moses shows these and tells of the tour.

27: The House of Wonders

gazed around the room...
The description of the cottage and its layout, furniture, Hetty's knitting etc. are from relatives, who had visited there on many occasions and could recall things vividly. Randolph's friend Mr Marshall helped Randolph get the cottage ready, according to the interview he did in 1987.

planned it all for ages...
Randolph had long wanted a collection. In an interview in The Sheffield Telegraph, August 2, 1932, it says, 'His main desire, however, was to obtain a unique collection of locks and keys, and he seems to have succeeded, for he has over 1,000 specimens of the locksmith's art, ranging over a period of 4,000 years. There are big ones, some nearly two feet long, small ones, thick ones, and thin ones".

the museum began to take shape...
The items in the museum and where they are placed is based on photographs of the museum rooms and also the list of the House of Wonders contents which was written down when the museum closed, reproduced in this book.

28: The last escape

unexpected blow...
This blow, and a later one in a hotel lobby, is

thought by some to have been dealt by people working, or supporting the cause of,spiritualists.

tired of fighting...
According to many books and articles about Houdini, these were said to be his last words, to his brother Hardeen.

would never see it...
Houdini died on October 31st 1926, Randolph bought the cottage in November 1925 and opened the museum at Eastertide 1926. After Houdini and Randolph saw each other at the Empire in 1920 Houdini did not come to Sheffield or the UK again- unless it was unrecorded.

In the interview with Randolph's sister, she says that 'after Randolph's marriage the Houdini's were regular visitors to Castleton when in this country.' and a newspaper article in The World's Fair, May 13th,1933, says that Houdini used to visit Randolph in Castleton when in Manchester or Sheffield.

Whether this is time mixing memory or a mistake, or if Houdini indeed managed to fit in visits to Castleton between November 1925 and his death, as well as battle spiritualists, I am not sure.

milk can escape...
Goldin died in 1939 and the whole of his show was bought by Cecil Lyle and some of the principal illusions then incorporated into Lyle's new show, Cavalcade of Mystery, which opened in 1940. Murray was an escapologist and so the milk can would be a natural purchase for him as a young man recently arrived in the UK from Australia.

The Milk Can was a Houdini idea from many years earlier, but because it was copied and had become a "standard" by the1920s, there were a number of variations on it. When Goldston asks about an inside lining, he's asking about a specific method. Murray's letter implies that Douglas had another variation on the method (or at least, one that was new to Murray), as he's commenting specifically on the design. Goldston was a magic dealer and, because of this, was often in the middle of a lot of deals. He was a friend of Murray and would have brokered props or tried to be aware of what was available for his customers, et cetera. (Thanks to Prof. E Dawes and Jim Steinmeyer for the above information).

Bess was drinking heavily...
Bess and her life after Houdini's death is described in The Secret Life of Houdini, by William Kalush and Larry Sloman.

and that was that...

These words are said by Hetty near the end of a taped tour she gave around the Douglas Museum on January 2nd 1979. with Ambrose recording. The tape is now in the hands of Hetty's relatives and there is also a copy in the Douglas Collection at the Buxton Museum and Art Gallery.

Hetty says, when asked by Ambrose if she and Randolph had kept in touch with Bess after Houdini's death: *"We exchanged Christmas cards but not for long. His secretary didn't like her with Randolph you know. He was a bit jealous. And that was that."*

29: A model career

warmly eulogised his work...

Noted in an interview headed 'Young Sheffielder outrivals Lilliput. Miniature marvels. Flowers in a Tom Thumb Greenhouse.' in the Sheffield Daily Independent, Wednesday 29th June 1927.

In the same interview the reporter mentions Randolph's range of models and attention to detail: "He can make a model of anything from a battleship to a sewing machine.

"There is a model of Ann Hathaway's cottage at Stratford on Avon, drawn exactly to scale - 1 inch to 16 feet - which means that the building is reduced nearly 200 times. Yet not a detail is missing, every flower is there in the garden, and even the separate bushes which comprise the hedge can be distinguished.

Ever since he was a lad Mr. Douglas has been fascinated by the making of tiny models.

"The detail work appeals to me," he said, "I am never satisfied unless I have included everything. Look at this model I am working on now, for instance."

It was a model of a cotton factory; a peep through the little windows showed the furniture inside the office and the machinery inside the 'shops.' There was even a pressure gauge on the boiler".

hired a cafe at Castleton...

Mentioned in the interview with his friend Mr Marshall, mentioned previously

crosswords...

This conversation is from an interview in The Leader, August 4th, 1931

Nettlepot and Perryfoot...

Nettle Pot was discovered by Derbyshire Pennine Club in the 1930s. It is above Oxlow House Farm, Winnats. A deep system, the first vertical pitch being 160 feet and tight in places. Followed by further deep shafts.GR 126819. Perryfoot Cave is at GR09898127 near Torr

Top Farm Perryfoot (beyond Winnats) Quoting from the guide book " After short crawl and walk, small chamber has a choice of two ways on, which link up. At floor level a tight crawl in a passage with small pools leads to Iron Maiden Squeeze, which is very tight and must not be attempted by large persons. Beyond the passage leads onto final chamber....." Information from Derbyshire Pennine Club.

cats...

mentioned in Randolph's letter.

hospital centenary...

The Royal Hospital, now demolished, stood on West Street, Sheffield. It was opened on July 2, 1832.

outing...book...

Details of the Guild outing and the book are from the Guild records at Sheffield Archives. The book is also mentioned on the Sheffield Millennium Gallery website.

J.B Himsworth...

Work by this man and his daughter Joyce can be seen in the metalwork room of Sheffield Millennium Gallery.

World's Fair article...

Printed on Saturday, May 13th, 1933

tiger ran amok...

Printed in The Times, 4th December 1933

another talented Douglas...

The article about Robert was in Sheffield Daily Independent, October 6th, 1933

quite a genius...prototype...

These words are used by the reporter in the World's Fair article, May 28th, 1938

ever since..meals with us..

These words and those of Kitty, are from the same interview.

30: War work

programme...

The acts on the bill are taken from the newspaper and and from the programme, in The Douglas Collection.

treasure for a lifetime...

Randolph's niece still has the little match holder cottages and does indeed treasure them

theatres closed...

The Sheffield Daily Independent reports this on September 5.

8.04 train...
A Castleton resident who knew Randolph remembers him getting this train every morning, carrying a case.

Clayton Hutton...
May 2nd 1913 was the date of the challenge in Birmingham, by Clayton Hutton, which Hutton mentions in his book 'Official Secret.'
May 2nd (but no year) is the date on Randolph Water Torture Cell diagram.
If Randolph went to see Houdini in Birmingham after making friends, he could have been there that night and met Clayton Hutton at the same time as he gave Houdini a copy of the dated Water Torture Cell drawing.
It is also a tenuous possibility that when Hutton came to Sheffield to get the steel their paths crossed. as Randolph was doing his repair jobs in the steelworks at the time.
It was a double take for a minute when one of Randolph's jobs on his worksheet was listed 'South Kens. T223 T224'. London.. it sounded familiar. Clayton Hutton's office was London.. with a similar room number... but it was room 424. and the hotel, The Metrolpole Hotel, was not in Kensingon.

Henry Hall...
Described in the book 'Sheffield's Lost Theatres' by Bryen Hillerby.

The morning after was chaos...
Descriptions of the blitz are taken from the book 'Sheffield Blitz' by Paul License.

decoy city...

Randolph's niece told me that there was a wake after Randolph's funeral, held at the Bulls Head public house in Castleton, pictured here   *Author*

More about the decoy city can be found in Peeks at the Peak,' Volume 2, (author) and 'Sheffield's Golden Frame' by Bill Bevan.

open the odd safe..
Anecdotal from a Castleton resident, who was told that Randolph was called in to open

doors with lost keys and safes with lost combinations.

a letter to Hadfields...
Randolph wrote to the Ministry of National Insurance on 25th July 1949, saying that on 5th July 1946, he had 'handed his cards in to the Bamford Exchange on the termination of my employment with Messrs Hadfields Ltd.'

31: Endings

skeletons..
According to the transcript of Mr Marshall's interview, Randolph had at one time two skeletons under the bed he used to sleep in when visiting the Douglas household.
A Mrs Grayson had given them to Randolph. It was said they were those of Alan and Clara, lovers murdered in Winnats Pass when on their way to marry at Peak Forest, the local version of Gretna Green.
More can be read of this sad tale in Peeks at the Peak,' by Ann Beedham and Murder and Mystery in the Peak, by Roly Smith.

cruise ship...
A relative of Hetty's remembers Randolph working on a 4ft model of the " Windsor Castle " cruise ship for Union Castle line in the 50s and that It used to take him about a year to make one.

whittling...
A lady, still living in Castleton, used to go down to the cottage with her parents when she was little. She told me she remembered Randolph whittling wood as he told them stories. She also said Hetty made good cakes.

likes me free...
A charming anecdote told to me by a Castleton resident who knew the couple.

they would have a favourite exhibit...
On a radio interview I did, asking about the House of Wonders, three people rang in. They all said they liked the Lord's Prayer passing through the eye of a needle. Likewise after an appeal in the newspaper for memories of Randolph, people described the museum and the same exhibit mainly. No one mentioned Houdini, or locks. So it seems Randolph's model making was remembered, even more by some than his Houdini connection and lock collection he most prized.

surrounded by all that was dear to him...
Randolph's death certificate shows that he died at home at the Douglas Museum, with Hetty there by his side.

Foil pictures by Randolph *Private Collection*

After

apoplexy and emphysema...
These are given as cause of death on the death certificate.

'just a boy'...
Words Hetty uses in the taped tour around the museum which was recorded by Randolph's step-brother Ambrose.

Colour section
Spirit cabinet
Here Randolph depicts an illusion where the manacled and chained escapologist seems to disappear into thin air.

Stage setting
This modern-looking stage setting seems to show a ball hovering. A hoop to the right of it may have been used to pass around the ball to show 'no strings'. Whether it is an idea by Randolph, or a show he had seen and noted, is unclear.

Randolph Mokana
On this imaginary stage setting by Randolph, the back cloth has two sections, one marked 'Mokana' and one marked 'Randolph.'
  'Mokana' was the stage name of James Meyer Goldston, an escapologist and the younger brother of the magic dealer Will Goldston. He died of Malaria whilst performing in India in 1905.
  Boards with handcuffs, set at either side of the stage, and a curtained cabinet with the initials 'M' and 'R' seem to imply that the two escapologists will share a display and maybe even try to out challenge each other

Randolph's autograph book drawing of Zakaree Ermakov, January 1st 1914
A preview in The Sheffield Daily Independent of Thursday December 23rd, 1915 tells that

Randolph would have seen Ermakov on the bill with a show called 'Red Heads'. The show was about 'Kaufski the amusing gentleman who hits upon the idea of exhibiting his fashion models upon a bevy of wonderful girls, each of whom has flaming hair'.
  "A novel item is the risky looking show of Ermakov, the giant Cossack, whose work is done with a collection of death defying weapons from bow to battleaxe, and includes some fine trick shooting.'
  The reviewer on the 28th described the show:
  'The main attraction is a show called 'The Red Heads' a 'vivacious and gorgeously dressed revue parade of ladies in Kaufski's show, a feast of colour and fascinating gowns. It makes a great appeal to the ladies'
  'Zakaree Ermakov presents a series of clever feats which show off the Cossack's warlike sports, his shooting being especially good.'

From an entry found on The Australian Dictionary of Biography on the internet, it seems that Ermakov was married to one Julia Gibson (1872-1953) who was a fortune teller with the stage name 'Madame Ghurka.'
  In 1903, in Warsaw, Julia (Morrison) married the Australian born Vaudeville artist and circus performer called Henry Gibson, whose stage name was 'Zakaree Ermakov.' By day she worked as a fortune teller and by night she was Ermakov's stage assistant. It is probably Julia that Randolph has put in the inset in his Ermakov drawing.
  In later years, after they divorced, Julia told people she had been a revolutionary and had a Cossack bullet in her body due to these activities. Her estranged husband, however, wrote to the newspapers in 1922, saying this was 'all bunkum' and that he had in fact accidentally shot her during a circus performance in Russia.
  In 1917 they moved to Australia, where they then split up. Julia became a fortune teller in Melbourne's Eastern Arcade.
  She was later involved in a murder case. A man who ran a wine saloon in the Eastern Arcade, Colin Ross, was accused of murdering a 12-year-old named Alma Tirtschke, in 1921. He was found guilty and hanged, though Julia was one of the witnesses and was accused of being unreliable and fabricating evidence against him.
  In May 2008, 86 years after his hanging, Ross was posthumously pardoned after a new enquiry found him innocent and subject to miscarriage of justice.

Clempert's stage setting
This seems to be a depiction of Clempert's version of the Water Torture Cell.

Author's note

It has been a fascinating and enjoyable journey finding out about Randolph's life. From the first sight of his incredible models and his tantalising link with the enigmatic Houdini, to the last sadly typed sentence telling of his death, it has felt like time travelling.

By the time the book was finished, Randolph and Hetty, and even Houdini, felt like old friends. I was seeped in their world and times. Wandering around Greenhill I saw it how Randolph would have seen it, almost heard the forge still pounding and ghostly children chatter in the schoolyard.

In Carrington Road I could see the young Randolph wandering down to the postbox to send Hetty a letter, or half convince myself his face was at the window still.

I have marvelled with him over the acts once treading the Empire's boards, visualised the hills and caves he found sparkling natural treasures within, felt his humour and felt his ambition. That ambition was to be like his role model Houdini, but like so many of us, his plans, and life, never worked out quite as he expected. He found himself doing jobs he didn't like, hands getting sore whilst his head was full of a hoped for, more adventurous life. I went through it with him, and hoped that this time he would triumph, that Randini would break free and prosper, though I already knew the end of the story.

It's an odd feeling knowing to the hour where a person was over a century ago. It is as if standing in those places you can connect with them. And even more so if you handle their letters and drawings, put the tiny greenhouse on your thumbnail and imagine the holding of breath as a tiny plant is glued in place.

I found I had a lot in common with Randolph. No, not the escapology part...but I too sketched daydreams, sent painted envelopes and cryptic symbol letters to loved ones. I also had an illustrated autograph book I eagerly thrust into the hands of favourite stars, though none so lofty as Houdini. And if I had added to their lives in some way, as Randolph did to his favourite star, it would have been a heady and delighted feeling.

I have pieced together Randolph's life mainly from the fond memories of generous relatives, fading photographs and his long still tools and work boxes. I perused the contents from his House of Wonders, for now homed partly in Castleton Information Centre, and in rows of boxes at Buxton Museum, where they are sometimes brought out to daylight for more eyes to be amazed at. I also used letters which he wrote to Hetty and Houdini and the Magic Circle's Randolph Douglas collection of letters and books.

The moves, words and thoughts of Randolph are mostly based on these sources, as well as birth death and marriage certificates and the census records.

In some places, however, for example when he wipes his breath from the attic window, or dreams of his mother during Devant's performance, it is an attempt to imagine myself in his place, to give the story some immediacy.

So now I leave Randolph between these pages, his life and works pinned like his butterflies. His dreams, of becoming the Great Randini, almost forgotten forever, are set down. Houdini is a famous name that is known the world over. Randolph Robert Osborne Douglas was part of that fame, the man in the shadow of Houdini's limelight. It is time he saw a little fame of his own.

Bibliography/further reading/sources

The Secret Life of Houdini
William Kalush & Larry Sloman
ISBN 978 1 8473 9082 0

The Glorious Deception.
The Double Life of William
Robinson aka Chung Ling Soo
the Marvellous Chinese Conjurer
Jim Steinmeyer
ISBN 978 0 78671 770 5

Houdini Speaks Out
Arthur Moses
ISBN 978 1 4257 6740 2

Houdini's Escapes
Walter B Gibson
ISBN 0 553 10398 9
Originally published 1930s

Houdini The Movie Star
Three DVD collection, Kino

Sheffield's Golden Frame
Bill Bevan
ISBN 978 1 85058 846 7

Lost Theatres of Sheffield
Bryen D Hillerby
ISBN 1 871647 53 3

St Vincent's: History of
A Parish 1853 - 2003
Derek R Cullen

The Sheffield City Battalion
Ralph Gibson & Paul Oldfield
ISBN 1 84415 423 8

Murder and Mystery
in the Peak, Roly Smith
ISBN 1 84114 369 3

A short history of The
Sheffield Royal Hospital
E.F Skinner 1932.
Sheffield Local Studies Library

Peeks at The Peak, vol 2
Ann Beedham
ISBN 9781905278244

House of Wonders
(Poems about Randolph
Douglas) John Lindley
ISBN 978 0 9559251 0 8

Jim Puttrell, J.P.Craddock
ISBN 9781848761803

British Mountaineering
Council (for Derbyshire
Pennine Club)
The Old Church 177-179
Burton Road, W.Didsbury,
Manchester M20 2BB
0161 445 6111

The Magic Circle
12 Stephenson Way
London NW1 2HD
Tel: 0845 006 2500
e mail: mail@magiccircle
venue.co.uk

Buxton Museum and Art Gallery
Terrace Road, Buxton
Derbyshire SK17 6DA
01298 24658
buxton.museum@
derbyshire.gov.uk

Sheffield Archives
52 Shoreham Street,
Sheffield S1 4SP
Tel: 0114 203 9395
email:
archives@sheffield.gov.uk

Sheffield Local
Studies Library,
Surrey Street, Sheffield S1 1XZ
Tel: 0114 273 4753
email: localstudies.library
@sheffield.gov.uk

Sheffield Newspapers
York Street,
Sheffield ,S1 1PU
0114 276 7676

Acknowledgements

My thanks go to the following people for their generous help in many practical ways,
and also for their time, expertise and enthusiasm:

William Kalush, Jim Steinmeyer
Dr. Bruce J. Averbook,

The Magic Circle, *especially Prof.Edwin*
A. Dawes and David Hibberd

Buxton Museum and Art Gallery,
especially Ros Westwood and Ben Jones

Anne - Marie Knowles, Chesterfield Museum
Sheffield Local Studies Library,
especially Michael Spick and Graeme Siddall
Brenda Simpson, Chris Emmerson
Mo Coleman, Malket and Tom,
Janet Harrison, John Lindley, Russell
of Magick, Christine Peacock,
John Craddock Geoff Peppit, Sheffield
Newspapers, David Sears, Edward Baker,
Catherine Parker, Jill Wright, Trevor Prew,

Nicola Hale, Judith Reading, Ben Hale,
Karl Noble, Maria Kenyon, Peter Harrison,
Mrs Haddock, Ken Pearce, Frank W. Adams,
Prof. Brian Robinson, Barry Richardson,
John Taylor Firth, Peter Higginbotham,
John Hinson, Barrie Duncan, Cameronians
Museum, June Morwood, H Harrold & Sons
ltd locksmiths, Sheffield, Graham Lawson,
Durham County Record Office, Andrew
Cormack, RAF museum, Aileen Anderson,
Clare Starkie, Millennium Gallery Sheffield,
Royal Air Force Museum London, David
Beasley, The Goldsmiths' Company,
...and to The Author's Foundation, for their
help with this book in the form of an award
granted towards research costs.

Index

The Douglas collection was purchased from Hetty's estate in 1979 by Derbyshire County Council. The county received a grant from the Fund for the Preservation of Technological and Scientific Material (currently known as the PRISM fund) to assist in this purchase, in respect of 'the interesting collection of

Buxton Museum and Art Gallery

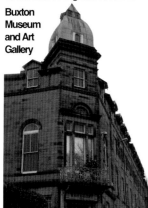

locks, manacles and handcuffs, some presented by Harry Houdini... and 'geological material...with particular relevance to Derbyshire caves, rocks and minerals and the activities of the lead miner.'

The whole collection is now housed at Buxton Museum and Art Gallery. This museum has extensive collections relating to Derbyshire and the Peak District and limited exhibition space, so the collection is not permanently on display. It is used regularly in temporary exhibitions, either specifically about Randolph Douglas and his museum, or to support other exhibition themes.

The collection is available to researchers for access with prior appointment. Small groups may have access to the collection in

the store; larger groups may make arrangements to have specific items available for inspection in the museum. All arrangements should be made in the first instance with the Derbyshire Museums Manager.

Information about visiting the museum, the exhibition programme and the collections (including the Douglas collection) is available on line at the county council's website:
www.derbyshire.gov.uk

Buxton Museum and Art Gallery
Terrace Road, Buxton
Derbyshire SK17 6DA
01298 24658
buxton.museum@
derbyshire.gov.uk
Information correct at the time of publication.